Hinduism and Human Rights

LAW IN INDIA SERIES

Series advisors: Rajeev Dhavan, Marc Galanter, S. P. Sathe, and Upendra Baxi

As well as catering to professional lawyers, advocates, and judges, the *Law in India* series is aimed at legal academics and students whose engagement with the law, in South Asia particularly, reaches beyond standard black letter law towards an understanding of how laws and legal institutions have an impact upon society as a whole.

The series includes high quality, authoritative texts by leading lawyers and academic across the globe. Each volume is vetted and approved by international legal experts chosen to ensure the highest levels of scholarship and accuracy under general advice from the series advisors.

Other books in the series:

S.P. Sathe
Judicial Activism in India:
Transgressing Borders and Enforcing Limits
Second Edition
(Oxford India Paperbacks)

Chiranjivi J. Nirmal (editor)
Human Rights in India
Historical, Social and Political Perspectives
(Oxford India Paperbacks)

Flavia Agnes
Law and Gender Inequality:
The Politics of Women's Rights in India
(Oxford India Paperbacks)

Stanley Yeo
Unrestrained Killings and the Law:
Provocation and Excessive Self-Defence in India, England, and Australia
(Oxford India Paperbacks)

Hinduism and Human Rights

A Conceptual Approach

ARVIND SHARMA

OXFORD
UNIVERSITY PRESS

OXFORD
UNIVERSITY PRESS

YMCA Library Building, Jai Singh Road, New Delhi 110 001

Oxford University Press is a department of the University of Oxford. It furthers the University's objective of excellence in research, scholarship, and education by publishing worldwide in

Oxford New York

Auckland Bangkok Buenos Aires Cape Town Chennai
Dar es Salaam Delhi Hong Kong Istanbul Karachi Kolkata
Kuala Lumpur Madrid Melbourne Mexico City Mumbai Nairobi
Sao Paulo Shanghai Taipei Tokyo Toronto

Published in India
By Oxford University Press, New Delhi

First published 2004

ISBN 0 19 566585 6

Typeset in Naurang
By Guru Typograph Technology, Dwarka, New Delhi 110 045
Printed at Pauls Press, Delhi 110 020
Published by Manzar Khan, Oxford University Press
YMCA Library Building, Jai Singh Road, New Delhi 110 001

Contents

Introduction

Academics rush in where angels fear to tread. Although the difficulties of discussing Hinduism and human rights may not require the same measure of subtlety as the calculation of the number of angels who can dance atop a pin, the complexity of the subject does approach the realm of conceptual difficulties symbolized by the metaphor. Many of these no doubt stem from the ambiguity which surrounds the terms themselves, to say nothing of the relationship.

If used as a Rorschach test of all that ensures human flourishing, human rights become as broad in scope as human suffering itself and its alleviation or amelioration (except perhaps in its spiritual and theological aspects). The term has indeed at times been so used.[1] However, if human rights as a term becomes so universal in its benevolence, it is hardly actionable in the usual sense and becomes more of an attitude than a programme. At the other extreme lies the possibility of too restricted a conception of human rights—such as its identification with civil and political rights in a purely legal way. The term has indeed been so used as well—a usage which has been criticised as too narrow, just as its use as a shorthand for human well-being has been criticized as too broad. These extreme positions in their own way do point to a truth though encrusted with exaggeration—that neither a sense of moral idealism nor legal realism can be entirely divorced from human rights discourse. In this book the term has been employed to cover the middle ground that lies between the two extremes—a place so dear to Buddhism, without however excluding the extreme points but also taking them into account when required, a position which some would identify with that of Jainism. We believe that such indeed is the ground covered by the various human rights documents which have been identified as such, documents which may be traced back, if not to the Magna Carta, then surely to the British Bill of Rights of 1689. This ongoing process is by no means over and the future will doubtless lift the curtain over many new formulations.

For the purpose of this book we have identified human rights discourse mainly as the discourse which has emerged around this documentary heritage. In this tradition the adoption of the Universal Declaration of Human Rights in 1948 is considered pivotal. One might say with only slight fear of exaggeration that most, if not all, previous human rights discourse flows into it and most, if not all, subsequent human rights discourse flows out of it.

The discourse around Hinduism, as that around human rights, also has its more extreme formulations. The term Hinduism is sometimes used so broadly as to virtually take the entire religious heritage of humanity within its ample embrace, as when one is epigrammatically told that a Hindu is most a Hindu when least a Hindu; or that there are only two kinds of people in the world: those who are Hindus and know themselves to be so, and those who are Hindus and do not know it yet. At the other extreme, the word Hinduism can be used to describe exclusive adherence to only those elements of it which are potentially quite exclusionary, a semantic direction in which its use is being increasingly propelled by recent political events on the subcontinent according to many observers.

The discourse around Hinduism is capable of enormous variation in historical and geographical terms even when these two extremes are eschewed. Even when we adopt an Indo-centric approach to control its global variability, the fact remains to be confronted that the historical vicissitudes undergone by it in India itself have led to its characterization successively as Vedic (and pre-Vedic) Hinduism, classical Hinduism, medieval Hinduism, and modern Hinduism. Which of these incarnations then is engaged in this book? This point needs to be clarified.

This book adopts a conceptual approach to the issue of Hinduism and human rights in a cultural ethos in which they are perceived, at least initially, as antithetical, if not antagonistic to each other, perhaps even displaying an aversion to each other bordering on hostility. Such a description best applies to classical Hinduism. Hinduism as such is too inchoate and pluripotent an entity in the Vedic period, while in the medieval period some of its sharper edges in relation to human rights were smoothened out by the leavening presence of Islam and the spread of the Bhakti movement. The modern period, of course, cannot be ignored but one is in it and this book itself is a product of it. All this is then by way of saying that it is Hinduism in its classical form, which it assumed and displayed between c. 400 BC and c. AD 1200, which will be primarily drawn upon in the following pages as representative of Hinduism, under the belief that it is best to confront Hinduism conceptually in the form least likely to be amenable to human rights discourse, as an example of the illuminating power of the extreme case.

Note

1. Lal Deosa Rai, *Human Rights in the Hindu-Buddhist Tradition*, Jaipur: Nirala Publications, 1995, passim.

CHAPTER 1

Bases of Human Rights in Hinduism

I

It might be useful to begin by examining the foundations of human rights in the Western world, as a prelude to identifying their bases, if any, in Hinduism. Four foundations of human rights can be identified in the current literature on the subject in the West. These may briefly be described as *legal*, *moral*, *ethical*, and *religious* in nature or conception.

Legal View of Human Rights

According to the positivistic or legal view of human rights, human rights are legal entities—no more, no less. Thus according to this view human rights are 'what the laws say they are'.[1] This raises two questions: what do the laws say they are; and what are the laws which say so? Minimally, these laws include the Universal Declaration of Human Rights, adopted and proclaimed by the General Assembly of the United Nations on 10 December 1948 (see Appendix I). Maximally, 'in practical terms if a subject is in a treaty, it is an issue of human rights'.[2] More concretely, the term human rights is used in this chapter to cover the provisions pertaining to rights provided for in the following documents: the Universal Declaration of Human Rights (1948); the International Covenant on Economic, Social and Cultural Rights (1966); the International Covenant on Civil and Political Rights (1966), and the two optional protocols to the latter Covenant.[3]

Such a view of human rights naturally follows, for instance, from the following comment of James Nickel: 'The formulation by the United Nations in 1948 of the Universal Declaration of Human Rights made possible the subsequent flourishing of the idea of Human Rights'.[4] Robert Traer thinks that the reasons responsible for the flourishing of human rights may be more complex.[5] Nevertheless the parturition, if not the conception, of human rights could perhaps reasonably be identified with the Universal Declaration of Human Rights.

Moral View of Human Rights

The moral view of human rights is grounded in the perception that human rights, as legal entities, stem from a moral vision of the world, of which they constitute a legal expression. From such a point of view, human rights, in the words of Louis Henkin, are 'simply those moral political claims which, by contemporary consensus, every human being has or is deemed to have upon his *society and government*'.[6]

It is possible to propose that the concept of human rights can be derived from a moral perspective rooted in the various religious traditions of humanity. This may be demonstrated by a series of logical steps. As a first step one could argue that

> The world religions do have a largely shared morality: murder, lying, stealing, sexual impropriety, and so on are universally prohibited. Moreover, even more general principles are often shared among the world religions. For instance, in the Chinese, Hindu, Buddhist, Zoroastrian, Christian, and Islamic traditions among others, we find a remarkably similar conception of how to treat others:
>
> Do not impose on others what you yourself do not desire.
>
> *The Analects*, XV:24, Confucius (551–479 BC)
>
> One should never do that to another which one regards as injurious to one's own self. This, in brief, is the rule of dharma. Yielding to desire and acting differently, one becomes guilty of adharma.
>
> *Mahabharata* XII: 113,8
>
> He who for the sake of happiness hurts others, who also want happiness, shall not hereafter find happiness.
>
> He who for the sake of happiness does not hurt others, who also want happiness, shall hereafter find happiness.
>
> *The Dhammapada* 131–2
>
> The nature only is good when it shall not do unto another whatever is not good for its own self.
>
> *Dabistan-i-dinik* 94:5
>
> Love your neighbour as yourself.
>
> *Gospel of Mark* 12:33 (RSV)

> No man is a true believer unless he desires for his brother that which he desires for himself.
>
> Muhammad, from the *Hadith*[7]

Joseph Runzo has identified the following four constituents of the moral point of view in general:

> (1) taking others into account in one's actions because one respects them as persons; (2) the willingness to take into account how one's actions affect others by taking into account the good of everyone equally; (3) abiding by the principle of universalizability—that is, the willingness to treat the actions as morally laudable or permissible only if similar acts of others in comparable circumstances would be equally laudable or permissible, and to treat the actions of others as morally impermissible only if similar acts of one's own would be equally morally culpable; (4) the willingness to be committed to some set of normative moral principles.[8]

As a third step, the presence or prevalence of these elements in the various religious traditions could be demonstrated as follows:

> Taking these in reverse order, of course, different religious traditions and different cultures will specify the normative principle in (4) differently. But all traditions share universalizability (3), for as we saw when we distinguished Kant's ethics, this is a logical feature of any morality. The willingness to take others into account (2) is a psychological feature of the moral life, and it, too, is shared by all the World Religions. This brings us to the key shared element of the religious ethics of all the World Religions: (1) taking others into account in one's actions because one respects them as persons. This is the crux of taking the moral point of view and so the crux of the shared ethics of the World Religions.[9]

As a fourth step, the key element underlying all of these may then be identified as consisting of relationality. Thus relating to other persons becomes a key factor in moral agency. This is most obvious in the Kantian dictum that one should 'always treat others as ends in themselves and not merely as means to an end'. It is also obvious in the Buberian 'I-thou' formulation: 'When I confront a human being as my You and speak on the basic word I-You to him, then he is no thing among things nor does he consist of things.' In other words, there is a radical difference between treating people as things and treating them as persons. To treat persons as things amounts to treating them as an 'it' rather than as 'you' according to Buber. It also means to treat human beings as less than human.[10]

This brings the argument into the moral sphere. However,

> The obligation to take the moral point of view is not a moral obligation, for that would be circular. However, relationality is a religious obligation, for on the view of World Religions, one cannot relate to the Transcendent unless one relates to

other persons. Hence taking the moral point of view is a religious obligation. Consequently, religion supervenes on morality. That is, religion encompasses but is more than a 'religious point of view'. Just as the moral point of view functions as the wellspring and the point of commonality and universality for moral value and truths, so too the religious point of view is the wellspring, the point of commonality, and the manifestation of universality in religion, even though the adherents of the World Religions have quite a different specific religious world-view.[11]

The final step consists in recognizing that a belief in the intrinsic worth of persons is a crucial component of this point of view:

In *Relationship Morality* James Kellenberger explains the moral point of view by arguing that 'the ultimate grounding of obligation, and finally of all morality, is a single but universal relationship between each and all,' suggesting that it is a realization of this 'person/person relationship' to others which creates 'a sense of duty grounded in a recognition of the intrinsic worth of persons'. Since religion supervenes on morality, to be genuinely religious is to realize the person/person relationship Kellenbeger identifies, but with the added or supervening dimension of the realization of a single universal relationship both among all persons as spirits and with the Transcendent. I call this universal religious relationship a 'spirit-spirit' relationship.

Such a belief constitutes the core moral concept of human rights.

Ethical View of Human Rights

If we may trace the moral view of human rights to Locke although elaborated above in the context of world religions, we may trace the ethical view of human rights to Bentham, despite his description of human rights as 'nonsense on stilts',[12] especially as his successor, John Stuart Mill, argued that 'a perceptive and far-sighted utilitarian supports strong rights both of democratic participation and of individual freedom of action'.[13]

However, utilitarianism may not always represent a dimension of virtue or ethics; it might even subvert it. Consider, for instance, the following social Darwinian perspective:

Judgements passed in a primitive society on the conduct of its members are related, as far as we can see, not to the betterment of their inner nature, but only to collective well-being; and it is argued, on this basis, that those forms of conduct which make for the survival of society are alone praised, and those that do not are condemned. What is good or bad for the hive is precisely what is good or bad for the bee. This originally *utilitarian* motive is, in course of time, forgotten; but the modes of conduct remain, it is explained, constituting what is now styled 'virtue'.[14]

In other words, we feel right talking about rights because by insisting on them for others we are only securing our overall protection. This line of reasoning is attractive but, according to the Indian philosopher, M. Hiriyanna, specious. He goes on to explain that even when we grant that:

What we term the 'higher values' have originated from modes of behaviour which once served only utilitarian purposes, there is one peculiarity about them which requires proper explanation. It is that, at one stage in this process of transformation, they have come to manifest a qualitative distinction, with the implication that they ought to be sought in preference to those that are purely utilitarian in their character. The genetic theory has nothing to say about the emergence of this distinction or, 'the growth', as it has been well put, 'of what was into what was not'. That is to say, it leaves wholly unexplained what, as pointed above, is essential to the very nature of value. It should therefore be concluded that there is something unique in the constitution of human nature, which serves as the necessary condition of the ideal life, which, as already stated, is intrinsic to the nature of man, and accounts for his feelings that he is not merely a finer kind of animal . . .[15]

Axiological space is thus created for the emergence of human rights. But we also notice that this move away from the utilitarian calculus points in the direction of morality.

The Religious View of Human Rights

The moral vision as a backdrop of human rights was referred to earlier. Such a moral vision could emerge on its own off and on, or from a secular view of the world; or it might be grounded in a religious vision. Robert Traer seems to incline towards this last view when he writes:

In fact, human rights are at the center of a global moral language that is being justified, elaborated, and advocated by members of different religious traditions and cultures. This is true not merely in the West but also in Africa and Asia. It is true not only in the First and Second Worlds, where liberal and socialist human rights theories have evolved, but in the Third World as well. Jews, Christians, Muslims, Hindus, Buddhists, and advocates of religious traditions indigenous to Africa and Asia fundamentally agree about human rights.[16]

Hence human rights can also be derived, at least potentially, from the different religious traditions of the world, and not just from their shared moral universe.

II

The relative merits and demerits of grounding human rights on these four foundations may now be considered. The great merit of the legal view of human rights is that they are thereby made justiciable, and can be enforced in a court of law. The great danger of adopting the legal view of human rights is that what is conferred by law can be taken away by law. The Indian experience in this respect is salutary. The fundamental rights of the Indian Constitution were in effect suspended during the proclamation of the Emergency by Mrs Gandhi in 1975.

The merit of the moral view of human rights is that they are, on that account, natural and therefore inalienable. In 1977, a questionnaire was circulated among the leaders of the Philippines by the University of the Philippines Law Centre and the Philippines Council of Policy Science. It included the following question: *What do you understand by 'human rights'? Do you believe that human rights are inherent in man or that they are granted by the state? What is your view on the subject?*

The reply given by Reynaldo S. Capule, a political leader, reflects the strength of the moral basis of human rights:

> Human rights are inherent or natural and are not granted by the state. Even at the beginning of history, people existed in a society where every member had equal rights, for example, equal rights in making use of the land, equal rights to the products of labour, equal rights in the protection of the security of the individual or of the society as a whole and other rights needed in order to live.[17]

The weakness of the moral basis of human rights lies in the disputed nature of a universal morality, a concept which must be carefully distinguished from that of universal moral consciousness. It can perhaps be reasonably claimed that moral consciousness is a universal phenomenon; that is to say, everyone possesses a sense of right and wrong. However, everyone may not agree on what is right and what is wrong, and the question of a universal morality can thus become an issue. The belief is widespread among American businessmen, for instance, that the Confucian ethic sets China apart from other civilizations, a view sometimes shared by Chinese Communists.[18]

The merit of the ethical view of human rights consists in the corrective it provides against taking too individualistic a view of human rights, by appealing to the common good. Some of these are reflected in Articles 22–27 of the Universal Declaration of Human Rights. Such provisions enable a Third World perspective to be recognized in the Declaration, a perspective rooted in its more communal forms of social organization, a history of collective struggle against imperialism in the colonial era and, subsequently, the widespread adoption of a socialistic orientation (now in the process of reassessment) in the post-colonial era. The shortcoming of the ethical approach is the objectification it involves of the individual in the interest of an abstract common good. An extreme example might be of help. As the per capita income is calculated on the basis of income divided by the population, it might be conceivable that reducing population could raise per capita income. Thus one must distinguish between genocide and family planning as ways of raising per capita income.

The strength of the religious view of human rights lies in its ability to tap into the deeply and widely held beliefs of the various religious traditions and even help provide a common platform around which religious zeal could be mobilized. However, its very strength can turn into a weakness, if that religious enthusiasm has already been channelled into a legal or quasi-legal structure, parts of which are antithetical to human rights. The obvious examples of such a development are the *sharī'ah* in Islam and the caste system in Hinduism. These obstacles may not be insuperable,[19] but they are obstacles nevertheless, although Robert Traer has recently argued vigorously for anchoring the human rights tradition in the rights-positive dimensions of the various religious traditions.[20] It is in this light that the following intriguing question deserves to be pursued:

> An intriguing question arises as to whether differing cultures can arrive at a similar conclusion about rights by rather different routes—some via explicit philosophizing, as with Locke, Kant and others in the West; others by contemplating religious texts and duties (as here, the Mīmāṁsā and the Gītā); others again by exploiting ideas of ritual and performative behaviour towards others (e.g. *li* in China as a source of rights). It would be a happy outcome if so: since it would allow a confluence model of world society to establish itself—differing civilizations like so many rivers coming together, like the reverse of a delta.[21]

III

From the Hindu point of view, each of these bases of human rights could be aligned to one of its four fundamental axiological orientations called *puruṣārtha*s. These are *kāma*, *artha*, *dharma*, and *mokṣa* and for our purposes may be translated as referring to the sensate, politico-economic, moral, and metaphysical dimensions of human existence. The ethical view of human rights connects with the dimension of *kāma* in the sense that it involves the assessment of the relative merits of the elements desired (*kāma* = desire) by the individual vis-à-vis the community. The legal view can be linked with *artha*, which takes a positivistic view of law.[22] The moral view of human rights can similarly be connected to *dharma* and the religious view with *mokṣa*.

All these links will be developed in detail in what follows but the conclusion may be anticipated. Hindu thinking is strongly in favour of grounding human rights in morality or *dharma*. For grounding it in *kāma* would be too hedonistic, in *artha* too positivistic and arbitrary, and in *mokṣa* too remote and even transgressive. Grounding human rights in a moral vision would mean grounding them on their home ground. The task of the rest of the section is to make this point apparent.

It was claimed above that the ethical grounding of human rights can be seen as corresponding to the Hindu value of *kāma*. At first blush this might seem somewhat odd for several reasons. For one, *Kāma* is the god of love in Hinduism so that when Śiva is 'dwelling on his sacred mountain in the Himalayas in deep yogic trance' and 'the Hindu god of lust, *Kāma*, tries to distract him from his meditation, Shiva burns him to ashes'.[23] Similarly, when the affection the female devotee Āṇṭāḷ has for Kṛṣṇa 'eventually turned into a desire to marry him,' then, 'in her devotional hymns, Āṇṭāḷ entreats *Kāma*, the Hindu god of love and desire, to attract Kṛṣṇa to her, to make him her husband'.[24] What has all this to do with human rights? So far nothing except perhaps her right to marry under Article 16 though we are not sure whether she had the 'free and full consent of the intending spouse', namely God. However, *kāma* or 'the quest for pleasure',[25] as a value, usually considered an inferior value, was raised to the highest when directed towards God. This creates room for translating *kāma* in our own context as the satisfaction of desired ends. This enables the utilitarian calculus to be brought into play, as well as the lapidary utterance, which evokes the right not only to life and liberty but also 'the pursuit of happiness'. What is right and wrong with this grounding of human rights in *kāma* becomes clear if we follow the example of Gilbert Harman as applied by James Fishkin:

> Let us first imagine a doctor who must choose between concentrating on one patient to the exclusion of five others in an emergency situation or saving the five others. In this simplified situation, if we must choose between saving one life and saving five, many of us would support the utilitarian calculation that the five be saved. I say 'utilitarian' because in introducing no further facts about the six patients, I am making it easy for a utilitarian to count them equally and to treat the

saving of life as a placeholder for the production of a future stream of utility. Furthermore, this calculation would appear quite favourable to utilitarianism because by counting lives rather than utilities or dollars, I am permitting the utilitarian to avoid the well-known Paretian difficulties with interpersonal comparisons.

The second step in the example is to imagine the same doctor with five patients, each of whom require a different organ (one a kidney, another a lung, another a heart, etc.). Without the required transplants, they will each die in the immediate future. The difficulty is that there is no available donor.

There is, however, a patient in room 306 who has all the required characteristics and organs in good condition. He has checked in for a routine set of physical exams. If he were killed and the required organs redistributed, five lives could be saved at the cost of one lost.

Now, this is the point in anti-utilitarian horror stories when the rejoinders focus on the dangers of exceptions, the value of maintaining ongoing practices, and the disutility of a climate of fear that might be created if exceptions to an ongoing practice—such as those defining the routine physical exam—were permitted. Much that Gibbard says along these lines is persuasive. Furthermore, his proposed right to protection from arbitrary loss of life or liberty might be held to protect the patient in room 306—even when the utilitarian calculations might support taking his life in the interests of saving five others (and even when secrecy and deception might be employed to prevent fear and other forms of disutility from entering the calculation).[26]

This scenario is not inconsistent with the picture of the Indian materialists who acknowledge only *kāma* as the primary value,[27] for whom 'the morality of an action depends on the quantity of pleasure it yields',[28] this pleasure principle being elevated to a communal level in our context, which requires a move from a hedonistic to a utilitarian interpretation of *kāma*.

The legal view of human rights pertains to the Hindu value of *artha*, especially as elaborated in the*Arthaśāstra*,[29] a famous text on polity, and sections dealing with similar topics in allied literature.[30] The value of *artha* is held to be supreme by the 'legalists',[31] taking precedence over *dharma* or morality per se.[32] This trend culminates in the *Nāradasmṛti*, which establishes the royal command as the ultimate source of*dharma*.[33] It has even been maintained that in the light of this value:

The state is welcomed by those who wish prosperity and property. Private property is a creation of the state. Through fear of the king the property of the weak is secured: 'If the king did not exercise the duty of protection, the strong would forcibly appropriate the possessions of the weak, and if the latter refused to surrender them with ease, their very lives would be taken. Nobody then, with reference to any article in his possession, would be able to say "this is mine".'[34]

The religious view of human rights pertains to the value of *mokṣa*. The difficulty in sustaining this view as a basis of human rights is both sublime on the one hand and mundane on the other, specially when viewed from the perspective of a major school of Hindu thought known as Advaita Vedānta. The person who, in this life, has attained the summum bonum of life, although active in life, no longer acts 'from any selfish impulse or even from a sense of obligation to others'. In fact, 'the common laws of social morality and ritual which are significant only in reference to one striving for perfection are meaningless to him'. So much so that 'impulse and desire become one to him. He is not then realizing virtue but revealing it'.[35] It is clear that in this form of liberation (*mokṣa*) the liberated person may see no 'other' vis-à-vis whom rights may be asserted.

The whole issue of human rights is predicated on distinctions among human beings and objects, but this whole worldview tends to be undermined by this version of the liberative vision of Hinduism, which possesses a pronouncedly unitive character. M. Hiriyanna highlights this point with exceptional clarity:

> What is the bearing of such a view of ultimate reality on our everyday life? The most striking feature of the latter is the conviction, which it involves, viz., that diversity is real and ultimate. The presupposition of most, if not all, of the activities of life is that one man is different from another. The very efforts made through social and political organizations to unify men imply that they regard themselves as distinct. If man is distinct from man, his distinction from his physical environment is even clearer. It is not merely man that is distinct from matter; matter itself, whether it serves as an adjunct of the self like the physical body and the organs of sense or as its environment, seems to be diverse in its character, each object having its own individuality or, as the Upanishads express it, its own name (*nāma*) and its own form (*rūpa*). It is obvious that, if monism is the truth, no part of this diversity can be ultimate. That is the significance of the teaching of the Upanishads, so far as our common beliefs are concerned.[36]

On the mundane side, the liberated person, under the influence of his or her previous *karma* being worked out, may not respect the rights of others as in the case of a figure called Alarka[37] but this is rare though qualitatively significant.

It is the axiological orientation of Hinduism provided by the value of *dharma*, which seems to hold the best promise in offering a solid grounding of human rights, but only after some caution has been exercised in this respect. Although the term *dharma* has a multitude of meanings and associations, one needs to identify and distinguish between three senses in the present context. The first is the use of the word *dharma* in a ritualistic context, as in the school of Mīmāṁsā. The point to be specially kept in mind is the Mīmāṁsā view

> that the Veda teaches *dharma* (religious duty). What is *dharma*? It is what is enjoined in the Veda . . . [However] *the commands of the Veda should not be mistaken for those of ordinary morality* [although] it is true that ordinary morality is required for a man before he gains competence to perform the rituals enjoined in the Vedas.[38]

The word *dharma* has another meaning as well. From another perspective the duties [*dharma*] are 'those of the castes *(varṇa-dharma)*,' and 'those of the stages in life (*āśrama-dharma*)'.[39] These two are jointly referred to as *varṇāśrama-dharma* and are not likely to carry us very far in the present context as they are specific to class and station in life.

We are now left with the third sense of the word *dharma—sādhāraṇa-dharma*, or duties common to all irrespective of class or station in life. Their presence in Hinduism has not received the recognition it deserves. They have been living, as it were, under the shadow of the *varṇāśrama dharma* and often considered secondary to it,[40] although this is a moot point. Let us therefore first give them the recognition they deserve. P.V. Kane, the noted authority on Hindu texts dealing with *dharma*, writes:

> Apart from the specific qualities required to be possessed by the members of each of the four varṇas, all Dharmaśāstra works attach the highest importance to certain moral qualities and enjoin them on all men. Manu X. 63, Yāj. I.2, Gaut. Dh. S. VIII. 23-25, Matsya 52. 8-10 (quoted above on p. 1652) prescribe for all varṇas a brief code of morals, such as ahiṁsā, truthfulness, non-stealing (i.e. no wrongful taking of another's property), purity and restraint of the senses. The Mitākṣarā on Yāj. I. 22 explains that the word 'sarveṣām' therein states that these moral qualities if practised are the means of Dharma for all men from brāhmaṇas to caṇḍālas.[41]

It is these qualities which establish a person as a virtuous, self-regarding human being who regards others as well. The ability to practise such virtues is a special feature of being human—a sign of human worth and dignity. This consideration is further enhanced by the fact that, among all creatures, human beings are said to be the ones best poised for salvation. The quest for such salvation requires five negative and five positive observances, which are unaffected by considerations of time and space and therefore truly universal (*Yogasūtra* II.30 - 1). *These are virtually identical with the* sādhāraṇa dharmas.[42] It is therefore our view that a Hindu perspective on the bases of human rights would recommend their grounding in morality, the brand of universal morality just mentioned.

One might also add that Hinduism displays a special consciousness of the weaknesses associated with other groundings of human rights—the utilitarian, the legal, and the religious (i.e., metaphysical). A popular didactic verse considers the utilitarian approach as crass. It declares that 'it is the small-minded who calculate on the basis of his and mine, for the large of heart look upon the whole world as a single family'. Moreover, the utilitarian willingness to sacrifice the person for 'the larger calculation' (read institution) does not sit well with Hinduism.

A theme running throughout Hinduism is that institutions exist for the sake of man. The state is to serve the best interests of individual human beings. Somehow nations tend to lose this simple truth. Brotherhood becomes a United Nations rather than a united people. Nations become competitive rather than co-operative, and the game of nations becomes too expensive and too dangerous to play. How much longer can nations spend over half their wealth and production for the weapons of war? What is the point of wars in which everyone loses? Why wage a war in which no one survives? Can the authority of nations be based on *dharma* rather than on *danda* (coercive power)? India has raised such questions, and she has refused to enter into the cold war. She has chosen an international policy of nonalignment. This is an expression of a universal humanism or a human Catholicism, which has been at work in India for many hundreds of years. India out of her Hindu tradition may yet lead the nations of the world into a new form of nationalism, which is more humanistic than nationalistic. Hinduism speaks for humanity against the nation. Mankind awaits the implementation of the ancient Vedic admonition:

One and the same be your resolve, and be your minds of one accord.
United by the thought of all that all may happily agree.[43]

Hinduism in general also recoils from the purely legal approach. The concept of the golden age in Hinduism is one in which everyone performs his or her duty, so that everyone's rights are simultaneously honoured. Human rights thus are our rights as human beings. This ties into another dimension of *dharma* which equates right with rights, and sees no need for a positivistic affirmation, an attitude which according to Troy Wilson Organ is quite consistent with democracy with its emphasis on rights:

Two aspects of Hinduism may be mentioned as relevant to the democratic experience. One is the doctrine of *dharma*. The possibility of organizing a state composed of people for whom duty is the way things are done rather than an obligation one assumes under coercion is very appealing. The Hindu does his *dharma* not because he is forced to, not because he is afraid not to, not because he enjoys it, but because one's *dharma* is just what one does. The notion of not doing one's *dharma* is almost incomprehensible to the Hindu. *Dharma*-motivated people ought to make good citizens in a democracy. The other aspect of

Hinduism, which is important for democracy in India and in the world, is what may be called humanism.[44]

As for the *mokṣa* or religious orientation, Troy Wilson Organ once again highlights the fact that humanism suffices for Hinduism. Hence the title of his book: *The Hindu Quest For The Perfection Of Man*, from which we cite:

The Perfected Man is the Universal Man. Individuality is not lost but is elevated and dignified as each man mirrors the Ideal Man according to his own talents. Both the Man and all men participate in the goal of the perfecting process; thus catholicity is manifested idealistically and pluralistically. Hinduism so conceived is *Visvajanina*, a catholic religion. The *Bhagavad Gita*, the one scripture common to all Hindus, is sometimes referred to as 'the gospel of humanity'. Rabindranath Tagore was characterized by Nehru as 'the great humanist of India'. A fine Baul song celebrates the glories of man, and sets the theme for this final chapter:

> Man, man, everyone speaks of man!
> What is man?
> Man is health, man is life, man is the jewel of the Heart;
> Very few on earth know the truth of Man.
> Man knows a love, which other creatures know not,
> Man's love helps him to know the Real Man,
> Thus man knows Man;
> The strength of man-in-Man is understood by man alone.

Troy Wilson Organ then proceeds to point out how Vedic thought becomes progressively anthropocentric. While the Vedic hymns treat of the gods and the *Brāhmaṇa* texts deal with ritual, the focus of the Upaniṣads is increasingly the human being. This then becomes a constant feature of Hindu thought. In the *Mahābhārata* it is disclosed as the truth of truths by Bhīṣma, as the supreme secret doctrine: 'This is the secret and supreme doctrine I announce to you. There is nothing in the universe higher than man.' In the same spirit Tulsīdās declares in the *Rāmcaritamānas*: 'know that devotee of Rāma to be greater than Rāma', while Caṇḍīdāsa, another famous medieval poet declares: 'Listen, brother man; the truth of man is the highest truth, there is no truth above it.'[45]

After all, it is morality which sets human beings apart anyway, according to the popular Hindu view.

IV

The point is not without contemporary significance. The central consideration one must take into account here is the fact that although the

'Indian constitution lists an impressive series of "fundamental rights" . . . it does not ground them in anything, whether in individual human nature, the requirements of human community, or the creative intention of God. What can be created by legislative fiat can be altered or abrogated in the same way.'[46] The practical significance of this observation is illustrated by P.V. Kane's observation that so far as the Indian Constitution is concerned,

> from 1950 there have been ten amendments [this was written in 1962] while in the USA there have been only 22 amendments during a period of about 170 years. The very first amendment was made within less than a year and a half from the day the Constitution came into force. It affected about a dozen Articles, among which there were three Articles dealing with fundamental rights, viz., 15, 19, 31. One fails to understand the meaning of the words 'fundamental rights' in a Constitution which took over two years of deliberations, if they could be changed within [*sic*] a year and a half.[47]

Professor J.B. Carman observes very pertinently, while assessing Professor P.V. Kane's negative verdict:

> It has been pointed out in another critical analysis of these fundamental rights that the Indian equivalent of 'due process' in American law is legislative enactment. There is therefore no explicit appeal to that which is right (*ius*) beyond the letter of the enacted law (*lex*). This is a point that Professor Kane does not make, but it is not very far away from his major concern, that the constitution does not recognize the fundamental *dharma* affirmed by the Hindu tradition and sets no spiritual obligation for the state itself or for the people.[48]

He is also quite correct in his observation that 'this is a point on which scholars of the Hindu tradition, both inside and outside it, are likely to agree, even if they have difficulty in agreeing on the content of *dharma*'.[49]

Those who have pursued this line of thought, however, have tended to show a striking tendency in the present context towards understanding *dharma* in the sense of duty. One may give the pride of place here to Mahatma Gandhi (1869–1948) who declared, when asked what he thought of the Universal Declaration of Human Rights, before it was adopted in 1948:

> I learnt from my illiterate but wise mother that all rights to be deserved and preserved came from duty well done. Thus, the very right to live accrues to us only when we do the duty of citizenship of the world. From this one fundamental statement, perhaps it is easy enough to define the duties of Man and Woman and correlate every right to some corresponding duty to be first performed.[50]

We found that although human rights can be connected with each of the four components of the Hindu doctrine of *puruṣārtha-catuṣṭaya* or *catur-varga* (the doctrine of the four ends of life), it is arguably the dimension of*dharma* or morality which seems to provide the most secure anchor for it. The word is usually understood in its sense of duty when so employed. Elsewhere also Gandhi remarks on the 'validity only of those rights which were directly derived from duty well performed'.[51] His political heir, Pandit Nehru, lamented, while delivering the Azad Memorial Lectures on 'India Today and Tomorrow' in 1959:

> All of us now talk of and demand rights and privileges, but the teaching of the old *dharma* was about duties and obligations. Rights follow duties discharged.[52]

The pre-eminent modern scholar of classic Hindu law, Professor P.V. Kane, shared this sense of grievance and articulated it at some length. He remarked that 'the Constitution makes a complete break with our traditional ideas. Dharmasūtras and smṛtis begin with the dharmas (duties) of the people (varṇas and āśramas)'.[53] He goes on to cite Pandit Nehru as noted above, and after pointing out that according to him 'rights follow duties discharged' he adds: 'unfortunately this thought finds no place in the Constitution'.[54] It is significant, though, that when he actually addresses what kinds of *dharma* should be invoked in the context of the Constitution, he turns not to *varṇāśrama*, but *sādhāraṇa dharmas*, or duties common to all:

> It is remarkable that the directive principles of state policy mostly contain provisions on the economic system for raising people's standard of living (Art. 43, 47, &c.), i.e. it lays emphasis only on the material things for the people. It seems to be assumed that if material prosperity or benefits are assured for, then there is nothing more to be done by the State. The present author feels that the Directive Principles should also have put equal or greater emphasis on moral or spiritual values and should have called upon the State to promote among the people high moral standards, self-discipline, co-operation, sense of responsibility, kindliness, high endeavor. Man is a many-sided being. The satisfaction of mere physical needs is not enough. Man has intellectual, spiritual, cultural and social aspirations also. The socio-economic pattern for the future must be based on the foundation of the best part of our traditions, the rule of dharma, the duties common to all as declared by Manu X. 63 and Yāj. I. 122. A secular state should not and does not mean a godless state or a state that has nothing to do with moral and spiritual values.[55]

One way to take this comment is to look upon it 'as the overly idealistic and impractical reflection of a retired professor—Kane was then eighty-two',[56] as J.B. Carman suggests. But he also hints that P.V. Kane may be expressing a concern here with the fact that the Constitution does not appeal to anything beyond the letter of the law, that this is a shortcoming and that it could perhaps be rectified by an appeal to *dharma*, not to the *dharma* specific to the stations and stages of life, but to the *dharma* which consisted of 'duties common to all'.

What is implicit in Kane is made explicit by R.C. Pandeya, who 'stresses that for the Indians all rights are derived from duties', and thus suggests that 'the first principle of human rights is buried in Article 29 of the Universal Declaration of Human Rights: 'Everyone has duties to the community in which alone the free and full development of his personality is possible'.[57] This shift in emphasis from the individual to communal dimension of *dharma* is to be welcomed and constitutes a major transformation in Hinduism wrought by Mahatma Gandhi through precept and practice. Nevertheless, it also poses a difficulty in the present context. To the extent rights are made dependent on duties, they remain vulnerable to abridgement. It could be argued that rights represent aspirations, which may never be fully achieved. Our point is that if they are not considered inalienable, they become vulnerable to abridgement both in principle and in practice. One must distinguish here between the principle and practical promise of rights. Our fear is that they become liable to being compromised even in principle, if linked to duties as a matter of principle. Howsoever wholesome this connection might seem on the face of it, nevertheless, it seems desirable that rights must have more than merely a reciprocal existence and that they must possess a moral location where they could continue to reside despite any breach in theory or practice. Our objection is that morally locating them in duties leaves them vulnerable in the very manner from which we wish to protect them most. This point may be strengthened with the help of a contemporary example. An amendment was introduced in the Indian Constitution during Mrs Indira Gandhi's Emergency as Article 51-A detailing the duties of Indian citizens. While it is tempting to think that this could be an attempt to ground the Constitution in something beyond it, like *dharma*, the facts indicate otherwise. During this Emergency, many of the fundamental rights were suspended and it could be argued persuasively that the intention here was to make people more duty oriented so that they become *less* assertive of rights, many of which were suspended during the Emergency. If this was indeed the reason, the insertion of the section on duties was more than just a political act, it might well have constituted a profound attempt at cultural and even religious manipulation, which had gone unnoticed and remains undetected.

Once it is conceded that human rights, in the Hindu context, should be grounded in morality and not left free-floating as it were, the next question which arises is: should they be tied to a specific moral value or be left to free-associate, as it were, with the whole range of moral values in Hinduism? Our reluctance to tie them with duty as such suggests the need to be more specific in this respect. At this point the suggestion could be made, on the basis of the following passage in the *Bṛhadāraṇyaka Upaniṣad* (I.4.14) that human rights could be tied to the ultimate reality or truth, that is, *satyam*, with justice as the vital link between the two:

> Verily that which is justice (*dharma*) is truth (*satyam*). Therefore they say of a man who speaks the truth, he speaks justice or of a man who speaks justice, that he speaks the truth. Verily, both these are the same.[58]

This thread, while it is being relinquished here, will be picked up in a later chapter.

Conclusion

Hindu axiology has been closely associated with the fourfold grid of the *puruṣārtha*s. In this chapter we discovered that the various connections which can and indeed have been made, both in terms of Indian and Western thought, between human rights and values in each of the quadrants below.

Dharma	*Artha*
Kāma	*Mokṣa*

After an analysis of the connections which can be forged between human rights and each of the values, it was felt that *dharma* or morality provides them with the safest anchor in Hinduism, when the term is understood to represent the category of *sādhāraṇa dharma* or *sāmānya dharma*.

This conclusion, however, is open to some criticisms which must be met before it can be accepted. It could be argued that such a conclusion relies excessively on the fourfold division of the goals of human endeavour known as the *puruṣārtha*s. According to this view such a classification lends a certain neatness to the argument but at the cost of oversimplification. There is considerable merit in this criticism and it could be plausibly maintained that the fourfold classification is an attempt to reduce the teeming plurality of human aspirations to manageable proportions. It could even be urged that the number four here is merely a numerical code for many and further that this logic may apply not only to the doctrine of four *puruṣārtha*s but also to the doctrine of four *varṇas* (or classes); four *āśrama*s (or stages of life); and four *yuga*s (or ages). Thus these expressions could be read as alluding to many classes, many periods of life, and multiple divisions of time. The fact that the expression *nānāvarṇa* also appears in Hindu literature along with *caturvarṇa* lends further credence to this view. The conclusion is also capable of being questioned from another perspective as well. One could ask 'whether such distinctions are really productive in view of the more integrated approach taken by Hindu philosophy and the conceptual categories themselves'. According to this view the categorization of human endeavour into *dharma*, *artha*, *kāma*, and *mokṣa* is no doubt a feature of Hindu axiology but

> This categorisation does overlook the fact that there are not such clear divisions in Hindu thought or, rather, that these divisions exist in the Hindu mind and the interpretations of scholars, but there is more to be said about the interrelationship of those four categories. The problem that is not discussed, whereas it should at least be raised, is that in Hindu thought of all orientations and descriptions, *dharma* is more or less explicitly seen as a super-category comprising all four elements. Indeed this term has many meanings. All the aims of human life are linked to *dharma* as the central cultural expectation that everyone and everything should be conducive to maintenance of a higher order, maybe the Hindu 'rule of law', but certainly not a modern human rights agenda.[59]

These criticisms are helpful as warnings against an over-reliance on the fourfold classification but it is possible to maintain that the significance of these criticisms in terms of the main argument is rather limited for the following reason. The basic point that the concept of human rights can be related to the concept of human aspirations in Hinduism remains unscathed. What is at issue is the level of categorization. When looked at in this way the criticisms actually end up by strengthening the conclusion. When it is argued that human ends may be more than just four, or rather many, the justification for human rights can similarly be broadened in line with the recognition of their plurality. For instance, the category of *artha* alone can include the case for both kinds of human rights—the political-civil and the socio-economic. Similarly, the category of *kāma* can cover reproductive as well as cultural rights. Thus the link between human rights and the doctrine of human aspirations in Hinduism is not snapped, rather it is so close that it can stretch or contract as the terms of reference are modified. Telling evidence in favour of this comes from the suggestion that the primary focus on *dharma* should not be allowed to be obscured by other *puruṣārtha*s. It has already been pointed out that the justification for human rights in Hindu terms is most solidly forthcoming from *dharma* itself.

A more substantial critique has to do with the understanding of *dharma* as 'an idealistically self-controlled order . . . grounded in the individual and the local, not in some national or even international sphere [as the] primary locus for the production of human rights principles in the Hindu context'.[60] The concept of *dharma* includes this view but is not confined to it or confined by it, as will be demonstrated amply in subsequent chapters, just as human rights discourse cannot be confined to or confined by one dimension of it.[61]

Derogability of Human Rights

Current political and legal discourse is so replete with appeals to human rights as to leave the impression that human rights discourse does not provide for their derogation in any context. This may indeed be true in the sense that human rights represent norms which we would ideally never like to see compromised. A reading of the 1948 Universal Declaration of Human Rights reinforces such an impression. However, the Declaration receives its concrete form in the Covenants which were adopted by the various nation states comprising the UNO. These documents yield to realism in recognizing that under certain conditions it may be permissible not to hold the states accountable to the ideal level of performance. In other words, human rights could be considered derogable under certain circumstances.

This is an issue which must now be faced squarely for both practical and theoretical reasons, specially as two relatively recent events, one more recent than the other, serve to highlight such vulnerability of human rights discourse. The first of these is the Emergency imposed by Mrs Indira Gandhi, as India's Prime Minister, in 1975 and the second is the war against terrorism on which the USA has embarked after 11 September 2001. The fact that India and the USA constitute the largest democracies in the world may help exalt them to the status of paradigm cases, which actually cuts to the heart of the matter. Human rights first emerged as citizens rights against the power of the state, but what if the state itself feels threatened either through actual or perceived danger to its existence, by internal rebellion as was the case with the Emergency imposed by Mrs Gandhi, or by external terror as is the case with the war against terrorism currently being conducted by the USA? The immediate effect in both the cases was the curtailment of citizens' rights and, therefore, human rights. This happened quite explicitly during the Emergency in India from June 1975 to March 1977,[62] and also seems to be a likely fallout of the current war on terrorism in the USA, given the regnant mood that 'national security trumps human rights'.[63] What is one to make of such developments as they seem to strike at the very basis of human rights?

What makes the issue particularly important is that it is not an unanticipated one. Both the Covenants referred to in the earlier part of this chapter provide for derogations to be made in times of emergency, just as all constitutions provide for the suspension of rights in the case of internal rebellion and external aggression. In such a context it seems only fair to ask: if Hinduism could provide bases for human rights, does it also provide for their derogation?

Hindu ethics and jurisprudence do indeed possess a category which broadly conforms to that of derogability, namely, that of *āpad-dharma* or simply *āpat*. J. Duncan M. Derrett explains:

> An entire chapter of the *śāstra* (supposedly obsolete today—or perhaps, on the contrary, the only justification in the eyes of the orthodox for their own anomalous proceedings) is devoted to *āpat*, 'time of distress'. It throws light on the character of the injunctions themselves. This is a law of exceptional circumstances. The theory was that restrictions on powers and the seriousness of social misconduct and crimes were automatically modified in a time of distress. This usually meant public distress, such as invasions by the enemy, drought, famine, plague and the like. In such circumstances marriages otherwise improper could be entered into, improper adoptions could be performed and, most striking of all, the normal precaution against crime and sin might be relaxed.[64]

He goes on to say:

> Moreover, as we see from Manu XI, 16-18, which enables a Brahman to steal from a person of lower caste enough to stay his hunger if he has not eaten in three days, even a personal distress, not really qualifying for the relaxations appropriate to *āpad,* which should be a general misfortune, may serve to vary the normal rigour of the law. It must therefore be borne in mind that the interpretation of the law was never complete unless the surrounding circumstances of the alleged offender had been taken into account. The full rigour of the *śāstra* unmodified by *āpad-dharma* would seem to most Hindus of today unreasonable, though the courts have never applied that system of modification consciously.[65]

A typical example of its application would be the following: a member of a 'caste' is normally expected to follow one's own allotted vocation, but in a time of crisis (*āpad-dharma*) one may adopt the mode of living of another, usually lower caste. Certain rules are meant to be observed sometimes even in the process of such 'derogation' but the main point should be obvious. By analogy then one could argue that *āpad-dharma* conforms in its essentials to the concept of derogability. Nevertheless there is need to proceed with caution.

The discussion of *āpad-dharma* in Hindu jurisprudence typically proceeds in the context of caste, or what is called *varṇa-dharma*. The category of *varṇa-dharma*, however, thus typically applies to all the four *varṇas*: those of priest (*brāhmaṇa*); warrior (*kṣatriya*); agriculturalist and trader (*vaiśya*); and labourer or servant (*śūdra*); while that of derogability applies to the state. The general treatment of *āpad-dharma* in Hindu literature thus suffers from overdetermination in the present context. The proper parallel here, it seems, is not provided by the *varṇa* system in general but the category of what is called *rāja-dharma* or duties of the king in terms of Hindu taxonomy, a category which properly constitutes a subject of *kṣātra-dharma*. So the question one now needs to ask is: what do Hindu texts say about the role of *āpad-dharma* in the context of *rāja-dharma* rather than in the context of *varṇa-dharma*?

It is interesting then that the category of *āpad-dharma* is not applied to *rāja-dharma* as such. It is rather the duty of the king to assist people in times of crisis. Thus if the *varṇas* cannot follow their vocations, it is the duty of the king to maintain those *brāhmaṇas*, *kṣatriyas*, *vaiśyas*, and *śūdras* who could not maintain themselves.[66] This is not to say that the texts take a Pollyannaish view of politics, for it is interesting in this context that the Twelfth Book of the *Mahābhārata* deals simultaneously with *rāja-dharma* and *āpad-dharma*.[67] The possibility that a dynasty may be threatened is visualized. Thus 'when the survival of a dynasty is threatened, actions which would otherwise be unrighteous (*adharma*) could be righteous (*dharma*) and vice versa'.[68] It is perhaps also instructive that 'this reversal is compared to the dispensation from dietary laws during famine, such as approval of Viśvāmitra's stealing dogmeat [*sic*] from an untouchable'.[69] The typical example is provided by the possibility that 'a king may ruin his enemy's state by the killing of people and destruction of roads and mines . . .'

This provision however refers to the king's behaviour towards the subjects of *another* kingdom. The proper example to consider then would be the steps the king could take in the event of a crisis in his own kingdom, for example, a financial crisis. P.V. Kane notes that

> Kauṭ (V.2), Manu (X.118), Śānti 87, Śukra IV.2.9-10 permit the king to take even one-third or one-fourth part of the crops in time of distress (*āpad*). It has however to be noted that Kauṭilya requires the king to beg (*yāceta*) of the people for this heavy taxation, he employs the word (*praṇaya*) request for such demands, such taxation was not to be levied from inferior lands, and he expressly says that such

a demand for excessive taxation is to be made only once and not twice in the same distress. Śānti (87.26-33) contains a specimen of a long address to be given to the people when a king demands higher taxation in danger (such as 'if the enemy invades you, you will lose all including your wives, the enemy will not restore to you what he robs you of' &c). The word 'praṇaya' occurs in this sense in the Junagadh Inscription of Rudradāman (E. I. vol. VIII. p. 36 II 15-16).[70]

These measures, though burdensome, are hardly violative of the rights of the citizens. A *sūtra* of Pāṇini (VI.3.10) also refers to certain specific taxes.

These appear to have been customary levies imposed by the king on special occasions to meet urgent expenditures. Some of these taxes in modern terms are *pāg* (per head), *tāg* (per adult of poll tax), *hār* (per plough), etc. It may be noted that Pāṇini does not name them by the usual word *kara* for 'tax', but they are known by the more emphatic word, *kāra*. Pāṇini mentions a special class of officers named *Kāra-kara* (III.2.21), who it appears, were entrusted with the raising of these taxes. The *Samañña-phala Sutta* mentions an officer called *Kāra-karaka* (II.38).[71]

A provision in the *Arthaśāstra* of Kauṭilya (V.2) does allow seizure of wealth from seditious or irreligious elements in a crisis, which is violative of human rights. It should however be set alongside the fact that the *Yājñavalkya-smṛti* (II.192) requires the king to respect the usages of heretical sects presumably in normal times,[72] although sometimes this instruction is restricted to sects not opposed to the Vedas.[73] These examples serve to illustrate the operation of the principle of *āpād-dharma* in the context of *rāja-dharma*.

The concept of *āpad-dharma* in the context of *rāja-dharma* is also conceptually matched by the *āpad-dharma* as it applies to *prajā-dharma*, or the rights and duties of the citizens. The *Mahābhārata* (*Anuśāsanaparva* 61.32-33) exhorts the people to 'gird themselves up and kill a cruel king, who does not protect his subjects, who extracts taxes and simply robs them of their wealth . . .'[74] Provisions in *Śānti-parva* (92.6), *Manu* (VII.27.34), and *Yājñavalkya* (I.356) are less drastic and 'appear to justify at least deposing a king if not tyrannicide'.[75] A notch less drastic is just driving the king away. *Taittirīya Saṁhitā* (II.3.I) provides early evidence of kings being driven away and in fact the 'Sautrāmaṇi *iṣṭi* is prescribed as a rite for a king to regain a kingdom from which he has been driven away'.[76]

If for some reason the king proved irremovable, the subjects could simply leave his kingdom, following the line of least resistance. In fact the 'most potent independent action of the people . . . was emigration to another kingdom'.[77] Thus in 'the fifth century AD a whole silk-weavers' guild moved from a town in Lāṭa (southern Gujarat) to Daśapur (modern Mandasor) in Mālvā (Madhya Pradesh)'.[78] In one instance from south India under the Hoysalas (c. twelfth and thirteenth centuries), 'the government yielded in its tax demands, and the people returned'.[79]

Hindu jurisprudence thus provides for the exceptional case in the context of the caste duties; the duties of the king towards the subjects and of the subjects towards the king in a way, comparable to that of derogation in the context of human rights—and may therefore be judged hospitable to such a concept.

Notes

1. David P. Forsythe, *Human Rights and World Politics*, Lincoln: University of Nebraska Press, 1983, p. 3.
2. Robert Traer, *Faith in Human Rights*, Washington D.C.: Georgetown University Press, 1991, p. 11, note 7.
3. *The International Bill of Human Rights*, New York: United Nations, 1993, p. 1.
4. James W. Nickel, *Making Sense of Human Rights: Philosophical Reflections on the Universal Declaration of Human Rights*, Berkeley: University of California Press, 1987, p. xi.
5. Robert Traer, op. cit., p. 15, note 58: 'For instance, Amnesty International, which today provides invaluable advocacy in defence of the human rights of prisoners of conscience, was founded by Peter Berenson. Why did he do it? "We know from things he's said that Eleanor Roosevelt and Martin Luther King were influences, yet in his own chemistry there was his Jewish background, the bell of the Holocaust still tolling, and his Catholic belief, shaped in part by the peasant Pope, John XXIII, who stripped layers off an ossified, even corrupt church and revealed the freshness of the liberating teaching of Jesus of Nazareth beneath", Jonathan Power, *Against Oblivion: Amnesty International's Fight For Human Rights, 218.*'
6. Louis Henkin, 'Rights: American and Human', *Columbia Law Review* 79:3:405, April 1975, emphasis added.
7. Joseph Runzo, *Global Philosophy of Religions: A Short Introduction*, Oxford: One World, 2001, pp. 187–8.
8. Ibid., p. 188.
9. Ibid.
10. Ibid.
11. Ibid., pp. 188–9.
12. Ellen Frankel Paul et al. (eds), *Human Rights*, Oxford: Basil Blackwell, 1986, p. 11.
13. Allan Gibbard, 'Utilitarianism and Human Rights' in op. cit. (eds) Ellen Frankel Paul et al., p. 92.

14. M. Hiriyanna, *Indian Conception of Values*, Mysore: Kavyalaya Publishers, 1975, p. 11.
15. Ibid.
16. Robert Traer, op. cit., pp. 10–11
17. Cited in Robert Traer, op. cit., p. 163.
18. Wm. Theodore de Bary and Tu Weiming (eds), *Confucianism and Human Rights*, New York: Columbia University Press, 1998, p. xiii.
19. See Abudallahi Ahmed An-Na'im, *Toward An Islamic Reformation: Civil Liberties, Human Rights and International Law*, Syracuse: Syracuse University Press, 1990.
20. Robert Traer, op. cit., passim.
21. Ninian Smart and Shivesh Thakur (eds), *Ethical and Political Dilemmas of Modern India*, New York: St. Martin's Press, 1993, p. xi.
22. The extent of which Hindu Law can be considered positivistic in a technical sense is a debatable point but the germ of the idea that the state can intervene to establish what we would now call a human rights regime over against anarchy is clearly present (see R.P. Kangle, *The Kauṭilīya Arthaśāstra*, Delhi: Motilal Banarsidass, 1988 (1965), Part III, p. 230; P.V. Kane, *History of Dharmaśāstra*, Poona: Bhandarkar Oriental Research Institute, 1973, Vol. III, p. 892; Ainslie T. Embree, ed., *The Hindu Tradition*, New York: Random House, 1972, Chapter V).
23. David R. Kinsley, *Hinduism: A Cultural Perspective*, second edition, Englewood Cliffs, NJ: Prentice Hall, 1993, p. 93.
24. Ibid.
25. Louis Renou, *The Nature of Hinduism*, tr. Patrick Evans, New York: Walker and Company, 1951, p. 106.
26. James Fishkin, 'Utilitarianism Versus Human Rights', in op. cit., (eds) Ellen Frankel Paul, et al., pp. 105–6.
27. T.M.P. Mahadevan, *Outlines of Hinduism*, Bombay: Chetana Limited, 1971, p. 67.
28. Ibid.
29. Hartmut Scharfe, *The State in Indian Tradition*, Leiden: E.J. Brill, 1989, p. 21.
30. Ibid., p. 22.
31. P.V. Kane, op. cit., Vol. III, p.9.
32. Harmut Scharfe, op. cit., p. 215. Also see A.L. Basham, *The Wonder That Was India*, New Delhi: Rupa & Co. 1999, p. 114.
33. R.C. Majumdar (ed.), *The Age of Imperial Unity*, Bombay: Bharatiya Vidya Bhavan. 1968, pp. 348--9.
34. Troy Wilson Organ, *The Hindu Quest For the Perfection of Man*, Athens, Ohio: Ohio University, 1970, p. 124.
35. M. Hiriyanna, *Outlines of Indian Philosophy*, London: George Allen & Unwin, 1932, p. 381.
36. M. Hiriyanna, *Essentials of Indian Philosophy*, London: George Allen & Unwin, 1949, pp. 24–5.

37. S.K. Ramachandra Rao, *Jīvanmukti in Advaita*, Madras: JBH Prakashana, 1979, pp. 49, 62.
38. T.M.P. Mahadevan, op. cit., p. 135, emphasis added.
39. Ibid., p. 69.
40. See A.L. Basham, op. cit., pp. 113, 137, 340.
41. P.V. Kane, op. cit., Vol. V, Part II, p. 1637.
42. Barbara Stoler Miller, *Yoga: Discipline of Freedom*, Berkeley: University of California Press, 1996, p. 53.
43. Troy Wilson Organ, *Hinduism: Its Historical Development*, Woodsbury, NY: Barron's Educational Series Inc., 1974, pp. 372–3.
44. Ibid., p. 372.
45. Troy Wilson Organ, *The Hindu Quest for the Perfection of Man*, pp. 333–4.
46. John B. Carman, 'Duties and Rights in Hindu Society', in *Human Rights and the World's Religions*, (ed.), Leroy S. Rouner, Notre Dame, Indiana: University of Notre Dame Press, 1988, p. 120.
47. Cited, ibid.
48. Ibid.
49. Ibid., p. 119.
50. See Robert Traer, op. cit., pp. 131–2.
51. M.K. Gandhi, *Hindu Dharma*, Ahmedabad: Navajivan Publishing House, 1958, p. 351.
52. Cited by John B. Carman, op. cit., p. 119.
53. P.V. Kane, op. cit., Vol. V, Part II, p. 1664.
54. Ibid.
55. Ibid,. pp. 1669–70.
56. John B. Carman, op. cit., p. 120.
57. Robert Traer, op. cit., p. 132. See R.C. Pandeya, 'Human Rights: An Indian Perspective', in*Philosophical Foundations of Human Rights*, Paris: UNESCO, 1986.
58. S. Radhakrishnan, *The Principal Upaniṣads*, Atlantic Highlands, NJ: Humanities Press, 1992, p. 170.
59. Anonymous referee's remarks.
60. Ibid.
61. See Michael Ignatieff, *The Rights Revolution*, Toronto: Canadian Broadcasting Corporation, 2000.
62. Girilal Jain, *The Hindu Phenomenon*, New Delhi: USPBD Publishers Distributors Ltd., 1994, p. 142. Also see p. 101.
63. Michael Ignatieff, 'Is the Human Rights Era Ending?', *The New York Times*, 5 February 2002, p. A29.
64. J. Duncan M. Derrett, *Religion, Law and State in India*, New York: The Free Press, 1968, pp. 95–6.
65. Ibid., p. 96.
66. P.V. Kane, op. cit., Vol. III, p. 59.
67. Hartmut Scharfe, op. cit., p. 18.

68. Ibid., pp. 211–12.
69. Ibid., p. 211, note 60; see *Mahābhārata* XII. 139.36ff.
70. Ibid., p. 211.
71. V.S. Agrawala, *India as Known to Pāṇini*, Varanasi: Prithvi Prakashan, 1963, pp. 416–17.
72. P.V. Kane, op. cit., Vol. III, p. 158.
73. Ibid., p. 104.
74. Ibid., p. 26.
75. Ibid.
76. Ibid.
77. Hartmut Scharfe, op. cit., p. 68.
78. Ibid., p. 171.
79. Ibid., p. 171, note 406.

CHAPTER 2

Hinduism and Human Rights Discourse

It was the thesis of the previous chapter that conceptions of human rights can be recognized within Hinduism, once the categories which correspond to them in the Hindu tradition are identified. One must now contend with the fact that human rights discourse in the West is neither monolithic nor static. The introduction of this consideration into the discussion complicates matters. The argument evolved in the previous chapter may be sound so far as it goes but it no longer suffices, for the fact that human rights discourse is neither monolithic nor static raises the following question: does the Hindu tradition also possess the resources to interact with these diverse and evolving patterns of human rights discourse?

Such a question needs to be understood less ambiguously before it can be answered adequately. When one moves forward from a simple discussion of human rights as such to engage the complexities which surround the discourse, at least three such vectors of engagement come into clear view.

I

The first consists of the consideration that the Universal Declaration of Human Rights embodies two distinct traditions. As Mary Ann Glendon points out, the Universal Declaration of Human Rights did not suddenly drop from heaven engraved on tablets but rather was a milestone on a path on which humanity had already been travelling for at least the past few centuries.

> The Declaration marked a new chapter in a history that began with the great charters of humanity's first rights movements in the seventeenth and eighteenth centuries. The British Bill of Rights of 1689, the U.S. Declaration of Independence of 1776, and the French Declaration of the Rights of Man and Citizen of

1789 were born out of struggles to overthrow autocratic rule and to establish governments based on the consent of the governed. They proclaimed that all men were born free and equal and that the purpose of government was to protect man's natural liberties. They gave rise to the modern language of rights.[1]

It is important to refer to this historical background of the Universal Declaration of Human Rights because it helps explain a special feature of the modern language of human rights.

From the outset, that language branched into two dialects. One, influenced by continental European thinkers, especially Rousseau, had more room for equality and 'fraternity' and tempered rights with duties and limits. It cast the state in a positive light as guarantor of rights and protector of the needy. Charters in this tradition—the French constitutions of the 1790s, the Prussian General Code of 1794, and the Norwegian Constitution of 1815—combined political and civil rights with public obligations to provide relief for the poor. In the late nineteenth and early twentieth centuries, as continental European Socialist and Christian Democratic parties reacted to the harsh effects of industrialization, these paternalistic principles evolved into social and economic rights.[2]

On the other hand,

The Anglo-American dialect of rights language emphasized individual liberty and initiative more than equality or social solidarity and was infused with a greater mistrust of government. The differences between the two traditions were mainly of degree and emphasis but their spirit penetrated every corner of their respective societies.[3]

The language of human right continued to reflect these two dialects.

When Latin American countries achieved independence in the nineteenth century, these two strains began to converge. Most of the new nations retained their continental European-style legal systems but adopted constitutions modeled on that of the United States, supplementing them with protections for workers and the poor. The Soviet Union's constitutions took a different path, subordinating the individual to the state, exalting equality over freedom, and emphasizing social and economic rights over political and civil liberty.[4]

Mary Ann Glendon situates the Universal Declaration of Human Rights in this context as follows:

In 1948 the framers of the Universal Declaration achieved a distinctive synthesis of previous thinking about rights and duties. After canvassing sources from North and South, East and West, they believed they had found a core principle so basic that no nation would wish openly to disavow them. They wove those principles into a unified document that quickly displaced all antecedents as the principal model for the rights instruments in force in the world today.[5]

The complexity introduced into human rights discourse, by the recognition of the presence of these two elements within it, did not come to an end with their synchronic incorporation in the Universal Declaration of Human Rights. Modern human rights discourse also recognizes their dynamic character by referring to these two kinds of rights as first-generation and second-generation human rights. As Paul Gordon Lauren notes:

> Reform liberalism claimed that the rights of men and women could be obtained best by working to protect personal life, liberty, equality and ownership of property by individuals through the existing political process. Marx and his followers, on the other hand, emphasized the group rather than the individual. They argued that the most important human rights were not those of a civil or political nature, hopelessly individualistic, and part of 'bourgeois democracy,' but rather those that focused on real human social and economic needs and that these rights could be secured only through revolution. Such different visions between those first-generation and political rights initially arising out of the eighteenth century and those second-generation social and economic rights emerging from the nineteenth century, and the often sharply different methods to achieve them, would play powerful roles in shaping the evolution of international human rights until our own day.[6]

The introduction of this dynamic element enables one to identify a second vector of complexity in human rights discourse, introduced by the identification of various generations of human rights over and above the idea of an inner dialectical variation in the language of modern human rights. Before turning to a consideration of the conceptualizations of generations of human rights, however, it might be of interest to examine the dialectical variation in the modern human rights discourse from a Hindu perspective, specially as articulated in terms of duties and rights. It is clear that from a Hindu perspective the word *dharma* could be used in both the contexts, both at the level of the individual and the community. It is well known that the word *dharma* is used to refer to duties or moral obligations. Thus it is the *dharma* of the *kṣatriya*, or ruler, to protect.[7] It is also the *dharma* of the *kṣatriya* to subsist through agriculture in a time of crisis, but engaging in agriculture is the duty of a *vaiśya*. Hence in such a context, to say that it is the *dharma* of a *kṣatriya* to engage in agriculture in a time of crisis, is tantamount to saying that the *kṣatriya* enjoys this 'right' in such troubled times. Similarly, at a collective level, it is the duty of the king to provide protection to workers, widows, the poor, and the like. That is to say, it is his *dharma*. But it is also stated that should the king not succeed in protecting the people, he has to compensate the victim of a robbery by right (*dharmeṇa*). It is also worth mentioning, as an additional point, that the Hindu perspective would tend to accord primacy to the dialect of duty.

K.B. Panda notes that, from a Hindu point of view, as mentioned earlier, Article 27 of the Universal Declaration of Human Rights (according to which 'everyone has duties to the community'), should have been placed towards the beginning rather than the end of the Universal Declaration of Human Rights. The following remark of Mary Ann Glendon becomes highly significant in this context:

> The human rights Commission's desire for consistency of style—specifically, to use the formulas 'Everyone has the right to . . .' or 'Everyone is entitled to . . .'—ruled out a common alternative approach to this group of issues: At the national level, welfare principles are sometimes framed as obligations of society and the state rather than entitlements of individuals. With hindsight, it is perhaps regrettable that the framers, in dealing with these provisions, did not adopt the obligation model. To couch the social security and welfare principles in terms of common responsibility might have resonated better than rights in most of the world's cultures and would still have left room for experiments with different mixes of private and public approaches.[8]

Another point is perhaps even more significant. It is often claimed that Hindu ethical thought is duty-oriented rather than rights-oriented. It has even been claimed, perhaps as an extreme formulation of this view, that Hindus had no conception of rights, a view K.B. Panda challenges head on when he remarks that while Hindu texts are

> replete with one's duties rather than rights, from this let no one misunderstand that Hindu society did not recognise any rights. For instance, in a joint family, one has a right to hold certain property, and if the husband has the right over the wife's person and property, yet the wife has her absolute right over her *stridhan* property.[9]

This impression that Hinduism fights shy of a discussion of rights has elements of truth in it but when Hinduism is analytically mined further, it seems capable of providing a rich vein in this respect. Such an analysis would proceed by drawing three kinds of distinctions: (1) a distinction between individual rights and group rights, (2) a distinction between individual duties and group duties, and (3) a distinction between our duties to ourselves—at both the individual and group level—and a similar distinction between our rights in relation to others and their rights in relation to ours. Finally, one needs to stir this soup with the realization that rights and duties are often correlational. As this correlationality of rights and duties is a subject of much discussion and exploration in ethical discourse, it might be helpful to state the exact nuance of the relationship one has in mind here. It consists of the fact that someone's right tends to be someone else's duty. Hence it is my right to be protected and it is the duty of the state to protect me, or it is the right of the child to be taken care of and the duty of the parents to provide such care. In other words, my duties are someone else's rights and vice versa.

In such a context the statement that Hinduism focuses more on duties rather than rights takes on a new complexion, for it can be reformulated as follows: *Hinduism tends to accord greater recognition to the rights that others have in relation to us as compared to the rights we have in relation to them.* Thus the issue morphs from being one of rights versus duties into one of the rights of others over us and our rights over them. But we will always be a singular right-bearing entity in relation to others and others will numerically always exceed us existentially as multiple right-bearing entities in relation to us. In this sense then the statement that Hinduism favours duty discourse over rights discourse could be seen as taking a patently existential situation and charging it with ethical meaning. Alternatively, it could be read as reflecting a preference for the group over the individual in a perhaps utilitarian way, as thereby the good of a larger number is secured. These views are being proposed to indicate how a Hindu perspective can enable one to incorporate new accents in the dialectical variation which characterizes modern human rights language.

II

One may now revert to the consideration of an earlier point to move ahead, in the spirit of taking one step backwards to march two steps forward. It was noted earlier how the two kinds of rights—individual rights along with civil and political rights, and group rights along with social and economic rights—may be viewed as composing two fundamental elements in the formulation of human rights, or, more dynamically, as two stages in the growth and development of the discourse on human rights. This latter point of view leads one to examine how Hindu thought may be related to the idea of generations of human rights within human rights discourse.

One way of making a friendly entrée into the discussion would be to begin with the recognition of the presence of group rights within Hinduism. Caste rights of course constitute the obvious example here but some less obvious examples are equally instructive. Under Hindu law, women as a group were only liable to half the punishment for the same crimes, just as old men and children as a group were exempted from culpability for crime on account of age. Thus not just caste but gender and age also provided the axes for group rights. From this perspective the development of the various generations of human rights could be viewed as a struggle on the part of human rights discourse in the West to break out of the conceptual shell of its obsessive concern with individual rights.

Nowhere are these difficulties more apparent than in the current discourse on human rights. On account of the individualistic starting point of modern human rights discourse, such discourse runs into difficulties as soon as it attempts to embrace first socio-cultural and then environmental concerns, which extend human rights discourse beyond the individual. This is not to say that such an attempt has not been made. The scheme of the three generations of human rights, even though the three generations are not always uniformly stated, constitutes precisely such an attempt. According to one version, civil and political rights constitute the first generation; social, cultural, and economic rights the second; and environmental and developmental rights the third.[10] This attempt to enlarge the circumference of human rights from its individualistic centre leads precisely to the kinds of difficulties one would expect on the basis of the foregoing analysis. John Witte Jr. draws attention to one such difficulty as follows:

> The simple state vs. individual dialectic of modern human rights theories leaves it to the state to protect rights of all sorts—'first generation' civil and political rights, 'second generation' social, cultural, and 'third generation' developmental rights. In reality, the state is not, and cannot be, so omnicompetent—as the recently failed experiments in socialism have vividly shown. A vast plurality of 'voluntary associations' or 'mediating structures' stands between the state and the individual, religious institutions prominently among them. Religious institutions, among others, play a vital role in the cultivation and realization of all rights, including religious rights. They create the conditions (if not the prototypes) for the realization of first generation civil and political rights. They provide a critical (and sometimes the principal) means to meet second-generation rights of education, health care, childcare, labour organizations, employment, and artistic opportunities, among others. Religious institutions offer some of the deepest insights into norms of creation, stewardship and servanthood that lie at the heart of third generation rights.[11]

Carol S. Robb similarly draws attention to another difficulty which has to do with the concept of group rights vis-à-vis individual rights, just as the earlier difficulty had to do with the state vis-à-vis the individual. She writes:

> It is common to speak of the development of arguments in the domain of human rights in terms of the first, second, and third generations of proposed rights. The first-generation rights are the civil and political rights, the protection against coercion. The second-generation rights are the economic, social, and cultural rights, or positive rights, which usually involve outlays or expenditures. The third-generation rights are group rights, which are hardly digestible in the United States legal tradition which is heavily rooted in the first generation. Group rights tend to be associated with claims of peoples in the two-thirds world, particularly indigenous peoples claiming rights to land and culture. Such rights are focused largely on a people's right to self-development, which involves both claims for the positive provision of certain goods and also restraints on the conduct of economic relations between poor and rich countries. The two Covenants of the United Nations Declaration seem generally to discuss and protect, separately and respectively, rights of the first and second generations. However, since both Covenants have articles promoting the inherent right of all people to enjoy and use fully and freely their natural wealth and resources, there already exists the basis for group rights, though this generation is still developing.[12]

The point then is that on account of the original individualistic orientation of human rights, extensions of it to cover society or social groups and the environment are not achieved without struggle.

One may now turn to the Hindu view which starts out not with the individual but from the cosmos. If the modern secular view takes the individual as the starting point and then expands beyond this point to embrace society and environment, the traditional Hindu view starts out from the cosmos and then zeroes in on the individual through the intervening layer of society. A movement of this kind is also not without its problems, for while this ensures that such a perspective is relatively more at ease in dealing with ecological and social and cultural rights and so on, it becomes a struggle to do full justice to the individual's rights, as *distinguished from duties*, in such a framework.[13]

Nevertheless, just as human rights discourse in the West has tried to overcome its individualistic orientation, by evolving the concept of different generations of rights, *dharmic* discourse in India is also trying to overcome the overshadowing of the individual by the collectivities which surround it and of his or her rights by an emphasis on duties, by reviving and moving the concept of *adhikāra* or entitlement into a moral and legal realm and then privileging it. In this respect

> The Indian constitution (which as a whole is termed '*Adhikāra-patra*') draws attention to what it calls 'Fundamental Rights', reinforcing the view of the progressive realisation for all citizens of something to which they are entitled. It was,

however, Gandhi's strong influence which led to the inclusion of special rights for the 'Harijans' and the extension of certain fundamental rights for all individuals, regardless of whether they are citizens of the nation or not. Several amendments have since been introduced or mooted to iron out certain deficiencies and inadequacies in the constitution on issues of rights and their implementation, or to curtail certain rights which the government (or rather elite) of the day felt were being misappropriated by one group or another.[14]

III

In extending the engagement of Hindu thought with human rights discourse beyond merely the Universal Declaration of Human Rights document we first took a closer look at the document itself, as woven out of two strands of human rights discourse and examined this aspect of it in a Hindu light. This provided one vector of extension for the discussion. A second vector was provided by taking a dynamic view of this distinction, which led to the identification of 'generations' of human rights and the assessment of their significance in a Hindu context. A third vector of further discussion is provided by our effort to answer the question: what forces propelled the human rights discourse in a direction which required the formulation of these new generations of human rights? We shall discover, in answering this question, that while the first two vectors involved the question of the existing and evolving *structure* of human rights, the third vector involves the question of their *scope*.

The point is best made by turning to the historical documents which launched human rights on their present course and noticing whom they excluded from their ambit. Thus the American documents excluded 'at least four categories of Americans: slaves, women, the unpropertied, and the indigenous peoples'.[15] Paul Gordon Lauren has pointed out how both George Washington and Thomas Jefferson owned slaves, how fugitive slaves could be returned to the owners and how the Congress was prohibited by the Constitution for twenty years from eliminating the slave trade. Similarly, women are not mentioned in the Constitution and as the qualifications for suffrage was a state subject women came to be denied the right for a century. The restriction on voting rights on the basis of age, race, and property meant that the unpropertied majority was excluded for a long time, while the general attitude towards the indigenous people offered little hope to them. Lauren pointedly notes that George Washington and Benjamin Franklin called them 'ignorant savages' and 'beasts' while Thomas Jefferson would pursue them to their 'extinction'.[16]

Even France, for all its revolutionary enthusiasm, had difficulty matching rhetoric with reality. Paul Gordon Lauren again notes that the equal rights granted to the blacks by the Declaration of the Rights of the Man and Citizen were rescinded within months; slavery was re-established soon thereafter in the colonies and the rights which were enjoyed by the people of France were never extended to the peoples in the French empire. Even in France a distinction was drawn between 'active' and 'passive' citizens and only those who passed a wealth test could be active citizens. Women were theoretically citizens but practically denied the rights of being one. Revolutionary leaders in both France and America 'understood that the extension of genuinely equal rights would entail vast social and political consequences that they were unwilling to accept'.[17]

In such a context, three major extensions in scope of human rights discourse in our own times are represented by (1) the International Convention on the Elimination of All Forms of Racial Discrimination (1966); (2) Convention on the Elimination of All Forms of Discrimination Against Women (1979); and (3) Convention on the Rights of the Child (1989).[18]

The significance of these developments tends to get obscured by a somewhat dull recitation of the titles of these documents. One needs to delve underneath to assess their significance. The abolition of racial discrimination may now sound like a cliché, but what an electrifying call it must have been—before it became a cliché—may be judged from the following words of Carlos Romulo, uttered at the first international conference of African and Asian Nations at Bandung in Indonesia in 1955.

> I have said that besides the issues of colonialism and political freedom, all of us here are concerned with the matter of racial equality. This is a touchstone, I think, for most of us assembled here and the people we represent. The systems and the manner of it have varied, but there has not been and there is not a Western colonial regime which has not imposed, to a greater or lesser degree, on the people it ruled the doctrine of their own racial inferiority. We have known, and some of us still know, the searing experience of being demeaned in our lands, of being systematically relegated to subject status not only politically and economically and militarily—but racially as well. Here was a stigma that could be applied to rich and poor alike, to prince and slave, bossman and workingman, landlord and peasant, scholar and ignoramus. To bolster his rule, to justify his own power to himself, the Western white man assumed that his superiority lay in his genes, in the colour of his skin. This made the lowest drunken sot superior in colonial society to the highest product of culture and scholarship and industry among subject people. . . . For many it has made the goal of regaining a status of simple manhood the be-all and end-all of a lifetime of devoted struggle and sacrifice.[19]

It is crucial to distinguish between casteism and racism in this context. Dr B.R. Ambedkar has convincingly demonstrated that casteism is not to be equated with racism and the attempt by Western scholars to establish such an equation only testifies to the strength of racism in the West.[20]

The incorporation of women's rights in the discourse on human rights has 'introduced unprecedented complexity in the theory and practice of human rights'. In this context a distinction must be drawn between a synchronic and a diachronic perspective on Hindu law in relation to women. The numerous legal disabilities from which Hindu women suffered in Hindu law have been widely documented, and the modern Indian state has been active in correcting these. A diachronic view of Hindu law in this respect generates the possibility that even traditional Hindu legal theory should not necessarily be viewed as opposed to the legal empowerment of women. Room for such a perspective is created by a consideration of the following facts. The foundational Hindu texts, the Vedas, also referred to as *śruti* or revelation, do not provide for proprietary rights to women, which is restricted to sons in these texts. In the course of Hinduism's chequered history, however, when the age of marriage of women was radically lowered between 200 BC and AD 300 and led to the emergence of the phenomenon of child widows, the right of the widow to inherit the share of her husband came to be eventually recognized all over the country by c. AD 1200. 'despite the fact that it went against *śruti*',[21] or sacred textual authority in Hinduism. Context trumped text.

The incorporation of the rights of the child has also extended human rights discourse further. This constitutes an extension of human rights discourse in a direction congenial to Hinduism. The conception of Kṛṣṇa as a child-god in the legends about him is not irrelevant here, as it represents a fundamentally positive orientation towards the child. The same positive orientation is also perhaps reflected in the fact that 'the cult of the child Kṛṣṇa made a special appeal to the warm maternity of Indian womanhood; and even today the simpler women of India, while worshipping the divine child so delightfully naughty despite his mighty power, refer to themselves as "the Mother of God" '.[22]

The attitude does not remain merely legendary; it also acquires a legal dimension in the story of Aṇī-Māṇḍavya, a cause célèbre of Hindu literature. Māṇḍavya, the sage, was practising austerities at the gate of his hermitage, with his hands raised upright, and observing the vow of silence, when a gang of robbers fleeing a posse of guardsmen in hot pursuit appeared at the gate. While passing through the hermitage the gang hid its plunder in the hermitage and fled. When the guardsmen arrived they questioned the sage about the whereabouts of the robbers. The sage, however, continued to observe his vow of silence, remaining fixed in his posture of self-mortification. The guardsmen thereupon searched the hermitage, and finding the loot, charged him with the crime. The silent sage was sentenced to death by impalement.

Sage Māṇḍavya, however, managed to survive his impalement long enough to attract the attention of other seers, and ultimately the king, mortified by the apparent miscarriage of justice when the facts became known, had him lowered from the stake. A piece of the stake however had become so firmly lodged in his flesh that it had to be sawed off. It became such a distinct part of his physiognomy thereafter that the sage himself came to be known as Māṇḍavya-with-the-stake or Aṇī-Māṇḍavya.

Once released from the stake, Aṇī-Māṇḍavya demanded an explanation of his condition from Dharma, or the God of Justice himself. Dharma pointed out that as a child Māṇḍavya had stuck blades of grass in the tails of little flies and had thus now got his karmic comeuppance. Aṇī-Māṇḍavya was however outraged by the disproportionate nature of the punishment and said:

> When I was a child I speared a little bird on a stock of reed. This sin I do remember, Dharma, but no other. Why have my thousand austerities not overcome it? The killing of a Brahmin is worse than the murder of any other creature. Therefore, because of your sin, you shall be born in the womb of a serf!

This story is told in the First Book of the *Mahābhārata* to account for the anomalous birth of Dharma in the form of Vidura, who in the epic is a person of low birth. After having reproached Dharma, Aṇī-Māṇḍavya also declared:

> Now I lay down the limit on the fruition of the law; nothing shall be a sin up to the age of fourteen years: but if they do it beyond that age it shall be counted an offence.[23]

A child thereafter was only liable for his actions on reaching the age of fourteen. The deeper significance of this case, however, which to us accounts for its celebrated nature, does not lie in its details but in the fact that it establishes the thoroughly empirical nature of the law within Hinduism, somewhat in the spirit of the Talmud. In a famous story in the Talmud it is stated that even a voice from heaven cannot override the majority opinion of the Rabbis because the Torah is no longer in heaven—as it was delivered to Moses, and thereafter all issues of law are to be settled by the majority opinion of the Rabbis.

IV

Human rights discourse has evolved in several directions as already noted since the landmark adoption of the Universal Declaration of Human Rights in 1948. It has since evolved new structures. It has greatly extended its embrace. It has also come to be distinguished by certain saliences represented by the Convention on the Prevention and Punishment of the Crime of Genocide (1948); the Convention relating to the Status of Refugees (1951); the Slavery Convention (1926), amended by the Protocol (1953) and the Supplementary Convention on the Abolition of Slavery, the Slave Trade, and Institutions and Practices Similar to Slavery (1956); the International Convention on the Elimination of All Forms of Racial Discrimination (1966); the Declaration on the Granting of Independence to Colonial Countries and Peoples (1960); the Declaration on Protection from Torture (1975); the Convention against Torture and other Cruel, Inhuman, or Degrading Treatment or Punishment (1984); the Convention on the Elimination of All Forms of Discrimination Against Women (1979);[24] and the United Nations Declaration on the Rights of Persons belonging to National or Ethnic, Religious, and Linguistic Minorities (1993). A United Nations Declaration on the Rights of Indigenous Peoples is on the anvil.[25]

The material from the history and philosophy of Hinduism which bears on genocide is such as tends towards its prevention. The caste system and the problems it raises from the point of human rights are discussed in a subsequent chapter. It is worth noting here that despite all that could be said against the caste system, according to many scholars it could be claimed in its favour that it may have prevented genocide. It is true that the *Arthaśāstra* recommends a price of twenty *paṇa*s upwards for the enemy's head but this is a far cry from the disbursements made from the state treasury for the scalps of 'red' Indians towards the end of the last century, which is a matter of public record in the state of California. It seems to be the clear implication of the following passage by S. Radhakrishnan that the caste system averted such outcomes in India:

> The trail of man is dotted with the graves of countless communities which reached an untimely end. But is there any justification for this violation of human

life? Have we any idea of what the world loses when one racial culture is extinguished? It is true that the Red Indians have not made, to all appearance, any contribution to the world's progress, but have we any clear understanding of their undeveloped possibilities which, in God's good time, might have come to fruition? Do we know so much of ourselves and the world and God's purpose as to believe that our civilization, our institutions and our customs are so immeasurably superior to those of others, not only what others actually possess but what existed in them potentially? We cannot measure beforehand the possibilities of a race. Civilizations are not made in a day, and had the fates been kindlier and we less arrogant in our ignorance, the world, I dare say, would have been richer for the contributions of the Red Indian.[26]

It would be wise however to temper this realization with the recognition that the lives may have been spared but at the price of dignity, if caste discrimination is also seen as part and parcel of the caste system. The humiliating details of some of the experiences of even a person of the stature of Dr B.R. Ambedkar are sobering in this regard.[27]

The evidence from the history of Hinduism on the question of colonization is similarly instructive. The political setbacks suffered by the Hindus in the last millennium, which saw them in a ruler-ruled relationship with first the Muslims and then the Christians tend to obscure the fact that the Hindus themselves in some sense were once a colonizing people. R.C. Majumdar may be faulted for making the following politically incorrect statement except for the fact that many would not consider it wide off the mark:

The most important remains of the Hindu colonists are Sanskrit inscriptions, written in Indian scripts, pure or slightly modified. They have been found all over the region, in Burma, Siam, Malay Peninsula, Annam, Cambodia, Sumatra, Java and Borneo. A perusal of these inscriptions shows that the language, literature, religion and political and social institutions of India made a thorough conquest of these far off lands and, to a large extent, eliminated or absorbed the native elements in these respects. The local peoples mostly belonged to a very primitive type of civilization, and it was the glorious mission of the Indian colonists to introduce a higher culture among them. In this task they achieved a large measure of success.[28]

Indic colonization, however, was of a markedly different character from Islamic and Christian colonization. Islamic imperialism advanced with the concept of one worldwide *umma* in the forefront, at least in theory, and Christian imperialism claimed the lands it conquered in the name of the conquering king and his religion. Both these imperialisms thus worked with a centre-periphery model, politically as well as culturally. Indic imperialism, however, only exhibited the cultural dimension, as the new kingdoms founded in such far-off lands as Cambodia and Java were independent kingdoms, for which the Indian counterparts may have served as models but in relation to which a ruled-ruler relationship never emerged. Hence Hindu concepts of colonialism are quite hospitable to the sentiments which actuated the Declaration on the Granting of Independence to Colonial Countries and Peoples (1960).

The Hindu position regarding the status of refugees as exemplified by its history is quite consistent with the provision of the Convention relating to their status which was adopted in 1951. The Jewish tradition of Malabar speaks of a community at Cochin in the first century AD which may have consisted of refugees after the Destruction of the Temple in AD 70. More certain is the arrival of Zoroastrians as refugees from Iran after the Arab invasion of Persia; 'according to the Parsis' own tradition one band of refugees settled first at Diu in Kathiawar, and then at Thana, near Bombay, in the early 8th century'.[29]

The Hindu attitude towards slavery seems to be one predisposed towards its abolition. Megasthenes even made the sensational claim that there were no slaves in India;[30] the claim is questionable but scholars think it was the mildness of the Indian phenomenon which made him presume its non-existence. It is a striking fact, given the caste system, that 'there was no caste of slaves'. This does not mean that slavery in its more sinister forms did not exist at all. *The Periplus of the Erythrean Sea*, an anonymous work of the first century of the Christian era, attests to trade in slave girls,[31] and slave markets are known to have existed in the sixteenth-century Vijayanagar empire. The Hindu position in the matter has basically been the one formulated in the *Arthaśāstra* which associates slavery with foreigners and states that the *ārya* (a category in which he explicitly includes the *śūdra*) may not be enslaved.[32] Once again one may wonder whether the caste system insulated Hindu society against slavery as it did against genocide.

As was the case with genocide and slavery, the Hindu milieu was also basically predisposed against racial discrimination. Once again the caste system may have been a factor, specially that dimension of it which explains the emergence of the various *jāti*s as arising out of the admixture of the various *varṇa*s. This may not be historically accurate but was sociologically revolutionary in that it made all the people of India theoretically of one blood and therefore race. Or in the words of Madhav Deshpande: 'By failing to recognize the foreign and racially different origins of the different peoples of India, and by focusing on their synchronic socio-religious positions, rights and duties, the classical Indian tradition brought about a wonderful racial and cultural synthesis of the

Indian people.'[33] He goes on to point out while 'classical India never saw the Aryan-Dravidian racial and cultural tensions', modern historical scholarship has destroyed 'the grand designs of Manu' by creating it.[34] Hindu attitudes by themselves then would not set much store by racial difference. The word *mleccha* is sometimes used to indicate its existence but its referent is cultural and linguistic rather than racial,[35] and a common humanity is never overlooked.[36]

V

In this last section of this chapter, one has now to discuss matters at the cutting edge of human rights discourse: those having to do with the evolution of international humanitarian law as it embodies the evolving tradition of human rights norms and standards. It has already been noted by scholars like Charles Alexandrowicz and Upendra Baxi that on this register Hindu laws and jurisprudence could be seen as anticipating modern developments rather remarkably. In the rest of this section one may travel down that road further by using the concept of a 'just war' as the starting point for developing an Indic perspective on humanitarian intervention.

The 'just war' doctrine has received considerable treatment in Christian literature.[37] It has also received some attention in the two other Abrahamic religions of Judaism and Islam.[38] The purpose of this section is to examine this topic in the light of Indic material.

At the most general level, the doctrine of war may be viewed as a way of limiting the use of war as an instrument of state policy. This element of the situation is most clearly expressed in the view that war must constitute a measure of 'last resort'. The temper underlying this view also finds expression within Indic civilization. Hartmut Scharfe writes that one approach to the resolution of conflicts within the Indic religions consists

> primarily of conciliation (*sāman*), gifts (*[upapra]dāna*), dissension (*bheda*), and force (*daṇḍa*), which are listed in order of declining value. It is widely agreed that conciliation is the best way to political success, force the worst. There were differences of opinion on the relative merit of gifts and dissension: Mānasollāsa II 972; 975 rates gifts as expensive and unreliable and puts them below the sowing of dissension. The important distinction is between the use of force and the other means: the force is recommended only as a last resort since war is always uncertain and the ideal conquest is attained without a fight. The KA takes a situational approach: one shall subjugate the weak with conciliation and gifts, the strong through dissension and force.[39]

At a less but still abstract level, the attitude underlying the doctrine of the 'just war', in a general way, is implicit in the typology of conquest in Indic political theory. Indic political thought classifies the nature of conquest resulting from the successful prosecution of war as follows:

According to the *Arthaśāstra*, there are three types of conquest: righteous conquest, conquest of greed, and demoniac conquest. The first is conquest in which the defeated king is forced to render homage and tribute, after which he or a member of his family is reinstated as a vassal. The second is victory in which enormous booty is demanded and large portions of enemy territory is annexed. The third involves the political annihilation of the conquered kingdom and its incorporation in that of the victor. The two latter types are generally disapproved of by all sources except the *Arthaśāstra.*[40]

The Sanskrit words for these three types are *dharma-vijaya*, *lobha-vijaya*, and *asura-vijaya*. The fact that *dharma-vijaya* came to be preferred seems to reflect a 'just war' mentality.

One may supplement the standard concept of *dharma-vijaya* with the version of it propounded by King Aśoka (r.c. 273–232 BC). The following passage from the Thirteenth Rock Edict enables one to form some concept of what he had in mind.

I have had this inscription of righteousness engraved that all my sons and grandsons may not seek to gain new victories, that in whatever victories they may gain they may prefer forgiveness and light punishment, that they may consider the only [valid] victory the victory of righteousness, which is of value both in this world and the next, and that all their pleasure may be in righteousness . . .[41]

This passage, upon investigation, discloses three dimensions of the concept of *dharma-vijaya* (or *dhamma-vijaya*) that Aśoka had in mind:

(1) abjuring further military conquest,
(2) mildness in such conquest when undertaken, and
(3) active benevolence.

This third sense is instantiated by the following passage in the Second Rock Edict:

Everywhere in the empire of the Beloved of the Gods, and even beyond his frontiers in the lands of the Cholas, Pandyas, Satyaputras, Keralaputras, and as far as Ceylon, and in the Kingdoms of Antiochus the Greek king and the kings who are his neighbours, the Beloved of the Gods has provided medicines for man and beast. Whenever medicinal plants have not been found they have been sent there and planted. Wells have been dug along the roads for the use of man and beast.[42]

It is also clear that the second of the three senses in which Aśoka uses the terms corresponds to the sense it possesses in the *Arthaśāstra* and Hindu *smṛti* literature. The two new senses Aśoka imparts to it are (1) pacifism and (2) humanitarianism.

Observations of foreign visitors of India during the period of its history represented by the Mauryan Dynasty enable one to define these senses further. Aśoka is explicit about abjuring *foreign* conquest under his policy of *dharma-vijaya*, but he does not rule out such 'conquest' *within* his empire:

> The Beloved of the Gods will forgive as far as he can, and he even conciliates the forest tribes of his dominions; but he warns them that there is power even in the remorse of the Beloved of the Gods, and he tells them to reform, lest they be killed.[43]

This further confirms the fact that he used the word *dharma-vijaya* in the context of areas lying within his territory, which might contain recalcitrant elements, in the traditional sense. It is in his extension of this concept to territories outside India that new features emerge. The first of these is a policy of non-aggression towards states lying outside his empire. This attitude, however, seems to be a manifestation of an attitude already present in Indic thought. Megasthenes, the Seleucid ambassador at the court of Candragupta Maurya (r.c. 322–298 BC) declared of India that 'Its people . . . never sent an expedition abroad',[44] according to the fragment preserved in Strabo (first century BC). The explanation of this attitude is provided in the fragment from Megasthenes preserved by Arrian (second century) that 'a sense of justice, they say, prevented any Indian king from attempting conquest beyond the limits of India'.[45]

The idea of carrying out humanitarian activities in other lands outside the empire—or even India—as part of *dharma-vijaya* then seems to be Aśoka's unique contribution to the concept.

A contribution to Indic thought in the context of contemporary international law from the Aśokan point of view would consist of the claim that, under international law, only humanitarian intervention is permissible, as distinguished from international intervention on humanitarian grounds. From the point of view of Aśoka, a humanitarian crisis would only justify humanitarian relief and not any other form of intervention such as military action on humanitarian grounds.[46]

These are just some of the ways in which discourses on Hinduism and human rights can be meaningfully aligned. One can go even further and suggest that the two may not merely stand side-by-side as in a garden, but may also be capable of cross-pollination. The reader might wish to review appendices II and III in this light.

NOTES

1. Mary Ann Glendon, *A World Made New: Eleanor Roosevelt and the Universal Declaration of Human Rights*, New York: Random House, 2001, p. xvii.
2. Ibid.
3. Ibid.
4. Ibid., pp. xvii–xviii.
5. Ibid., p. xviii.
6. Paul Gordon Lauren, *The Evolution of International Human Rights: Visions Seen*, Philadelphia: University of Pennsylvania Press, 1998, p. 57.
7. Hartmut Scharfe, op. cit., p. 41.
8. Mary Ann Glendon, op. cit., p. 189.
9. K.B. Panda, *Sanatana Dharma and Law*, Cuttack: Naitika Punaruthan Samiti, 1977, p. 18.
10. See Sumner B. Twiss, 'Moral Grounds and Plural Cultures: Interpreting Human Rights in the International Community', *Journal of Religious Ethics*, 26:2, Fall 1998, p. 272; Carol S. Robb, 'Liberties, Claims, Entitlements and Trumps: Reproductive Rights and Ecological Responsibilities', *Journal of Religious Ethics*, 26:2, Fall 1998, p. 286; John Witte Jr., 'Law, Religion and Human Rights', *Columbia Human Rights Law Review*, 28:1, Fall 1996, p. 13; Gregory Baum. 'Human Rights: An Ethical Perspective', *The Ecumenist*, May–June 1994, pp. 64–7; etc.
11. John Witte Jr., op. cit., p. 13.
12. Carol S. Robb, op. cit., p. 286.
13. See Purushottama Bilimoria, 'Rights and Duties: The (Modern) Indian Dilemma', in *Ethical and Political Dilemmas in Modern India*, (eds) Ninian Smart and Shivesh Thakur, New York: St. Martin's Press, 1993, pp. 35–6.
14. Ibid., p. 48.
15. Paul Gordon Lauren, op. cit., p. 31.
16. Ibid.
17. Ibid., pp. 31–2. Also see Michael Ignatieff, *The Warrior's Honor: Ethnic War and the Modern Conscience*, New York: Henry Holt and Company, 1997, pp. 12–20.
18. See Ian Brownlie (ed.), *Basic Documents on Human Rights*, third edition, Oxford: Clarendon Press, 1992, pp. 148–61; 169–81; and 182–202.
19. Cited in Mary Ann Glendon, op. cit., p. 216.
20. B.R. Ambedkar, *Who Were the Shudras?* Bombay: Thackers 1970 [1946], passim, specially see p. 104.
21. A.S. Altekar, *The Position of Women in Hindu Civilization*, Delhi: Motilal Banarsidass, 1995, pp. 353–4.

22. A.L. Basham, op. cit., p. 306.
23. J.A.B. van Buitenen, tr. & ed., *The Mahābhārata*, Chicago and London: The University of Chicago Press, 1973, Vol. 1, p. 134.
24. For the texts of the documents please consult Ian Brownlie (ed.), op. cit.
25. For the texts of the documents please see Tad Stahnke and J. Paul Martin (eds), *Religion and Human Rights: Basic Documents*, New York: Centre for the Study of Human Rights, Columbia University, 1998.
26. S. Radhakrishnan, *The Hindu View of Life*, New Delhi: Indus, 1993; first published 1927, p. 68.
27. Dhananjay Keer, *Dr Ambedkar: Life and Mission*, Bombay: Popular Prakashan, 1971 [1954], passim.
28. R.C. Majumdar, 'Colonial and Cultural Expansion in South-East Asia', in *The Classical Age*, Bombay: Bharatiya Vidya Bhavan, 1970 [1954], p. 654.
29. A.L. Basham, op. cit., p. 344.
30. F.W. Thomas, 'Political and Social Organisation of the Maurya Empire', in *Ancient India* (ed.), E.J. Rapson, Cambridge: Cambridge University Press, 1922, p. 481.
31. K.A. Nilakanta Sastri (ed.), *The Mauryas and Satavahanas*, Bombay: Orient Longman, 1957, p. 444.
32. A.L. Basham, op. cit., p. 152.
33. Madhav Despande, 'History: Change and Permanence. A Classical Indian Perspective', in *Contributions to South Asian Studies* (ed.), Gopal Krishna, Delhi: Oxford University Press, 1979, p. 21.
34. Ibid.
35. Romila Thapar, *Ancient Indian Social History: Some Interpretations*, New Delhi: Orient Longman, 1978, p. 156.
36. J. Duncan M. Derrett, op. cit., pp. 102–3.
37. According to Christian just war theory, a war is just if the following seven criteria are observed: (1)the cause must be just—and hence only defence is permitted; (2) war must be declared by a competent authority—and hence excludes surprise attack; (3) war must be chosen as a means of last resort; (4) the intention must be good—excluding vengeance or pride; (5) the immunity of non-combatants must be assured (many Christians argue that today's massive weaponry inevitably kills civilians, making just war an impossibility); (6) the principle of proportionality in the matter of damage inflicted must be respected so that the harm inflicted in self-defence may not exceed the harm caused by the attack; and (7) a speedy victory should be expected. I owe this summary statement to Professor Gregory Baum. For more details see James Turner Johnson, *Just War Tradition and the Restraint of War: A Moral and Historical Inquiry*, Princeton, NJ: Princeton University Press, 1981.
38. See John Kelsay, *Just War and Jihad: Historical and Theoretical Perspectives on War and Peace in Western Islamic Traditions*, New York: Greenwood Press, 1991; see also James Turner Johnson, *The Holy War in Western Islamic Traditions*, University Park, PA: Pennsylvania State University Press, 1997.
39. Hartmut Scharfe, op. cit., p. 209.

40. A.L. Basham, op. cit., p. 124.
41. Ainslie T. Embree, *Sources of Indian Tradition*, second edition, New York: Columbia University Press, 1988, Vol. I, p. 143.
42. Ibid., pp. 144–5.
43. Ibid., p. 142.
44. J.W. McCrindle, *Ancient India as Described by Megasthenes and Arrian*, Calcutta: Chuckervertty, Chatterjee & Co. Ltd., 1960 [1876–1877], p. 109.
45. Ibid., p. 209.
46. For future trends in human rights discourse see Upendra Baxi, *The Future of Human Rights*, New Delhi: Oxford University Press, 2002.

CHAPTER 3

The Caste System (*Varṇa*, *Jāti*) and Human Rights

I

The question of the caste system and its relationship to human rights is a complex one, even a vexed one. And yet it is possible that an exercise along these lines may be as rewarding as it is challenging. Nothing contributes to clarity so much as confusion. Such confusion, however, seems to be more characteristic of the caste system than human rights. Article 1 of the Universal Declaration of Human Rights states unambiguously and unequivocally:

> All human beings are born free and equal in dignity and rights. They are endowed with reason and conscience and should act towards one another in a spirit of brotherhood.[1]

How does the caste system fare in relation to this Article, which was adopted as part of the Declaration of Human Rights by the General Assembly of the United Nations on 10 December 1948, as a 'common standard of achievement for all peoples and all nations'.[2] How does the caste system fare by this yardstick? Before one can decide how it fares by this yardstick, we must first find out what it is.

II

What is the Caste System?

Caste (*varṇa, jāti*) is a phenomenon at once complex and widely distributed[3] and we would expect the discussion to be similar.

To begin with, the word caste is not of Indian origin. 'When the Portuguese came to India in the 16th century, they found the Hindu community divided into many separate groups, which they called *castas*, meaning tribes, clans, or families. The name stuck, and became the usual word for the Hindu social group.'[4] The problem is that the same word is often used to refer to two different concepts, those of *varṇa* and *jāti*, and the confusion is further compounded by the fact that these two are themselves conflated in the Hindu law-books.[5] This situation is further aggravated by an attempt (1) to explain the *jāti*s as social entities emerging from miscegenation among the former and (2) to subsume all the *jāti*s,[6] which number anywhere from three to five thousand, under the four *varṇas*.[7] 'This is false terminology; castes (*jāti*s) rise and fall in the social scale, and old castes die out and new ones are formed, but the four great classes (*varṇa*s) are stable.'[8]

These *varṇa*s, which are historically mentioned before the *jāti*s, constitute the fourfold division of society into: (1) *Brāhmaṇa*s, (2) *Kṣatriyas*, (3) *Vaiśyas*, and (4) *Śūdras* or the priestly, warrior, agriculturist and trading, and serving classes respectively. The *jāti*s constitute commensal, endogamous, craft-specific closed groups. What seems to have happened is that when the Indo-Aryans, with their *varṇa* system, intermingled with the indigenous peoples (who were most likely characterized by the *jāti* system) after entering India, they 'imposed their social system on the indigenous peoples, while aspects of the indigenous people in turn began to characterize the *varṇa* system. The end result is the caste system as we see it in India today'.[9]

Our discussion of human rights in relation to the caste system is crucially complicated by this fact, that the caste system braids these two strands almost inextricably. As David Kinsley points out:

> The *jāti* system is difficult to study apart from the *varṇa* system because for centuries the two have been seen as complementary in the Hindu tradition, or in fact as one and the same. However, the *jāti* system, the caste system proper as it operates at the village level, is quite different from the *varṇa* system as described in most traditional Hindu scriptures. The term *jāti* means birth and is the proper term for caste. A caste is a group into which one is born and within which one must marry, and it usually is characterized by a traditional, specialized occupation. Unlike a *varṇa*, a *jāti* is geographically and linguistically limited and in most cases has the characteristics of a large kin group with distinctive customs, dress, diet, and behaviour. A *jāti* is self-governing; being responsible for the behaviour of its own members, and only mingles with other castes in carefully circumscribed ways. Sometimes it is also characterized by a particular type of religious affiliation or behaviour. *Jātis* are ranked hierarchically vis-à-vis one another, and this ranking determines who may do what with whom under what conditions.[10]

For the sake of completeness, we must now add to this conglomeration of units the category of *untouchables*, who virtually formed a separate group at the bottom, and contact with whom was considered polluting. They had *jātis* among them as well. One prefers to use the past tense as untouchability was legally abolished in 1950.

This hyphenated *varṇa-jāti* system is what is known as the caste system and its significance for our discussion will become apparent as we proceed to examine the various views canvassed in the context of the caste system and human rights.

Before such an examination is attempted, however, attention needs to be drawn to another fact, which, if it does not complicate the situation further, at least laces it with irony. The nature of the social reality about human beings as expressed through the caste system is heavily at odds with the spiritual nature of human beings as understood within Hinduism.[11] At that level, 'theistic Hinduism upholds human equality on the basis that all are God's creatures. Non-theistic Hinduism emphasizes the identity of the essence of all humans'.[12] Hence the anguished words of Professor A.R. Wadia:

> The high metaphysics of the Upanishads and the ethics of the Gita have been reduced to mere words by the tyranny of caste. Emphasising the unity of the whole world, animate and inanimate, India has yet fostered a social system which has divided them from one another, generation to generation for endless centuries. It has exposed her to foreign conquests, which have left her poor, and weak and worst of all she has become the home of untouchability and unapproachability, which have branded her with the curse of Cain.[13]

These words echo those of Swami Vivekananda (1863–1902) in whom the same sentiment finds this mordant expression: 'No religion on earth preaches the dignity of humanity in such a lofty strain as Hinduism, and no religion on earth treads upon the necks of the poor and the low in such a fashion as Hinduism.'[14]

III

Human Rights and the Caste System: The Dismissive Approach

A question to which many scholars have addressed themselves in modern times is whether a human rights concept can be somehow extracted from the unpromising ore of the caste system? Surprisingly, many have thought that this is possible. One may, however, begin with a few who do not deem it possible.

B.R. Ambedkar

Dr B.R. Ambedkar (1891–1956), who was born an untouchable, played a major role in the drafting of the Indian Constitution, a Constitution whose 'elaborate statement of 'fundamental rights' far exceeds in detail the provisions of the American Bill of Rights'.[15] These include the Right to Equality, Right to Freedom, Right Against Exploitation, Right to Freedom of Religion, Right to Property, and Right to Constitutional Remedies. J.B. Carman points out that 'many of the rights enumerated directly challenge the unequal privileges to the traditional Hindu system of *varṇa dharma*, which, in practice, means the caste system'.[16] In fact he remarks that 'the explicit challenge to all forms of inequality may seem more prominent in the Indian Constitution than the issue of "fundamental rights".'[17]

Despite his role in the drafting of the Indian Constitution so committed to upholding human rights, Dr Ambedkar converted to Buddhism in 1956. It was a biographical statement: he had finally concluded that Hinduism, with its caste system, could not be reconciled with human rights.

S. Radhakrishnan

Dr S. Radhakrishnan (1888–1975) is perhaps the most persuasive spokesman of Hinduism that modern India produced. Nevertheless, towards the end of a long career, which he began[18] by defending an idealized version of the *varṇa* system as compatible with equality and human rights, he declared in 1950: 'If democracy is to be seriously implemented, then caste and untouchability should go.'[19] The statement is prefaced by numerous citations on how 'caste' should be based on worth and not on birth, as was the case with his early defence of the idealized *varṇa* system. At that time he had written: 'If the progressive thinkers of India had the power, as they undoubtedly have the authority, they would transform the institution out of recognition.'[20] But now he spoke not of its transformation but elimination, proof-texting his position in the usual way. The reference to democracy accords with Article 21 of the Universal Declaration of Human Rights.

K.M. Panikkar

K.M. Panikkar (1894–1963) clearly accepts the inequality of the *jāti* system,[21] but he exculpates the *varṇa* system,[22] and even suggests that 'if instead of being divided into sub-castes, the castes had been integrated into the four ideological divisions, this disastrous fragmentation of society would never have happened'.[23]

K.M. Panikkar was not concerned so much with human rights as with the consolidation of the Hindu community on the basis of equality. As this egalitarian thrust, however, is shared by the Universal Declaration of Human Rights, K.M. Panikkar's method of dealing with the caste system as a social rather than religious fact is not without interest. He finds support for it even in the words of Swami Vivekananda:

> Beginning from Buddha to Ram Mohan Roy, every one made the mistake of holding caste to be a religious institution . . . but in spite of all the ravings of the priests, caste is simply a crystallized social institution, which after doing its service is now filling the atmosphere of India with stink.[24]

IV

Human Rights and the Caste System: The Derivative Approach

According to the view adopted in the previous section, human rights could be advanced by doing away with the caste system.[25] There is, however, another approach, which has been advocated and adopted by some religious leaders and scholars of Hinduism. They maintain, in opposition to the views just expressed, that the concept of human rights could be derived from the caste system.

Mahatma Gandhi (1869–1948)

Mahatma Gandhi affirmed human rights both in support and in opposition to the caste system. Mahatma Gandhi asserted human rights in *opposition* to the caste system in his campaign against untouchability. As we shall soon see, Gandhi saw some point in the caste system, but he saw no point in untouchability or a class of outcastes. Robert Traer seems correct in his assessment that 'Gandhi considered himself an orthodox Hindu. He believed that God is understood in theistic or non-theistic terms, [and] Hindu theology could not be used to justify inequality of human beings'.[26]

The question arises: if Gandhi could not justify inequality, how could he justify the caste system, while denouncing untouchability? Contrary to the popular understanding of the caste system, Gandhi did not see it as advocating inequality. His views on this point are unusual and need to be understood with care. Gandhi defends the caste system but 'that does not mean that you and I may tolerate for one moment or be gentle towards the hideous travesty of *varṇāśrama* that we see about us today. There is nothing in common between *varṇāśrama* and caste. Caste if you will, is undoubtedly a drag upon Hindu progress, and untouchability is, as I have already called it or described it, an excrescence upon *varṇāśrama*'.[27] Then what is Gandhi defending? Curiously enough, *varṇa* based on birth. For Gandhi, one's birth determined one's *varṇa* and what it meant was that one might only earn one's livelihood through one's inherited profession. Any other talents one possessed had to be made available to society free of charge. This was Gandhi's solution to the problem of economic strife. He also said:

> I do not believe, that inter-dining or even intermarriage necessarily deprives a man of his status that his birth has not given him. The four divisions define a man's calling; they do not restrict or regulate social intercourse. The divisions define duties; they confer no privileges. It is, I hold, against the genius of Hinduism to arrogate to oneself a higher status or assign to another a lower. All are born to serve God's creation: a *brāhmaṇa* with his knowledge, a *kṣatriya* with his power of protection, a *vaiśya* with his commercial ability and a *śūdra* with bodily labour.[28]

Thus Gandhi accepts the idea of *varṇa dharma* or duty of one's *varṇa* as formulated in Hindu law-books such as that of Manu, and yet the idea lacks the rigidity of the formal concept.[29]

R.C. Pandeya (1932–)

R.C. Pandeya does not accept the unilateral view of *dharma* as duty per se, with rights to follow. He is more consciously reciprocal about their relationship. In regard to the favourite axiom of many Hindu thinkers that rights flow from duties discharged, he wants to know *which* duties generate human rights, having pleaded earlier that Article 29 in the Universal Declaration of Human Rights, which speaks of duties, should have preceded the articles which confer rights. While he faults the dharmic approach for not being specific on the point of the correlation of duties and rights, he appreciates its formulation of *duties in general terms*, which for him correspond with those of Buddhism and Vedānta:

> negatively formulated, it will state that a man ought not to act in such a way as to obscure his true nature. In other words his duty would consist in withdrawing or refraining from all such acts as were likely to obscure any aspect of the totality of his being. The same idea formulated in positive terms would amount to saying that man ought to act in order to fulfill his total nature. In this alternative formulation his duty would consist in a complete knowledge of self.[30]

One must immediately note though, that the duties have become general and no longer remain specific the way they are in the caste system; and that this loosens the link of specific reciprocity, it seems, which R.C. Pandeya was perhaps actually seeking.

R. Panikkar (1918–)

R. Panikkar (not to be confused with K.M. Panikkar) takes a slightly different but very Hindu tack, which warns against confusing equality with uniformity. He writes: 'All humans are equal as God's creation but are not the same; therefore, all should give and receive according to their own nature. These groups uphold the ideal of following one's own nature (*svadharma*) in the *Bhagavad-Gita*.'[31]

This has considerable support from within the tradition. S. Radhakrishnan pointed out in 1926 that 'it is not true that all men are born equal in every way and everyone is equally fit to govern the country or till the ground'.[32] P. Nagaraja Rao has vigorously articulated this position more recently as follows:

> The Hindu mind was not doctrinaire in its approach, and did not believe in the doctrine of absolute equality. It believed that each should develop to his best in the manner that suited his grain and *svahbhāva*. They knew the true implications of the doctrine of equality. They proclaimed an optimum ideal for mankind which is summed up in the Gita phrase: *sarva-bhūta-hite-ratāh*:—the good of all: *Sarvodaya*, of Gandhiji. The Hindu never declares that 'all men are equal' but that all men must be happy (*sarve janāḥ sukhino bhavantu*).[33]

P.V. Kane is perhaps trying to say something similar when he comments on the following famous line in the American Declaration of Independence: 'All men are created equal. They are endowed by their creator with certain inalienable rights, among them are life, liberty and the pursuit of happiness.' He remarks:

> Of course it is wrong and unscientific to say that all men are created equal if literally construed (as even children of the same parents are not equal in height, strength and mental equipment). All that is meant is that all are equal in the eye of the law or have the same rights before the law.[34]

J.B. Carman (1930–)

This idea is developed by John B. Carman to raise an interesting question: can privileges lead to the notion of rights, for if they can and the caste system is connected with privileges, then it could account for the emergence of rights, as a way of explaining how quickly the discourse could shift in India from *duties* to *rights*, as elsewhere.[35]

One obvious approach is to ask what rights are assumed from the listing of duties in the Dharmaśāstras. If we include special privileges for particular groups among rights, then there are many included in the discussion of duties. Most notable, of course, are the special privileges of the three 'twice-born' or 'noble' classes (*varṇas*): Brahmins (priests and scholars), Ksatriyans (rulers and warriors); and Vaiśyas (the Aryan commoners who became farmers and later merchants). With some exceptions there is a sharp hierarchical grading that applied not only to positive rewards but also to punishments meted out by the ruler. The Brahmin is most rewarded and most lightly punished. It is worth noting that our Western notion of right goes back much further than the affirmation of equal rights.[36]

But since we are looking for analogues for the generic category of human rights, J.B. Carman is led to ask: 'But were there any rights owed equally to all in any village? Yes, for there was one person in this traditional system who owed something to all: the ruler. What the ruler owed was protection to all.'[37] Professor Carman goes on to argue that the same applied to the ruler of all—God, in an interesting role reversal of 'king equals God' to 'God equals king', on whose behalf various temple honours (*maryādā*) were administered. These were also of the nature of privileges.

Thus apart from the restricted idea of caste duty or caste rights, 'for Gandhi and other Hindu reformers, both priests and rulers have duties that can be made the basis of universal rights, and all people have, in addition to their particular occupational duties, a common *dharma* of fundamental duties, of which the most important are truth telling (*satya*) and not harming living beings (*ahiṁsā*).'[38]

Klaus K. Klostermaier (1933–)

One scholar who makes a direct comment on the caste system in relation to human rights is Klaus K. Klostermaier. He writes:

> Basically the Brahmins did not develop 'human rights' but 'caste-rights', which had the side effect that, in the course of time, about one-fifth of the total population, as 'outcastes', had virtually no rights. They were treated worse than cattle, which even in legal theory ranked above them. People became casteless by violating the rules of their castes, either by marrying contrary to the caste regulations, by following professions not allowed by caste rules, or by committing other acts that were punished by expulsion from the caste. Some books give them the appellation of 'fifth caste', but that may leave a wrong impression. They were cut off from all the rights and privileges that caste society extended to its members, ritually impure and ostensibly the product of bad *karma* coming to fruition.[39]

He goes on to say:

Mahatma Gandhi fought for their rights, especially the right to enter Hindu temples (quite often they are still refused admission), calling them *Harijan*, God's people. But even he wanted to maintain the caste structure and was extremely angry with Dr Ambedkar, the leader of the outcastes, who severed all ties with caste society by turning Buddhist and drawing some 3 million of his followers with him. The casteism of the outcastes, however, is highlighted by the fact that, despised and humiliated as they are, they have established among themselves a caste structure analogous to the *cāturvarṇa* system and jealously observe their own ranking within it.[40]

This calls for some comment. If the earlier discussion about the distinctions between *varṇa* and *jāti* still holds good, it might be more accurate to say that the caste structure among the former untouchables are more akin to the *jāti* system. It is well known that the *jāti*s proliferate as one moves down the *varṇa* totem pole.

Ramesh N. Patel (1939–)

Whether human rights could be derived from the caste system is a question which, when placed in the context of the *Bhagavadgītā*, suggests some interesting possibilities. Although in the text itself Arjuna at certain points is asked to fight because it is his *duty* to do so, the context cannot be divorced from the issue of rights.

Ramesh N. Patel introduces the rights argument at two levels. At the first level, it is specific to the context. He presents the argument for Yudhiṣṭhira claiming the kingdom as of right:

We, being my brothers and I, have the right to our share of the kingdom. In terms of the accepted legal tradition, we have the right to inherit the entire kingdom, but in the interest of peace we will not claim more than a share of it. The share legitimately belongs to us and we ask that it be restored to us. True, we lost our rightful share in my gambling bout with Shakuni who played dice with me on behalf of Duryodhana. But because Shakuni won by deceit, Duryodhana was embarrassed to make an agreement with us whereby he was to look after our share of the kingdom till we returned from an exile in the forest of a number of years. The stipulated period for which our share was to be withheld has now expired. We scrupulously performed our part of the agreement; now, Duryodhana should do his. Since our right to the share is not questioned by anyone, there is no reason why the right should not be respected.[41]

At this level the issue is still pegged to the question of caste rights and duties. It is when Ramesh N. Patel lifts this argument to another level that a new possibility emerges. He goes on to say:

Being soldier-administrators happens to be our identity and not merely a socially imposed obligation. We have been nurtured with it as our identity from childhood. We always thought of ourselves as soldier-administrators. Our people, too, have always thought of us and recognized us as such. Since our particular identity is both expected of us and accepted by us, it is reasonable to sustain it by giving it a scope for functioning. All this, again, means that we need our share of the kingdom and just that. What can be conceivably wrong in our enjoying our identity and asserting our rights to it, specially when it neither disrupts social harmony nor usurps anyone else's rights.[42]

For once the concept of identity as a *kṣatriya*, and rights to be accorded as a *kṣatriya*, are introduced, one is not far from the concept of a human being, and rights to be accorded as a human being. If winter comes can spring be far behind?

V

The key word, which we have used only sparingly so far, is the word *dharma*. The word is as ambiguous as it is crucial. One must begin with its use in the present context as *varṇa dharma* or caste duty. When used only in this sense it points to specific duties but not to rights as such. Even in this sense it might embody a lofty ethical ideal, but not the one we want in the sense of the word, which has perhaps led Louis Renou to declare:

A factor in social and psychical equilibrium is found in the notion of *dharma* with its rigorous justice and the 'truth' which it implies (the Indians insist on an attitude of truthfulness as others insist on an 'attitude of consciousness'). An important consequence of this is tolerance, non-violence considered an active virtue; this is a manner of acting which must be respected—*even in the political sphere*—regardless of the attitude of others. In this perhaps is to be found the most spectacular contribution, which India has made to the modern world and the most worthy reply to Marxism and its materialism.[43]

However, the word itself possesses a far broader connotation in this context when it is applied not to *varṇa*s or specific castes, as *varṇa-dharma*, but to all human being as *sādhāraṇa dharma*. This move is so seminal in the context of human rights that the absence of the word or concept in the Indian Constitution is a source of genuine puzzlement to scholars like P.V. Kane, who held that plans of India's future should have been 'based on the foundation of the best part of our traditions, the rule of *dharma*, duties common to all'.[44] John B. Carman is similarly surprised, as noted earlier, by the omission when he declared: 'Most educated modern Hindus would agree theoretically with this emphasis on common *dharma*, not only of Hindus, but of all human beings. But the language of *dharma*, whether traditional or revised, is strangely absent from the Indian Constitution.'[45]

The source of human rights could be sought here, though some would like to seek it even further, not just in *mānava dharma* or in our moral obligations to all human beings, but in morality or *dharma* per se.

VI

This might not seem possible at first glance, unless one realizes that the word *dharma* is not just a lexical item but represents a cultural ethos of a very subtle kind. Of course all meaning has a cultural dimension to it and it *can* be restrictive, even in the case of the word *dharma*. Louis Renou explains:

> Inasmuch as social and religious duties depend on castes and the stages of life, morality, to the extent that it derives from these duties, follows the same divisions; *dharma* is not a universal *dharma* but one of 'caste and stage of life'. In addition, morality is subject to a subdivision that coincides only partly with the foregoing, namely of the 'three goals' of human activity, *dharma* (duty, religion or moral worth), *artha* (the pursuit of wealth), and *kāma* (the quest for pleasure).[46]

Renou, however, goes on to explain its deeper resonance, drawing both on the sacred and secular background of the term and its history in doing so. What he says must be cited in extenso as the point is often overlooked:

> At the same time it would be a mistake to overlook the implicit presence of a general morality the lines of which emerge more or less clearly in the archaic values of ritual exactitude and purity. The old term *rita*, 'cosmic order' became a synonym for truth, and its opposite, *anrita*, for falsehood. In the Epic and thereafter there is much moralizing to the effect that we must aspire to virtue even at the expense of worldly advantage; man's duty must be done. In our relations with other people, and even with animals, the prime virtue is non-violence, or *ahiṁsā* (a word occurring first in the *Chāndogya-Upanishad* and destined to reverberate again and again in modern India); according to Manu the practice of non-violence permits a man to escape from the cycle of *karman*. Certain heroic values are also advocated; true greatness demands suffering on one another's behalf and even saving one's enemy's life. One of the heroes of Brahmanism is Prince Vipashcit, who, when he finds on going down into hell that his presence solaces the damned, offers to stay there. From the moral point of view the *Mahābhārata* is a code of chivalrous virtue for the warrior, and court poetry and the *Rāmāyaṇa* claim to present the model head of a family and the ideal prince.[47]

What he says later reinforces what he has said earlier and must once again be cited in detail, as we have not encountered such a nuanced appreciation of the term elsewhere within memory.

It is by striking such notes as these that Indian poetry transcends religious divisions and endows the Indian sensibility with a broader resonance. Gnomic poetry, that typically Indian creation, celebrates all the 'profane' virtues and is the medium in which the man of humble circumstances edifies those above him, as the hunter teaches the Brahman in an episode in the *Mahābhārata* (III, 206). The moral virtues possess a divine power as a means of attaining deliverance (*Gītā* XVI, 5); they are as potent as religious donations in this respect (*Chānd. Up.* III, 17); and the corresponding vices condemn the individual to that 'demoniacal' destiny that is the way of transmigration. In short, a holy life without any religious exercises and without any definite religious attachment can produce the same result as devotional or mystical practice. We are told over and over again that what counts is not outward piety or the caste in which your destiny has caused you to be born, but conduct. Buddhism has no monopoly in urging this.[48]

One could therefore locate the idea of human rights in the general ethos of moral claims within Hinduism. But can one do better?

VI

There is a text in the *Bṛhadārayaka Upaniṣad* whose full significance in the context of the discussion of human rights has gone unrecognized. A part of it was cited in the first chapter and I would like to overcome this textual oversight by citing the full passage here. Its theme concerns the 'one Being' which failed initially to flourish, but then successively produced the *Brāhmaṇa*, *Kṣatriya*, *Vaiśya*, and *Śūdra* in order to do so.

11. Verify, in the beginning this (world) was *Brahman*, one only. That, being one, did not flourish. He created further an excellent form, the *Kṣatra* power, even those who are *Kṣatra* (rulers) among the gods, Indra, Varuṇa, Soma (Moon), Rudra, Parjanya, Yama, Mṛtyu (Death), Īśāna. Therefore there is nothing higher than *Kṣatra*. Therefore at the Rājasūya sacrifice the Brāhmaṇa sits below the *Kṣatra*. On Kṣatrahood alone does he confer this honour. But the Brāhmaṇa is nevertheless the source of the *Kṣatra*. Therefore, even if the king attains supremacy at the end of it, he resorts to Brāhmaṇa as his source. Therefore he who injures the Brāhmaṇa strikes at his own source. He becomes more evil as he injures one who is superior.
12. Yet he did not flourish. He created the *viś* (the commonality), [those] classes of gods who are designated in groups. The Vasus, Rudra, Ādityas, Viśvedevās and Maruts.

13. He did not still flourish. He created the Śūdra order, as Pūṣan. Verily, this (earth) is Pūṣan (the nourisher), for she nourishes everything that is.
14. Yet he did not flourish. He created further an excellent form, justice. This is the power of the *Kṣatriya* class, viz. justice. Therefore there is nothing higher than justice. So a weak man hopes (to defeat) a strong man by means of justice as one does through a king. Verily, that which is justice is truth. Therefore they say of a man who speaks the truth, he speaks justice or of a man who speaks justice that he speaks the truth. Verily, both these are the same.
15. So these (four orders were created) the Brāhmaṇa, the Kṣatriya, the Vaiśya and the Śūdra. Among the gods that Brahma existed as Fire, among men as Brāhmaṇa, as a Kṣatriya by means of the (divine) Kṣatriya, as a Vaiśya by means of the (divine) Vaiśya, as a Śūdra by means of the (divine) Śūdra. Therefore people desire a place among the gods through fire only, and among men as the Brāhmaṇa, for by these two forms (pre-eminently) Brahma existed. If anyone, however, departs from this world without seeing (knowing) his own world, it being unknown, does not protect him, as the Vedas unrecited or as deed not done do not (protect him). Even if one performs great and holy work, but without knowing this, that work of his is exhausted in the end. One should meditate only on the Self as his (true) works. The work of him who meditates on the Self alone as his world is not exhausted for out of that very Self he creates whatsoever he desires.[49]

Bṛhadāraṇyaka Upaniṣad, I.4 11–15

Passage no. 14 above contains the striking statement: 'So a weak man hopes (to defeat) a strong man by means of justice.' Thus even the weak possess rights in relation to the strong; an insight that paves the way for the individual possessing rights in the face of the power of the state. The philological point that the word for state—*rājya*—is derived from the word king—*rājā*—possesses clarificatory power here. It should however be further clarified that the word *rājya* also possesses allied meanings such as kingdom, government, and so on.[50] But scholars are agreed that '*rājya* is the Indian term closest to our "state" '.[51]

From the point of human rights, two crucial points emerge from this passage. The first is that this *dharma* is over and above the *varṇa*s. It is not a *varṇa dharma* but something above the *varṇa*s as *dharma*, and one should guard against semantic slippage here. The second point is not obvious from the passage but emerges from Śaṅkara's commentary on it. Śaṅkara notes that once the four *varṇa*s were created, one had to restrain the ruler from exercising power arbitrarily. Hence *dharma* was set above all. Such a sentiment must seem surprisingly modern to those familiar with the role of human rights as a check on the arbitrary exercise of power by the state. It is therefore best to cite Śaṅkara himself:[52]

> Even after having created the four *varṇas* it did not flourish on account of threat (of force) posed by the arbitrary exercise of power by the king. Then it created a splendid form. What was it? *Dharma*, it was such a splendid form that it could restrain even the king. More forceful than force. Because it is capable of restraining even the king, there is nothing greater than it. All are restrained by it.

Several points need careful attention in this pregnant passage. There is the clear sense of rule of law being established, whose primary significance consists in the fact that the ruler is also subject to it. The word*ugra*, which implies ferocity, and which is used by Śaṅkara in relation to the *kṣatriya,* is sometimes used to denote the savage condition of existence prior to the existence of kingship. Note how the ante has been upped here: if kingship emerges as a check against the violence of anarchy, *dharma* has now emerged as a check against the violence of kingship. This seems to be the significance of the expression *dharmeṇa yathā rājñā* in I.4.14.

VII

Varna System: A Modern Analysis

Popular impressions suggest that nothing could be more antithetical to human rights than caste. Yet the Indian Constitution and the Indian political system has made strange bedfellows of the two. Let us not pronounce them divorced even before their marriage, notwithstanding the obstacles to consummation.

Our first task is to make the caste system intelligible—neither acceptable nor damnable, but simply intelligible—to Western and westernized Indian readers. As the raison d'etre of caste is birth-ascription, we ask the reader the following question: which cultural (as distinguished from natural) dimension of human existence in the West is defined by birth?

The answer is evident: nationality. In the West, one's national citizenship is just as firmly based on birth as caste is. This concept is almost religiously binding. Couples from Hong Kong have been known to travel to Canada, with the wife in advanced pregnancy, so that their child could be born in Canada. The child is then a natural citizen who can, upon reaching the designated age, sponsor his or her parents as immigrants! Birth-ascribed nationality can make a child 'the father of man' in a way Wordsworth could not imagine. It is worth noting that a child born to US citizens in the United Kingdom is automatically a British citizen, even if the parents are not entitled to hold British passports. Such is the miracle of birth in the modern polity. Although citizenship can be acquired, birth still has priority, as shown in eligibility requirements for the US presidency. Note that the place of birth, then, constitutes a *political* space.

A citizen of a country is likely to marry a citizen of the same country and is likely to mix primarily, although not exclusively, with fellow citizens of that country when overseas. In other words, the circle of connubium and commensality tends to be constituted by one's nationality just as in the case of caste. To a lesser extent, one's predilection toward a certain career-orientation is often associated with nationality, as revealed by expressions such as Yankee ingenuity, German technology, British diplomacy, and so on. Nationality thus provides the proper analogue for caste with this important difference; the place of birth, in terms of caste, constitutes a *social* space.

We shall return to this important distinction between political and social space, but first let us consider some similarities. Notwithstanding the hierarchy *among* castes, all are born equal *within* a caste. There is a perfect democracy, and one is even judged by one's peers. Caste constitutes one's social security net, just as the nation, with its social services, constitutes a citizen's safety net. Indians have no social security number; they have their caste.

The popular imagination, especially in the West, overwhelmingly connects caste and hierarchy within a society. The case of nations is similar, however, outside each nation. Nations rise and fall from power. Political pundits who speak of a Third and a Fourth World are merely replicating the fourfold *varṇa* or class order of Hinduism, which subsumes all castes, just as the four 'worlds' subsume all the countries of the world. Consider that India perceived itself as the world to such an event that no classical Hindu 'universal' monarch militarily stepped outside India, prevented from doing so, we are assured by the Greeks, 'out of a sense of justice'. The *varṇa* system, said to be characteristic of such an India, was equated with the world.

A conclusion emerges in that both citizenship and caste membership are determined by birth, although differences develop when this shared starting point is applied in terms of *society* or in terms of *polity*. When applied societally, the birth determinant gives rise to the caste system. When applied politically, it gives rise to the nation state. In both Indian and Western societies, the principle of birth discrimination was applied at a particular point in time. This point is unknown in the case of India. In the West it followed the Reformation. Application of the principle produced comparable results, in keeping with its respective social and political idiom. Being stateless and being casteless are comparable misfortunes.

The emergence of India as a nation provides an important illustration. To begin with, the weakness of the Indian concept of nation state has often been remarked. However, when large numbers of people are organized as a society in terms of caste, many of the functions of a state come to be handled socially. Such functions include, to some extent, even aspects involving the administration of justice. Empires rise and fall; society continues, as it has in India. Whence follows the inadequate politicization of a people, from a modern point of view, and the weakness of national feeling. Second, while politically organized groups based on caste are involved in an external hierarchy of nations, socially organized groups based on caste are involved in an *internal* hierarchy. The former is fluid, and the latter is more or less fixed, at least in broad terms and for longer periods than the political eras of nations. Third, the direct relationship between the citizen and the state is mediated by a caste in societies organized by caste. In India today, the competing ideal of a nation has been placed alongside caste, although both are based on birth. The government is attempting to convert all Indians into one caste, the Indian caste, as it were.

India is caught, then, in the shift from 'society' to 'polity'. Inasmuch as the latter form of organization is very different from the former, India seems adrift. However, inasmuch as both are based on birth, India possesses a 'home-ground' advantage. In cases of both caste system and nation state, the scale has created the phenomenon, and the basis of the phenomenon in both cases is birth ascription. This example, we hope, illustrates that when the principles of otherwise apparently antithetical systems are uncovered, radical revisioning may be possible. A scalar shift in the operational locus of the basic premise of the caste system renders it 'rights-friendly'. Do I not destroy my enemy, Abraham Lincoln is believed to have asked, if I make him (or her) a friend?

Conclusion

There are thus various ways in which the caste system can be brought into relationship with human rights, through the twin concepts of *varṇa* and *jāti*. The concept of *varṇa* can be viewed as a system of balancing duties and privileges. Human rights can be brought into relationship with both sides of this scale. The point at which Hindu thought makes its own contribution to human rights discourse is when it proposes that the discourse must view rights and duties as an integrated whole. Moreover, the application of the *varṇa* model to the contemporary world results in a surprising extension of human rights discourse.[53]

VIII

It was pointed out at the very outset that the English word 'caste' does duty for two Sanskrit words, *varṇa* and *jāti*. The implications of the concept of *varṇa* for human rights discourse were explored in the preceding section. Attention may now be turned to the term *jāti* in this section. It might be useful, while doing so, to refresh our memory regarding the semantic fields of these two words and the area of semantic overlap. P.V. Kane explains the terms as follows:

> A few words must be said about the word *jāti*. The idea of varṇa was as we have seen based originally on race, culture, character and profession. It takes account mainly of the moral and intellectual worth of man and is a system of classes, which appears more or less natural. The ideal of varṇa even in the smṛtis lays far more emphasis on duties, on a high standard of effort for the community or society rather than on the rights and privileges of birth. The system of *jātis* (castes) lays all emphasis on birth and heredity and tends to create the mentality of clinging to privileges without trying to fulfil the obligations corresponding to such privileges. The word '*jāti*' in the sense of caste hardly ever occurs in the vedic literature . . ., the use of the word jāti in the sense of caste can be traced back at least to the times of the Nirukta.
>
> . . .
>
> Varṇa and jāti are sometimes clearly distinguished as in Yāj. II 69 and 206. But very often they are confounded. In Manu X. 27, 31 the word varṇa is used in the sense of mixed castes (*jātis*). Conversely the word jāti often appears to be used to indicate 'varṇa'. Vide Manu III. 15, VIII. 177, IX. 86 and 335, X. 41 and Yāj. I. 89 (in which latter sajāti appears to mean 'savarṇa').[54]

The etymologies of the two words are helpful here. The word *varṇa* is sometimes connected with the verb *vṛ*, which means to choose among other things; while the word *jāti* is derived from the root *jan*, to be born or produced. The point being made is simply this, that the concept of a *birthright* can perhaps be more clearly and unambiguously associated with the word *jāti* than *varṇa*.

The word *jāti* by itself stands for 'birth or social status based on lineage' and 'is one of the conditions which determines the position of the individual or family in the caste system', and thus starts out as being narrower in orientation in comparison to *varṇa*. This would seem to dim its prospects for contributing meaningfully to human rights discourse. The actual outcome, however, turns out to be the opposite of what one might expect.

Crucial to this development is the association of the word with the process of procreation. This association contributed to developments, which, while distinct by themselves, ultimately led to solidifying the concept of human, as in human rights.

The first line of development has to do with the concept of *varṇa-saṅkara* or *jāti-saṅkara*, both signifying marriage against caste lines. (The first form of the word is used more commonly;[55] although both are attested,[56] the second is rarely used). The fact that Hindu law books explain the various *jāti*s as a result of the intermarriage among the four *varṇa*s seems to imply paradoxically that a lot of *varṇa-saṅkara* must have been taking place (even if only in the imagination of the lawgivers) despite all the inveighing against it in these texts themselves. It must be assumed to have been going on all the time despite the scriptures speaking all the time against it, if the spawning of the numerous *jāti*s from the four *varṇa*s is to be explained. It is this *assumption* that holds the key to the next stage of the argument.

The stage of the argument is set in the *Mahābhārata* in the form of a conversation between a serpent and King Yudhiṣṭhira. The circumstances in which the conversation took place arose as follows:

> Yudhishthira found his brother Bhīmasena caught in the coils of a serpent, which, it turned out, was no other than the famous king Nahusha, who by his sacrifices, austerities, etc., has formerly raised himself to the sovereignty of the three worlds; but had been reduced to the condition in which he was now seen, as a punishment for his pride and contempt of the Brāhmaṇas. He promises to let Bhīmasena go, if Yudhishthira will answer certain questions. Yudhishthira agrees, and remarks that the serpent was acquainted with whatever a Brāhmaṇ ought to know. Whereupon the Serpent proceeds.[57]

In the course of this conversation Nahuṣa pointedly asks Yudhiṣṭhira for the basis of distinguishing between the *brāhmaṇa* and the *śūdra*, or the first and the last *varṇa*. In the course of his response, Yudhiṣṭhira maintains that the distinction rests entirely on the difference in moral and spiritual qualities possessed by the two. At this, Nahuṣa (in the form of the serpent) hastens to point out that 'if a man is regarded by you as being a man only in consequence of his conduct, then *birth is vain* until action is known'.[58] In his response to Nahuṣa, Yudhiṣṭhira relies on the phenomenon of *varṇa-saṅkara* to negate the role of birth in determining Brahminhood. He says in effect that because of rampant admixture of *varṇas*, caste is a poor yardstick in this matter. His actual words run as follows:

> Yudhishthira replied: O most sapient Serpent, birth is difficult to be discriminated in the present condition of humanity, on account of the confusion of all castes. All (sorts of) men are continually begetting children on all (sorts of) women. The text which follows is Vedic and authoritative: 'We who (are called upon) we recite the text.' Hence those men who have an insight into truth know that virtuous character is the thing chiefly to be desired.[59]

The first part of the answer is clear. It contains a clear allusion to the phenomenon of *varṇa-saṅkara,* from which Yudhiṣṭhira draws the logical conclusion that therefore Brāhmaṇahood, or *varṇa* distinctions in general, must be based on qualities or virtue since birth-criterion no longer applies in a situation of *varṇa-saṅkara.*

The second part of his answer, in which a Vedic text is quoted, also refers to the same fact but its cryptic formulation needs to be explained. The text quoted is *ye yajāmahe*: 'We who offer sacrifice'. The point is that those who are offering the sacrifice are saying in effect to the gods: accept these sacrifices from us such as we are, without going too deeply into the purity of our lineages (which are often recited at these sacrifices) since *varṇa-saṅkara* is a fact of life.[60] Professor P.V. Kane sheds light on the point when he writes:

> That varṇasaṅkara has gone too far in the opinion of the author of the Mahābhārata (Vanaparva 180.31-33) follows from the following words, which are despairingly put in the mouth of Yudhiṣṭhira. 'It appears to me that it is very difficult to ascertain the caste of human beings on account of the confusion of all varṇas; all sorts of men are always begetting offspring from all sorts of women; speech, sexual intercourse, being born and death—these are common to all human beings; and there is scriptural authority (for his view) in the word 'We, whoever we are, offer the sacrifice'. Hence those who have seen the truth regard character as the principal thing desired.' Saṁkarācārya is his bhāṣya on Vedāntasūtra I.3.33 remarks that, though in his day varṇas and āśramas had become disorganized and unstable as to their dharmas that was not the case in other ages, since otherwise the śāstras laying down regulations for them would have to be deemed purposeless or futile.[61]

Evidence from another part of the *Mahbhārata*, the *Śānti Parva*, also seems to suggest that 'varṇasaṅkara had gone too far in the opinion of the author of the Mahābhārata'. Sometimes an attempt is made to associate a particular colour with a *varṇa,* perhaps because the word literally means 'colour'. Under such a chromatic scheme 'Brahmins are fair, kṣatriyas reddish, vaiśyas yellowish and śūdras black'.[62] When Bhṛgu proposes this, sage Bharadvāja replies: 'If different colours indicate different castes, then all castes are mixed castes.'[63]

The upshot of the foregoing analysis is that at least according to these portions of the *Mahābhārata*, any rights or privileges based on birth cannot be entertained; they must be deserved. A *brāhmaṇa* to be a *brāhmaṇa* will have to possess the qualities of a *brāhmaṇa* and so forth. This may be described as the principle of *proportional egalitarianism*: status must equal or be in proportion to qualities or qualifications, not birth.

Mānava-jāti

The dialogue between Nahuṣa and Yudhiṣṭhira on this point also contains a seed of another kind for developing an argument based on the concept of *jāti* in the context of human rights. In the course of their conversation Yudhiṣṭhira also draws attention to the following fact: 'The speech, the mode of propagation, the birth, the death of all mankind are alike.'[64] Yudhiṣṭhira is highlighting the fact that all human beings, notwithstanding their classification into *varṇa*s or *jāti*s, share certain attributes in common, namely: (1) speech (*vāk*); (2) sexual activity (*maithunam*); (3) birth (*janma*), and (4) death (*maraṇam*). Thus all human beings are born, die, and have sex. Thus they are all the same, in this sense, at the physical level. Then they all possess the power of speech as well. In other words, since all these attributes follow from the fact of being *born* a human being, all of them belong to one *jāti*—the human race or *mānava-jāti*. The same line of argument is also developed elsewhere in the *Mahābhārata*. In the *Śānti Parva*, in the course of (yet another!) dialogue, this time between sage Bhṛgu and sage Bharadvāja, sage Bharadvāja remarks: 'We all seem to be affected by desire, anger, fear, sorrow, worry, hunger and labour; how do we have caste differences then?'[65]

This line of argument is different from the previous one, which was negative in nature. It negated any special privilege based on birth because *purity* of birth can no longer be established or claimed on account of *varṇa-saṅkara*. The present line of argument is positive in nature in that all human beings possess certain attributes in common by virtue of their common humanity—by being born human. So all are the same on account of this fact. As such (a) none can belong to a special class because (b) all belong to the same class.

One finds recognition of this position in both the popular and the philosophical traditions of Hinduism. The following four stanzas of the Telegu poet Vemana may be taken to represent the popular view.

CASTE

If we look through all the earth,
Men, we see, have equal birth,
Made in one great brotherhood,
Equal in the sight of God.

Food or caste or place of birth
Cannot alter human worth.
Why let caste be so supreme?
'Tis but folly's passing stream.

Empty is a caste dispute:
All the castes have but one root.
Who on earth can e'er decide
Whom to praise and whom do deride?

Why should we the pariah scorn,
When his flesh and blood were born
Like to ours? What caste is He
Who doth dwell in all we see?[66]

For the philosophical evidence one may turn to the *Sāṅkhya-Kārikā* of Īśvarakṛṣṇa, a text which Paramārtha carried with him to China in AD 546 where it was translated into Chinese.[67] Its fifty-third verse[68] contains a description of the entire world of the living (*samasto bhautikaḥ sargaḥ*). This world is said to consist of the gods, animals and human beings. The text then goes on to speak of eight kinds of gods (*aṣṭa-vikalpo daivaḥ*) and five kinds of animals (*tairyagyonayaśca pañcadhā*). But it speaks of all human beings as one (*manuṣyaścaikavidhaḥ*). It is also perhaps worth adding that the commentator Gauḍapāda (seventh century) explains the words '*manuṣyaścaika-vidhaḥ* by *manuṣyayonir ekaiva*, 'the source of production of mankind is one only' and that Vijñānabhikṣu (sixteenth century) 'the commentator on Sāṅkhya Pravacana iii.46, paraphrases the same words thus: *manuṣya-sargaścaika-prakāraḥ*, 'that human creation is of one sort.'[69]

Once the category of *jāti* is expanded to embrace the whole of humanity in this way, then from the *rejection* of rights of a specific *jāti* in the face of the fact that all human beings are similar, the *affirmation* of the rights of *mānava jāti* or humanity in general is but a step. We are now brought on the threshold of the concept of universal human rights. Thus whereas the first line of argument via *varṇa* had led to the direction of *proportional egalitarianism*, this second line of argument, proceeding from the concept of *jāti*, leads to *radical egalitarianism*.

Conclusions

(1) Hence one way in which the two discourses—Hindu religious discourse and human rights discourse—could be juxtaposed innovatively is by asking the question: is there some privilege claimed by one hierarchically superior group which deserves to be extended to all groups as a human right, as another example of the process by which privileges of a higher class are transformed into a human right?

One of these privileges the *brāhmaṇa*s claimed in ancient India was immunity from capital punishment.[70] It seems capable of such an extension. A movement for the abolition of the death penalty on the grounds that it constitutes a violation of human rights is already afoot in the West. It is a curious fact that despite its tradition of *ahiṁsā*, little thought was given towards extending it in the direction of abolishing capital punishment in ancient India.[71] By contrast, the famous Taoist Chinese text, the *Tao Te Ching* makes a strong case for it:

> The people are not frightened of death. What then is the use of trying to intimidate them with the death-penalty? And even supposing people were generally frightened of death and did not regard it as an everyday thing, which of us would dare to seize them and slay them? There is the Lord of Slaughter always ready for this task, and to do it in his stead is like thrusting oneself into the master-carpenter's place and doing his chipping for him. Now 'he who tries to do the master-carpenter's chipping for him is lucky if he does not cut his hand.'[72]

Human Rights discourse in general tends to favour the abolition of the death penalty.[73]

(2) Another aspect of the caste system is represented by the concept of *jāti*. This has two versions, one in which it refers to commensal, endogamous, and craft-exclusive units called *jāti*s (because one becomes a member of it by birth); and another in which it refers to the entire human race (*mānava jāti*) because one is born a human being.

The second understanding of *jāti* is in keeping with human rights discourse, for 'at the basis of the discourse on human rights there is the assumption of a *universal human nature* common to all peoples. Otherwise, a universal declaration could not logically have been proclaimed'.[74]

(3) The concept of the nation state can be identified as the hereomorphic equivalent of the caste system in the West. Once this equivalence is established, the barriers to the free movement of people across national

frontiers can be identified as the parallel to caste restrictions, and need to be done away with it, like them, for the flourishing of human rights.

(4) According to Dr B.R. Ambedkar, Western Indology has incorrectly identified the caste system as racial in origin (see Appendix IV). If the Western view, for which there is not much solid evidence, is abandoned, then the cause of human rights is advanced because as a result the caste system becomes functional rather than racial in nature, and discrimination based on functional differences are more easily eliminated than if based on racial differences.

Notes

1. *The International Bill of Human Rights*, New York: United Nations, 1993, p. 5.
2. Ibid.
3. Louis Renou, op. cit., p. 105.
4. A.L. Basham, op. cit., p. 148.
5. P.V. Kane, op. cit., Vol. V, p. 1633; but also see P.V. Kane, op. cit., Vol. II, Part I, second edition, p. 55, and Percival Spear (ed.), *The Oxford History of India*, fourth edition, New Delhi: Oxford University Press, 1994, pp. 63–4.
6. Ibid., Vol. II, Part I, p. 54.
7. David R. Kinsley, *Hinduism: A Cultural Perspective*, second edition, Englewood Cliffs, NJ: Prentice Hall, 1993, p. 155.
8. A.L. Basham, op. cit., p. 148.
9. David R. Kinsley, op. cit., p. 153.
10. Ibid., pp. 153–4.
11. See N.K. Devaraja, *Hinduism and the Modern Age*, New Delhi: Islam and the Modern Age Society, 1975, pp. 54–5.
12. Kana Mitra, cited in Robert Traer, op. cit., p. 131.
13. Cited in K.M. Panikkar, *Hindu Society at the Crossroads*, Bombay: Asia Publishing House, 1961, pp. 48–9.
14. *The Collected Works of Swami Vivekananda*, Calcutta: Advaita Ashrama, 1970 [Mayavati Memorial Edition], Vol. 5, p. 15.
15. John B. Carman, op. cit., p. 117.
16. Ibid.
17. Ibid.
18. S. Radhakrishnan, *The Hindu View of Life*, New York: The Macmillan Company, 1927, Lecture IV.
19. S. Radhakrishnan, *The Brahma Sūtra: The Philosophy of Spiritual Life*, London: George Allen & Unwin, 1960, p. 163.
20. S. Radhakrishnan, *The Hindu View of Life*, p. 93.
21. K.M. Panikkar, op. cit., p. 34: 'A man's caste is decided by birth. From one caste to another there is no passage for the *individual*, though the position is now changing a little for small, organized communities, as we shall show later. If a man is born a Sudra he remains a Sudra all his life. He must marry only a

Sudra and according to caste-theory he should only carry on the professions allotted to Sudra. How the Brahmin theorists justified the establishment of a society, based on irremovable *inequality* under which the vast majority of the population was forced to accept the stigma of inferiority, need not be discussed here. It constitutes the most interesting example of the overwhelming influence of institutions on the mind of man.'

22. Ibid., pp. 40–1. Also see p. 47: 'Recently Indian leaders have begun to realize the evils of 'caste-ism'. Now it will be seen that this *caste-ism has nothing to do with Chaturvarnya or the four-fold division of caste*. There is no common Sudra feeling, no appeal to Sudra unity, or even to Brahmin unity. *Caste-ism is the loyalty to the sub-caste translated into politics*' (emphasis added).
23. Ibid., p. 37.
24. Cited, ibid., p. 111.
25. On the implications of such a step see Pratima Bowes, *The Hindu Religious Tradition*, London: Routledge & Kegan Paul, 1977, p. 305 ff.
26. Robert Traer, op. cit., p. 131.
27. M.K. Gandhi, op. cit., p. 324. Diacritics added. *Varṇāśrama* refers to the two doctrines of the fourfold division of society and the four stages of life, which are characteristic of Hinduism.
28. Ibid., p. 333. Diacritics added.
29. How this could be achieved is explained by Kana Mitra as follows (cited in Robert Traer, op. cit., p. 131): 'The ideal of *svadharma*, if not understood as a rigid code or law, can be a contribution in the field of human rights in its suggestion that differences be taken seriously. Manu offers suggestions in taking it in a non-rigid way. *Dharma*, he says, is what "is followed by those learned of the Vedas and what is approved by the conscience of the virtuous who are exempt from hatred and inordinate affection". Traditions, conscience, and reason must all be consulted to determine the rights and duties of humans. Rights and duties of different people in different situations are different, but each human being deserves and should have equal consideration and concern.'
30. Cited in Robert Traer, op. cit., p. 132.
31. Cited in ibid., p. 130.
32. S. Radhakrishnan, *The Hindu View of Life*, p. 114.
33. P. Nagaraja Rao, *The Four Values in Indian Philosophy and Culture*, Mysore: University of Mysore, 1970, pp. 21–2.
34. P.V. Kane, op. cit., Vol. II, Part II, p. 1696.
35. John B. Carman, op. cit., p. 121.
36. Ibid.
37. Ibid.
38. Ibid., pp. 126–7.
39. Klaus K. Klostermaier, *A Survey of Hinduism*, Albany: State University of New York Press, 1989, p. 326, emphasis added.
40. Ibid., p. 327. Dr Ambedkar converted in 1956 and Gandhi died in 1948. So the statement of Gandhi's relationship with Ambedkar, though generally correct, may have to be corrected for detail.

41. Ramesh N. Patel, *Philosophy of the Gita*, New York: Peter Lang, 1991, p. 44.
42. Ibid.
43. Louis Renou (ed.), *Hinduism*, New York: George Braziller, 1962, pp.55–6.
44. P.V. Kane, op. cit., Vol. V, Part II, p. 1669.
45. J.B. Carman, op. cit., p. 127.
46. Louis Renou, op. cit., pp. 105–6.
47. Ibid., p. 106.
48. Ibid., pp. 106–7.
49. S. Radhakrishnan, *The Principal Upaniṣads*, pp. 169–71.
50. P.V. Kane, op. cit., Vol. III, pp. 19–20.
51. Hartmut Scharfe, op. cit., p. 2.
52. For Sanskrit text see *Ten Principal Upaniṣads with Śāṅkarabhāṣya*, Delhi: Motilal Banarsidass, 1987, p. 683. For a Vaiṣṇava Dvaita interpretation see Major B.D. Basu, *The Bṛhadāraṇyaka Upaniṣad with the Commentary of Sri Madhvācārya*, Allahabad: The Panini Office, 1916, p. 94.
53. This section draws heavily on the author's contribution found in John Kelsay and Sumner B. Twiss (eds), *Religion and Human Rights*, New York: The Project on Religion and Human Rights, 1994, Chapter 4.
54. P.V. Kane, op. cit., Vol. II, Part I, second edition, pp. 54–5.
55. Ibid., p. 59.
56. See R.P. Kangle, *The Kauṭilīya Arthaśāstra*, Delhi: Motilal Banarsidass, 1988 [1965], Part III, pp. 146–7: 'This theory of the origin of these communities is of extremely doubtful validity. There seems little doubt that some of these communities, for example, the Niṣāda and the Caṇḍāla, are aboriginal communities. Others, like Ugra and Kṣatta, seem to have been warrior clans. Names like Māgadha and Vaidehaka contain an obvious reference to the region from which the communities came, whereas names like Vaina, Kuśīlava, perhaps also Sūta, appear to be derived from the profession followed by the community. It is, therefore, hardly possible to believe that any of these communities really came into being as a result of mixed marriages among the four *varṇas*. To believe that, we would have to assume that inter-marriages among the four *varṇa*s, not only in the *anuloma*, but also in the *pratiloma* way, were quite common. Otherwise, it would be very difficult to explain the large number of Caṇḍāla, Vaidehaka, Sūta or other communities that are said to be the result of *pratiloma* unions. But if such inter-marriages are assumed to have been very common, that would mean that rules about marrying a girl of the same *varṇa*, which we find not only in the *Smṛtis* but also in the *Arthaśāstra* (1.3.9), were consistently ignored. In other words, we should have to believe that *varṇa-saṅkara* or mixing of the *varṇa*s, of which the theory shows such a pious horror, was in reality a fact of social life. Such a conclusion, however, is hardly acceptable. Evidence from all sources, Brahamanical, Buddhist and Jain, showing that marriages, say, between Brahmin girls and Śūdra boys on such a large scale as to bring into being the very numerous and widespread community of Caṇḍālas, are quite inconceivable. Illicit unions instead of marriages on this scale are, of course, still more inconceivable. It, therefore, appears clear

that this theory of the origin of these communities is merely a fiction, apparently a legal fiction, invented to bring them into relation with the *varṇa* system, which alone was regarded as valid in law.'

57. J. Muir, *Original Sanskrit Texts*, Delhi: Oriental Publishers, 1972, Part 1, p. 133.
58. Ibid., p. 135, emphasis added.
59. Ibid., pp. 135–6.
60. A more detailed explanation is offered below, vide J. Muir, op. cit., part 1, p. 137, note 243: 'To explain the last elliptical expression I will quote part of the Commentator's remarks on the beginning of Yudhishthira's reply: *Vāgādīnām iva maithunasyāpi sādhāraṇyāj jātir durjneyā / tathā chā śruṭiḥ 'na chaitad vidma brāhmaṉāḥ smo vayam abrāhmaṇā vā" iti brāhmaṉya-samśayam̃ upanyasyati / nanu jāty-aniśchaye katham 'brāhmaṉo'ham" ityādy abhimāna-purassaram yāgādau pravartteta ity āśankyāha 'idam ārsham" iti / atra 'ye yajāmahe, ity anena cha ye vayam̃ smo brāhmaṉāḥ anye vā te vayam yajāmhe iti brāhmaṉye' navadhāraṉam̃ darśitam / mantra-lingam api 'ya evāsmi sa san yaje" iti / . . . Tasmād āchāra eva brāhmaṇya-niśchayahetur veda-prāmāṇyād ity upasaharati* / 'As the mode of propagation is common to all the castes, just as speech, etc. are, birth is difficult to be determined. And accordingly, by the words: 'We know not this, whether we are Brāhmans or no Brāhmans,' the Veda signifies a doubt as to Brāhmanhood. Then, having raised the difficulty 'how, if birth is undetermined, can a man engage in sacrifice, etc., with the previous consciousness that he is a Brāhman, etc.?' The author answers in the words 'this text is Vedic, etc.' It is both shown by the words 'we who . . . recite (which mean) 'we, whoever we are,—Brāhmans or others,—we recite', that the fact of Brāhmanhood is unascertained; and this is also a characteristic of the formula, 'whosoever I am, being he who I am, I recite.'' The comment concludes: 'Hence he briefly infers from the authoritative character of the Veda, that conduct is the cause of certainty in regard to Brāhmanhood.' Prof. Aufrecht has pointed out to me that the words *ye yajāmahe* occur in S.P. Br.I.5, 2,16 and in Taitt. 2.I.16, 11,1. The Commentator on the last-named passage refers in explanation of them to Aśvalāyana's Śrauta Sūtras, I.5,4f., where it is said that these two words constitute the formula called *āguh,* which comes in at the beginning of all the *yajyas* which are unaccompanied by any *anuyāja.* The Commentator interprets the two words thus: *sarve 'ye' vayaṁ hotāro 'dhvaryuṇā 'yaja' iti preshitās te vayam 'yajāmahe" yājyām paṭhāmaḥ* / 'All we hotri priests who are called upon by the adhvaryu by the word 'recite', we recite, i.e. repeat the *yājyā.'* (See Haug's Ait. Br. II, p. 133 and note 11.), Prof Aufrecht thinks the words in the Commentator's note *ya evāsmi sa san yaje* may be a free adaptation of Atharva VI. 123, 3.42. It does not appear from what source the words *na chaitad vidmaḥ* etc. are derived.'
61. P.V. Kane, op. cit., Vol. II, Part I, second edition, p. 61.
62. K.M. Sen, *Hinduism*, Harmondsworth: Penguin Books, 1961, p. 28.
63. Ibid.
64. J. Muir, op. cit., Part I, p.137.

65. K.M. Sen, op. cit., p. 28.
66. Cited in Percival Spear (ed.), op. cit., p. 67.
67. T.M.P. Mahadevan, op. cit., p. 117.
68. J. Muir, op. cit., Part I, p. 158, note 285.
69. Ibid., pp. 81–2.
70. A.L. Basham, op. cit., p. 120; P.V. Kane, op. cit., Vol. III, pp. 398–9; etc. Although it is uncertain whether this privilege was always extended there is little doubt that the privilege was claimed and sometimes granted. See Samuel Beal, *Buddhist Records of the Western World* (translated from the Chinese of Huien Tsiang [AD 629]), Delhi: Oriental Books Reprint Corporation, 1969 [1884], p. 221.
71. A.L. Basham, op. cit., pp. 118–20. Also see P.V. Kane, op. cit., Vol. III, p. 399.
72. Arthur Waley, *The Way and Its Power: A Study of the Tao Te Ching and its Place in Chinese Thought*, New York: The Grove Press, Inc., 1958, p. 234.
73. K.P. Saksena (ed.), *Human Rights: Perspective and Challenges*, (New Delhi: Lancers Books, 1994, pp. 97–104.
74. Raimundo Panikkar, 'Is the Notion of Human Rights a Western Concept?', *Diogenes 120*, Winter 1982, pp. 80–1, emphasis added.

CHAPTER 4

The Stages of Life (*Āśrama*) and Human Rights

The concept known as the *āśrama* system, or the doctrine of the stages of life, developed early in the history of Hinduism, perhaps as early as the first millennium BC or soon thereafter.[1] According to this scheme, the life of a human being is notionally divided into four stages: (1) that of a celibate student (*brahmacarya*); (2) a householder (*gārhasthya*); (3) a hermit (*vānprasthya*), and (4) a renunciant (*sannyāsa*). The following is a summary statement of the four stages with their Sanskrit names.

> The four *ashramas* are the *brahmacharya* (student), *grihasthya* (householder), *vanaprasthya* (hermit), and *sannyasa* (wandering mendicant). . . . In the *Brahmacharya* the student receives instruction in the *Vedas*, learns meditative disciplines, develops self-control, and prepares himself for life's responsibilities. *Grihasthya* is the time of marriage, vocation, and family responsibilities. *Vanaprasthya* is the period for releasing attachments to worldly goods, for turning over the family vocation and possessions to sons, for guiding others on the basis of one's own experiences, and for paying more and more attention to the liberation of one's self from worldly attachments. In the *sannyasa* stage of life a break is made from all worldly ties, and full attention is given to the goal of *moksha.*[2]

There is an inner rhythm and logic to the scheme.[3] In the light of the normal Hindu expectation of a life of a hundred years, each stage is often assigned twenty-five years but really 'all that is meant is that a man may, if he lives long, pass through the four stages'.[4]

On the whole this aspect of Hindu social organization has caused less problems for Hinduism than the caste system[5] and has even been applauded.[6] In view of the fact that we discussed the *puruśārtha*s, or the *caturvarga* scheme, in relation to human rights earlier, it is worth noting that to pair the *puruśārtha*s and *āśrama*s in a mechanical way might be 'a mistake'.[7] Nevertheless while not all Hindus would follow this sequence of stages in their lives, the structure that the *caturāśrama* scheme suggests and the interests to be pursued according to the *caturvarga* scheme certainly have deeply influenced the personal and social history of Hindus and Hinduism. Its structure apparently reflects so well what Hindus understood to be the essence of Hinduism that R.N. Dandeker chose it as the schema for his representation of Hinduism in the influential *Sources of Indian Tradition.*[8]

From the point of view of Western culture, the striking aspect of the *āśrama* scheme is the provision found therein for the spiritual dimension of life:

> The doctrine illustrates the contrast between two ideals, works and asceticism, a contrast expressed in a man's lifetime as a continuous evolution. It should moreover be remarked that in the past the transition from a social to a contemplative life did in fact frequently take place; even today there is no lack of people who after being deeply involved in worldly life suddenly abandon all in response to the call of the spirit.[9]

Recent evidence confirms a strong ideological commitment on the part of the Hindus to this scheme.[10]

II

It is an interesting fact that many of the articles of the Universal Declaration of Human Rights could be distributed over the various stages of life. A tentative assignment would appear as follows:

Brahmacarya: Article 26

Article 26

(1) Everyone has the right to education. Education shall be free, at least in the elementary and fundamental stages. Elementary education shall be compulsory. Technical and professional education shall be made generally available and higher education shall be equally accessible to all on the basis of merit.

(2) Education shall be directed to the full development of the human personality and to the strengthening of respect for human rights and fundamental freedoms. It shall promote understanding, tolerance and friendship among all nations, racial or religious groups, and shall further the activities of the United Nations for the maintenance of peace.

(3) Parents have a prior right to choose the kind of education that shall be given to their children.

GĀRHASTHYA: ARTICLES 16, 23, AND 25

Article 16

(1) Men and women of full age, without any limitation due to race, nationality or religion, have the right to marry and to found a family. They are entitled to equal rights as to marriage, during marriage and at its dissolution.
(2) Marriage shall be entered into only with the free and full consent of the intending spouses.
(3) The family is the natural and fundamental group unit of society and is entitled to protection by society and the State.

Article 23

(1) Everyone has the right to work, to free choice of employment, to just and favourable conditions at work and to protection against unemployment.
(2) Everyone, without any discrimination, has the right to equal pay for equal work.
(3) Everyone who works has the right to just and favourable remuneration ensuring for himself and his family an existence worthy of human dignity, and supplemented, if necessary, by other means of social protection.
(4) Everyone has the right to form and to join trade unions for the protection of his interests.

Article 25

(1) Everyone has the right to a standard of living adequate for the health and well-being of himself and of his family, including food, clothing, housing and medical care and necessary social services, and the right to security in the event of unemployment, sickness, disability, widowhood, old age or other lack of livelihood in circumstances beyond his control.
(2) Motherhood and childhood are entitled to special care and assistance. All children, whether born in or out of wedlock, shall enjoy the same social protection.

VĀNAPRASTHYA

Article 24

Everyone has the right to rest and leisure, including reasonable limitation of working hours and periodic holidays with pay.

III

The juxtaposition of these articles with the *āśramas* produces some interesting results. Article 26, clause 1: 'Everyone has the right to education' should presumably be read as 'Everyone has the right to *every kind of* education'. This is important in the context of education because certain classes of people were barred from obtaining certain forms of religious education for several centuries in the history of Hinduism. As Professor K. Satchidananda Murty has remarked:

> For several centuries only the traivarṇika (men of the three upper castes) have been generally considered eligible to undertake Vedic study, but in effect it has been the exclusive privilege and prerogative of male Brāhmins only. Even today most Brāhmins who have learnt the Veda, either with or without meaning generally do not teach it to women, śūdras and others.[11]

He goes on to point out:

> But the Veda itself does not say that it is meant for any particular sex, caste or race. On the contrary, it declares that it is meant for all. There is the following Yajurvedic text: 'Just as I have revealed this auspicious word to all human beings, so must you. I have revealed the Vedic truth to Brāhmins, Kshatriyas, Śūdras, Āryās, personal servants (*svāya*) and to the lowest of Śūdras (*araṇyāya*) also.' There is also the following Atharvavedic text: 'O Man, I, being of the nature of truth and being unfathomable, have revealed the true Vedic knowledge; so I am he who gave birth to the Veda. I cannot be partial either to a Dāsa (slave) or an Ārya; I save all those who behave like myself (i.e. impartially) and follow my truthful commands.' The Veda is a universal scripture.[12]

Thus while the position adopted in classical Hinduism *about* the Vedas violates human rights, the position of the Vedas themselves is apparently consistent with Article 26 of the Universal Declaration of Human Rights. Modern Hinduism is virtually unanimous in upholding full access to Vedic studies on the part of all.

In the matter of *secular* education, the *śūdras* had more freedom even in the past. For instance, the medical text, *Suśruta Saṁhitā* mentions *śūdras* of good families with good qualifications as fit students for medicine, which ironically is itself classified as a kind of Veda (*āyurveda*).[13] The thrust of the Universal Declaration of Human Rights seems primarily directed at secular education but it is important to bear in mind that it must also be extended to sacred education, if its spirit is to be honoured. This is how the human rights issues interact with the first *āśrama*.

In the case of the second *āśrama*, the main point of interaction is provided by the mode and manner of marriage. Most of the marriages in Hinduism, as they take place today, are 'arranged marriages', that is, arranged by the parents. One should, however, not leap to the conclusion that this fact violates Section 2 of Article 16. For it might be possible, even within the framework of arranged marriages, to secure 'full and free consent of the intending spouses'. In the light of this right one may wish to assess all the forms of marriage referred to in the Hindu texts, 'which enumerate eight types of marriage, named after various gods and supernatural beings:

(1) *Brāhma,* marriage of a duly dowered girl to a man of the same class.
(2) *Daiva*, when a householder gives a daughter to a sacrificial priest as part of his fee.
(3) *Ārṣa*, in which, in place of the dowry, there is a token bride price of a cow and a bull.
(4) *Prājāpatya*, in which the father gives the girl without dowry and without demanding the bride price.
(5) *Gāndharva*, marriage by the consent of the two parties, which might be solemnized merely by plighting troth. This form of marriage was often clandestine.
(6) *Āsura*, marriage by purchase.
(7) *Rākṣasa*, marriage by capture.
(8) *Paiśāca*, which can scarcely be called marriage at all—the seduction of a girl while asleep, mentally deranged, or drunk.[14]

The application of the human rights criterion will rule out the last three and accept the first four, if in the process of arranging them 'the full and free consent of the intending spouses has been secured'. However, its enthusiastic approval will be preserved for the *fifth* type, preferably without its clandestine character.

Another perspective may be brought to bear on the issue to present marriage by mutual consent in a more favourable light. Yāska, the ancient Vedic exegete (700–500 BC) declares in the *Nirukta* (11–4):

They give away to others the female children. There exist *dāna*, *vikraya* and *atisarga* of the female but not of the male. *Dāna*, means gift, *vikraya* means sale, and *atisarga* means abandonment. Durgacharya, the commentator explains these three methods of the disposal of daughters as giving away in marriage (*dāna*), as acceptance of payment for marriage (*vikraya*), and freedom to choose (*atisarga*).[15]

The emphasis on freedom to choose, called *svayaṁvara*, is particularly associated with women, as the woman's right to choose her husband.

A special form of *gāndharva* marriage was the *svayaṁvara* or 'self-choice'. The law books lay down that if a girl is not married by her parents soon after attaining puberty she may choose her own husband, and evidently marriage by the choice of the bride sometimes took place. Epic literature shows that more than one form of *svayaṁvara* was practiced. Princess Sāvitrī toured the country in her chariot in search of a suitable mate, until she found Satyavant, the woodcutter's son. Damayantī chose her husband Nala at a great ceremony, at which she passed along the assembled ranks of her suitors until she found the man of her choice.[16]

In this respect perhaps Hindu men should catch up with Hindu women, and *svyaṁvara* may be advocated as the appropriate form of marriage in the light of the Universal Declaration of Human Rights.

IV

The Universal Declaration of Human Rights can be criticized from the perspective of the *āśrama* doctrine as not taking the full lifespan of a human being and the changes it undergoes in the course of its passage from one phase to another into full account. It does make a special mention of childhood (Article 23, Section 2) and education (Article 26) but it has little to say about the life of a senior citizen. Article 24 highlights this lack of perspective. It mentions rest, leisure, and holidays but they are aplenty upon retirement. This oversight may reflect the alleged Western preoccupation with youth, in contrast to the esteem attached to age in primal religions and in Chinese and Indian cultures. It is interesting that although the *śūdra* is at the bottom of the social totem pole, so to say, in terms of caste hierarchy, the great exponent of this hierarchy, the legendary lawgiver, Manu, states that the *śūdra* is venerable on account of his age (II.137). Thus, the process of aging, and its 'staging' as visualized in the *āśrama* scheme, may be worth reflecting on in the context of human rights as well as on its own. Modern Hindu thinkers sometimes cite, with obvious satisfaction, the following remark of C.G. Jung, in which they read a confirmation of the Hindu perspective as based on human nature:

After immense clinical experience over a period of thirty years, I find among those in the second half of life, that is, over thirty-five there has not been one whose problem in the last resort was not that of finding a religious outlook on life. When a modern physician is confronted with a neurotic patient he sees very clearly why his patient is ill, it arises from his having no love but only sexuality, no faith because he is afraid to grope in the dark, no hope because he is disillusioned by the world and life, no understanding because he has failed to read the meaning of his own existence. What the patient needs are faith, hope, love and insight.[17]

Conclusion

The four stages of human life are really an extension of a pivotal distinction drawn within Hinduism between *pravṛtti* and *nivṛtti*, where the first term stands for involvement in the affairs of the world and the second term for the disengagement therefrom. And the contribution Hindu thought makes to human rights discourse is to suggest that it has not paid enough attention to the *nivṛtti* phase of life.

Notes

1. P.V. Kane, *History of Dharmaśāstra*, Poona: Bhandarkar Oriental Research Institute, 1962, Vol. V, Part II, p. 1643; Patrick Olivelle, *The Āśrama System: The History and Hermeneutics of a Religious Institution*, New York and Oxford: Oxford University Press, 1993, passim.
2. Troy Wilson, Organ, *Hinduism: Its Historical Development*, Woodsbury, NY: Barron's Educational Series Inc., 1974, p. 203.
3. Ibid.: 'the *ashrama* program is a functional division. The four *ashramas* are in chronological order: preparation, production, service, and retirement. They constitute a rhythm of inner-direction and outer-direction. The student is inner-directed; his task is to prepare himself for the life ahead. The *grihastha* and the *vanaprastha* are both outer-directed: the former supports the entire society; the latter shares his experiences for the good of all. The *sannyasi* is inner-directed; having contributed to society at least as much as he received, he prepares himself for the final release.'
4. P.V. Kane, op. cit., Vol. V, Part II, p. 1644.
5. T.M.P. Mahadevan, op. cit., p. 75.
6. P.V. Kane, op. cit., Vol. V, Part II, p. 1646.
7. Troy Wilson Organ, op. cit., p. 203. But also see Arvind Sharma, 'The Puruṣārthas: An Axiological Exploration of Hinduism', *Journal of Religious Ethics*, 27:2, Summer 1999, p. 235.
8. Klaus K. Klostermaier, op. cit., p. 337.
9. Louis Renou, *The Nature of Hinduism*, tr., p. 100.
10. Philip H. Ashby, *Modern Trends in Hinduism*, New York: Columbia University Press, 1974, p. 62.
11. K. Satchidananda Murty, *Vedic Hermeneutics*, Delhi: Motilal Barnarsidass, 1993, p. 14.
12. Ibid.
13. Ibid., p. 20, note 31. It is a curious fact that the Chinese pilgrim Xuanzang (Hieun-Tsiang), who visited India in the seventh century, seems to include *Āyurveda* among the four principal Vedas. He writes in his Si-Yu-Ki (Samuel Beal, *Buddhist Records of the Western World*, Delhi: Oriental Books Reprint

Corporation, 1969 (1884), p. 79: 'The Brahmans study the four Veda Sastras. The first is called *Shau* (longevity); it relates to the preservation of life and the regulation of the natural condition. The second is called *Sse* (sacrifice); it relates to the (rules of) sacrifice and prayer. The third is called *Ping* (peace or regulation); it relates to decorum, casting of lots, military affairs, and army regulations. The fourth is called *Shu* (secret mysteries); it relates to various branches of science, incantations, medicine.'

14. A.L. Basham, op. cit., p. 168, with slight emendation.
15. K. M. Panikkar, op. cit., p. 57. We may disregard Panikkar's suggestion for our present purposes that *atisarga* really means abandonment.
16. A.L. Basham, op. cit., p. 169.
17. P. Nagaraja Rao, op. cit., pp. 48–9.

CHAPTER 5

The Four Ages (*Yuga*s) and Human Rights

I

Another well-known doctrine within Hinduism—along with that of the four ends of human endeavour (*puruṣārtha-catuṣṭaya* or *caturvarga*), the four classes (*caturvarṇa*), and the four stages of life (*caturāśrama*)—is that of the four ages (*caturyuga*). The details of it are somewhat complex, and are summarized below. The four *yuga*s are called *Kṛta*, *Tretā*, *Dvāpara* and *Kali*.[1] The following table specifies the allotment of 'divine' years to each *yuga* along with the preceding and succeeding periods called *sandhyā* and *sadhyāṁśa*:[2]

	god years (one god year = 360 solar years)	*solar or mortal years*	
kṛta-yuga saṁdhyā	400	144,000	
kṛta-yuga	4000	1,440,000	
kṛta-yuga saṁdhyāṁśa	400	144,000	1,728,000
tretā-yuga saṁdhyā	300	108,000	
tretā-yuga	3000	1,080,000	
tretā-yuga saṁdhyāṁśa	300	108,000	1,296,000
dvāpara-yuga saṁdhyā	200	72,000	
dvāpara-yuga	2000	720,000	
dvāpara-yuga saṁdhyāṁśa	200	72,000	864,000
kali-yuga saṁdhyā	100	36,000	
kali-yuga	1000	360,000	
kali-yuga saṁdhyāṁśa	100	36,000	432,000
	12,000		4,320,000

The world at the moment is passing through Kali Yuga, which commenced on Friday, 18 February 3102 BC. These four ages, however, are part of an even larger calculation in terms of which

> 1000 of these four yugas constitute a day of Brahmā, which is called kalpa. The night of Brahmā is of the same duration. At the end of a kalpa the universe is resolved into Brahmā (and this is called *pralaya*) and at the end of Brahmā's night the world is created again. In one day of Brahmā there are 14 Manus and therefore each Manvantara is equal to about 71 caturyugas (1000 divided by 14). The life of Brahmā is 100, out of which half is gone and therefore the present is said to be the 2nd or latter half (*dvitīya parārdha*) of the life of Brahmā and at the present the kalpa that is running is called Varāha. From the above it will be seen that, according to the Purāṇas, the universe has been created and dissolved many times and there have been numerous Manvantaras also (vide Manu I.80).[3]

From our standpoint the important point to note is that

> The four yugas in various ways differ in their characteristics. Kṛta is so called because it is an age in which everything is fulfilled by every one and nothing is left to be done. The symbolic colours of the four yugas are respectively white, yellow, red and dark (Vanaparva 189.32). In Kṛta, dharma prevails in all its perfection and it stands with all its four feet (dharma being figuratively spoken of as vṛṣa, a bull, in Manu VIII.16 and Vanaparva 190.9) and it declines or deteriorates by a quarter in each of the following yugas (Manu I.81-82 = Śānti 232.23–4), so that in Kali only one quarter (or one foot) of dharma remains and adharma occupies three quarters.[4]

The human condition also varies with the *yugas*:

> In Kṛta people are entirely free from diseases, secure all that they desire and the length of human life is four hundred years, all of which decline by one quarter successively in the following three yugas (Manu I.83 = Śānti 232.25). The dharmas in each of the four yugas are different; *tapas* was the highest in Kṛta, philosophic knowledge in Tretā, sacrifice in Dvāpara and charity alone in Kali (Manu I.85–86 = Parāśara I.22–23 = Śānti 232.27–28). Manu I.85, Śānti 232.27 and 261.8, Parāśara I.22 all have the same verse stating that the dharmas prescribed for men in each yuga differ.[5]

On the face of it this would seem rather unpromising material to advance a discussion of human rights! Nevertheless, scholarly perseverance might be in order, and its first reward might come in the form of reviewing this scheme as a Hindu perspective on the *nature of history*, as proposed by Ainslee T. Embree. He writes:

> While it is impossible to speak of a 'Hindu view of history', since this phrase implies a way of looking at the world that was foreign to Indian thought, there is,

however, an understanding of the nature of the historical process that is of fundamental importance for the Hindu tradition. The principal feature of this understanding, which is given an elaborate analysis in the *Purāṇas*, is that human existence must be seen against a background of an almost unimaginable duration of time. In contrast to other civilizations which have been content to see man's history in terms of thousands of years, Indians—Buddhists and Jains as well as Hindus—spoke of billions of years. But even these figures, which are nearly meaningless in their magnitude, are dwarfed by the concept of cycles of aeons, endlessly renewing themselves, without beginning or end. Time and the historical process are parts of a vast cyclical movement, but not, as in some cyclical versions of history, a simple cycle of birth, growth, death and then rebirth with a repetition of the past. The Hindu model is of concentric circles, moving within each other in a complex series of retrogressive movements. The vastest cycle was 'a year of Brahmā', which by some reckonings was 311 040 000 million years long, with Brahmā's life lasting for one hundred of these cycles. This was followed by dissolution of all the worlds—those of men and gods—and then creation once more took place.[6]

The next promising step might be to review the nature of present-day history in the light of this perspective. Once again we follow the lead provided by Professor Embree:

Within these cycles there were other cycles, which were of more imaginable dimensions, and it is these, which are of primary significance for human history. A *kalpa*, or day of Brahmā, was 4 320 million years long, and within this were the smallest cycles, the four yugas. The *Krita Yuga*, the golden age, lasted for 1 738 000 years; the *Tretā* for 1 296 000 years; the *Dvāpara* for 864 000 years; and the *Kali* for 432 000 years. The four ages are calculated as a descending arithmetical progression, marked by progressive physical and spiritual deterioration. Present history is taking place within the *Kali Yuga*, which explains the violence and evil of human history. When this age comes to an end, a new cycle will begin—one of the thousand cycles of yugas that make up a day of Brahmā.

Man cannot save the social process from the decay and dissolution that is an inherent part of its structure, but he can save himself from within the process. The point is made, indeed, that one mark of the wickedness of the *Kali Yuga* is that salvation has been made much easier than in the former ages, since men of this age could not be expected to fulfill the rigorous requirements of a better time.[7]

The point to note here is that from the point of view of human rights discourse, this will be an age in which human rights abuses will be rampant. Here, for instance, is an unappetizing account of what things will be like in the Kali age:

At that time there will be monarchs, reigning over the earth; kings of churlish spirit, violent temper, and ever addicted to falsehood and wickedness. They will inflict death on women, children and cows; they will seize upon the property of their subjects; they will be of limited power, and will for the most part rapidly rise and fall; their lives will be short, their desires insatiable and they will display but little piety. The people of the various countries intermingling with them will follow their example, and the barbarians being powerful in the patronage of the princes, whilst purer tribes are neglected, the people will perish. Wealth and piety will decrease day by day, until the world will be wholly depraved.[8]

II

The key question to be faced is: what is one supposed to do in the face of these human rights violations, laced with ecological disaster, according to Hinduism?

At one time it was thought that Hinduism had nothing to offer in such a situation except passive resignation and that the age must run its course and things go from bad to worse. It can now be clarified that such a conclusion, advocating historical pessimism, is based on a serious misunderstanding of Hinduism. It can be asserted on the basis of authoritative texts (e.g., Manu IX.301 and 302) that

> the yugas are not watertight parts of Time. It is the king who can by his conduct introduce the characteristics of one yuga into another. Medhātithi on Manu IX.301 explains that the king should not be misled into thinking that Kali is a historical part of Time and that he (the king) cannot therefore be Kali or Kṛta, but that it is the king's way of conducting himself that will produce the conditions of the several yugas among his people.[9]

In other words, the state can intervene to uphold human rights norms. The importance of this conclusion is easy to lose sight of, because these days claims of violations of human rights are often made *against* the state. Hindu thought in this context draws attention to the fact that the state originally arose in a situation in which human beings had no rights, so that its dual role in the context of human rights must not be lost sight of. This original state in which human beings had no rights is referred to by the expression *mātsyanyāya* in the Hindu texts. The expression, which literally means 'law of the fish' (i.e., 'big fish eat small fish'), metaphorically denotes that 'might is right' and thus describes a situation in which people have no rights.

> They who live in countries where anarchy prevails cannot enjoy their wealth and wives. During times of anarchy the sinful man derives great pleasure from robbing the wealth of other people. When, however, his (ill-got)wealth is snatched by others, he wishes for a king. It is evident therefore that in times of anarchy

the very wicked even cannot be happy. The wealth of one is snatched away by two. That of those two is snatched away by many acting together. He who is not a slave is made a slave. Women, again, are forcibly abducted.[10]

The insight, which lies buried in the mythos of Hinduism and has to be extracted therefrom, refers to the emergence of kingship sometimes even in the Kṛta Yuga, the *best* of the ages,[11] as well as to the constant need of royal protection.[12] In modern idiom, then, the state is there to enforce human rights norms.

One point, however, needs to be addressed, which, on the face of it, seems to reduce the force of this conclusion. If concepts of duty or *dharma* are couched in terms of cosmological time, the difference between them and human rights discourse is in danger of becoming so acute as to render them incommensurable. For human rights discourse is temporally typically confined to one life. This yawning chasm between the two may seem hard to bridge. It helps to invoke the doctrine of *karma* and its relationship to that of *dharma* in such a context. Just as the universe is reborn cyclically, as it were, so is the individual, who is constantly reborn in this universe which ceaselessly regenerates itself. But while the status of *dharma* in terms of its cosmological formulation is unidirectional and visualized in terms of decline from a previous golden age, the status of *karma* in relation to the individual is not so fixed. One is free to perform good or bad *karma* based on one's moral volition at all times; were it not so the whole doctrine of *karma* would be reduced to mockery. It is true that the degree of free will human beings possess in this respect is variously assessed in the different versions of this doctrine but in no version of the doctrine which may be identified as such within Hinduism (with the possible exception of the defunct sect known as the *Ājīvika*) is it denied in moral terms, and even less so in soteriological terms. In other words, the nature of *karma* in relation to the individual is on a different footing than the nature of *dharma* in relation to a cosmic age, and while the latter suffers from a certain entropy, it is totally inapplicable in relation to the individual's *karma*. The point becomes clear if the concept that the king as the maker of the age (rather than the age being the maker of the king) is understood as an example of the king's *karma* overcoming the cosmic *yugadharma*. And the king is after all, an individual. In Western terms this could be phrased as the overcoming of a kind of natural law with a kind of positive law. Now that the topic has been broached, one might also use this opportunity to examine a point of interface of this doctrine of the *dharma* of the *yugas* with one aspect of Western thought. Western thought as represented by Rudolph Stammler,

Gustav Radbruch, and also such theists as St. Thomas and Dunus Scouts can be said to present the model of a 'natural law' which possesses a changing content.[13] There is a tendency on the part of the human mind to equate the 'natural' with the invariable in such a context as the present. Both Hindu and Western thought patterns of the type under the lens here challenge this easy equation. But while the idea of cosmic *yugadharma* tends to predict the direction of this change, the doctrine of *karma* as outlined above renders it forever open. Thus while from one point of view the cosmos may tend one way and the individual another, it lies within the power of the state as represented by the king to bend, mend, and amend it. Individual soteriological optimism is thus transformed into a more generalized political optimism through the agency of the king.

III

Just as the concept of the four ages itself is usually misconstrued as a doctrine of historical pessimism, which is dissipated by its more nuanced understanding, similarly the doctrine of the decline of *dharma* through the cycle of the four ages needs to be revisited to achieve a better understanding of it.

The clarifying question to ask in this context is: what is the nature of this *dharma*, which is destined to decline through the ages? One component of this *dharma*, as conceived in the texts, apparently consists of the privileges of the higher castes. Along with physical and moral decline, the descriptions of this age refer to the rise of the lower classes, the *śūdras*:

> Brāhmaṇas will not engage in *japa* (muttering of Vedic mantras), while śūdras will be intent on *japa* . . .[14] Śūdras will employ the word 'bho' (in addressing others of higher classes) and brāhmaṇas will employ the word *ārya* (in addressing peoples other than Brāhmaṇas) . . .[15]

Some descriptions have been read by scholars as thinly veiled attacks on 'Buddhist monks taken from the class of śūdras'.[16] The point to note then is that part of the 'decline' consists of the loss of 'higher caste' privileges. One can see how the privileged might well bemoan the loss of privilege but it is not at all clear that this is to be regretted from an egalitarian point of view.

This point is more potent than it might appear. To realize its full significance one might refer to a well-known incident in the *Rāmāyaṇa*, which is regularly cited as an example of the tacit, or even explicit, sanctioning of the oppression of the lower castes by the higher, namely, the killing of Śambūka by King Rāma. Rāma is supposed to be an ideal king but even as he was reigning, the young son of a *brāhmaṇa* died prematurely. The *brāhmaṇa* approached and then reproached the king for such a happening. The king was told, upon inquiry, by the sages that this was the unfortunate outcome of a *śūdra* practising austerities in his kingdom, to which only the higher castes were entitled. King Rāma thereupon traced down the felon, Śambūka, and beheaded him for his transgression, whereupon the *brāhmaṇa*'s dead son did a Lazarus and came back to life.

The story thus is an open and shut case of oppression of the *śūdras* by the higher castes. There is, however, a section of the deliberation of King Rāma with the sages whose significance seems to have gone unnoticed. While explaining to Rāma that a *śūdra* cannot practise austerities, they point out that a *śūdra* cannot do so in the age in which Rāma was reigning, namely, in the Tretā Yuga. They also imply that this would *not* constitute an offence in Kali Yuga, that is, in our age, the age we are living in. This is how Nārada explains the situation to Rāma:

> Learn, O King, what has caused the untimely death of this child! When thou are conversant therewith, do what thou considerest to be thy duty!
>
> O Prince, Joy to the Raghus, formerly in the Krita Yuga, the Brahmins alone practised asceticism; he who was not a brahmin in no wise undertook it.
>
> In the Treta Yuga, brahmins and warriors practised asceticism and the rest were under the supreme obligation of obedience, proper to the Vaishya and Shudra classes; the Shudras' duty being to serve the other three.
>
> O Great King, in the Dwapara Yuga, untruth and evil increased, unrighteousness having placed a second foot on the earth, and then the Vaishyas began to practise penance, so that dharma, in the form of asceticism, was performed by the three castes, but the Shudras were not permitted to undertake it during that time, O Foremost of Men.
>
> O Prince, a man of the lowest caste may not give himself up to penance in the Dwapara Yuga; it is only the Kali Yuga that the practice of asceticism is permitted to the Shudra caste.[17]

The 'right to practising austerities' expands with each age, even as '*dharma*' declines! In other words, one needs to take the full picture into account with all the nuances. From one point of view, probably that of the composers of the texts, *dharma* declines in the sense that the higher castes *progressively* lose their *privileges*; yet from the point of view of the lower castes, *dharma* expands with each passing age, they gain more *rights*![18]

A comparison from the history of Judaism may be helpful here. The destruction of the Temple was a terrible setback for Judaism, a rude shock for Judaic *dharma*. But this destruction produced a startling egalitarian consequence. While in biblical Judaism the priests were a hereditary class, in Rabbinic Judaism 'maintaining oneself ritually pure became an obligation for every Jew, *whether descended from a priestly family or not*. And Rabbinic Judaism would think of the community as having a priestly role among the nations of the world'.[19]

Thus at least three facts have to be taken into account in the present context: (1) what does the word *dharma* signify in a particular context? (2) who constitutes the context? (3) what are the facts of the situation, once the theory-laden descriptions have been shorn of the presuppositions.

For instance, the Kali Yuga is said to be the worst of times because of the decline of traditional*dharma*. But what is traditionally negative can also be radically positive, for it is clearly maintained that the *same amount* of moral or spiritual effort undertaken in the Kali Yuga is far more efficacious compared to the previous supposedly holier ages.[20] Hermeneutical vigilance may be required in dealing with the semiotically rich valences of Hindu categories.

IV

It is the clear implication of the doctrine of the four *yuga*s as applied to the case of Śambūka that Hinduism will become progressively egalitarian, and will be most so in the Kali Yuga. In fact not only will all the *varṇa*s be entitled to performing *tapa*s, including the *śūdra*s, according to the *Matsya Purāṇa* there will be only one *varṇa* in the Kali Yuga, the *śūdra*.[21] This could well be a highly convoluted Hindu way of saying that universal human rights will prevail.

Notes

1. P.V. Kane, op. cit., Vol. III, second edition, p. 891.
2. Benjamin Walker, *The Hindu World*, New York: Frederick A. Praeger, 1968, Vol. I, p. 8.
3. P.V. Kane, op. cit., p. 891.
4. Ibid., pp. 891–2.

5. Ibid., p. 892.
6. Ainslee T. Embree (ed.), *The Hindu Tradition*, New York: Random House, 1972, p. 220. One should avoid concluding that each cycle constitutes merely an exact replication or carbon copy of an earlier one; see Lyn Thomas, 'The Nature of Cyclical Repetition in the Indian Idea of Cyclical Time', in *Indian Insights: Buddhism, Brahmanism and Bhakti* (eds), Peter Connolly and Sue Hamilton, London: Luzac Oriental, 1997, pp. 83–9.
7. Ibid., pp. 220–1.
8. Ibid., p. 222.
9. P.V. Kane, op. cit., Vol. III, p. 892.
10. Ainslie T. Embree, ed., op. cit., pp. 107–8.
11. Ibid., p. 104.
12. Ibid., pp. 106–8.
13. I owe this point to Professor Upendra Baxi.
14. P.V. Kane, op. cit., p. 893.
15. Ibid.
16. Ibid., p. 895, note 1754.
17. Hari Prasad Shastri, tr., *The Ramayana of Valmiki*, London: Shanti Sadan, 1992 [1959], Vol. III, pp. 580–1.
18. This mythical pattern actually seems to conform broadly in outline with historical facts if they are presented and interpreted as follows (P.V. Kane, op. cit., Vol. V, Part II, pp. 929–30): 'The Viṣṇupurāṇa emphasizes that each one must do one's duty in the society in which one is born or one's duty which one has undertaken, that, if a person does this, he reaches the same higher worlds, whether he be a brāhmaṇa or a śūdra. This doctrine is the same as taught in the Bhagavadgītā18.45 and 46 "a person secures the highest perfection (final emancipation) by being intent on carrying out the duties appropriate to him; man secures perfection (or bliss) by worshipping with the performance of his peculiar duties (not with flowers and the like or by words) Him from whom all beings proceed and by whom all this (world) is enveloped." Ancient works like the Vedas, Jaimini's sūtras on Mīmāṁsā and the Vedāntasūtra (1.3 34–8) denies to the śūdra the right to study the Veda and the Upaniṣads. Buddha's teaching held out the same promise of liberation from suffering to all men irrespective of class or caste and was therefore more attractive to the śūdras. The Bhagavadgītā and the Purāṇas changed the whole outlook of Indian society, high or low, and promised the same higher spiritual life or worlds to all who did mundane work under a sense of social duty, did not hanker after mundane rewards and brought all their actions, in whatever avocation they might be engaged, as an offering to God. In the Padmapurāṇa Vyāsa is made to say to Yudhiṣṭhira: "It is not possible to observe a Fast on Ekādaśī in both fortnights (of a month), which is an easy means (that) requires little wealth, that entails little trouble, but yields great rewards, that is the very essence (of the teaching) of all Purāṇas, he should be pure and on Dvādaśī after worshiping Keśava with flowers he should first feed brāhmaṇas and then himself take his

meal. Those who desire to secure heaven should perform this vrata throughout their lives; even persons of evil conduct, the greatest sinners devoid of dharma, do not go to Yama (do not fall into hell) if they fast on Ekādaśī," The Sūtasaṁhitā states "effort for acquiring true knowledge (of the Self) is meant for all (for persons even lower than śūdras), that effort made by explaining in a different language (than Sanskrit) and by the lapse of enough time will tend to the good (of the lowest)". This clearly shows how the Purāṇas put before all people easy ways whereby they could attain bliss in the Hereafter.'

19. Alan F. Segal, 'The Jewish Tradition', in *World Religions: Western Traditions* (ed.), Willard G. Oxtoby, Toronto: Oxford University Press, 1996, p. 76, emphasis added.
20. P.V. Kane writes (op. cit., Vol. V, Part II, pp. 928–9): 'The Purāṇas introduced several striking changes in the religious rites, practices and ideals of the people. The most characteristic thought and the keynote of the Purāṇas is to declare how great rewards and results could be secured with little effort. The Viṣṇupurāṇa (VI. 2) narrates how sages approached Vyāsa with the question "in what age does a little dharma yield very great rewards?" Vyāsa was bathing in the Ganges; he came out, uttered "śūdra is good and Kali is good" and then again plunged into the river; then he again came out and said "well done, O śūdra! You are blessed"; he again plunged into the river came out and said "women are good and blessed; who is more blessed than they". When he finished his bath and performed his morning rites, the sages asked him to explain what he meant by calling Kali, śūdras, and women good and blessed. He replied: "a man secures in a single day and night in Kali age as much reward of *tapas*, celibacy and *japa* as is obtained in ten years in Kṛta age, in one year in Tretā and in a month in Dvāpara; therefore, I spoke of Kali as good; in Kali age a man secures merely by the glorification or incessant repetition of the name of Keśava what he would secure by deep meditation in Kṛta, by sacrifices in Tretā, and by worship in Dvāpara; I am pleased with Kali because a man secures great eminence of dharma with a little effort. Persons of the three higher varṇas have to study the Vedas after observing many strict rules, then they have to perform sacrifices which require wealth; they incur sin if they do not perform their duties properly; they cannot eat and drink as they please, but are dependent on the observance of many rules as to food etc.; dvijas secure higher worlds after great trouble; the śūdra secures his worlds by serving the three varṇas, he has the right to offer the pākayajñas (without mantras) and therefore he is more blessed than a dvija. He has not to observe strict rules about proper and disallowed food or drink and therefore he was declared 'good' by me. A woman by serving her husband in thought, word, and deed secures with less trouble the same worlds that her husband secures with great effort and trouble and therefore I said a third time about women that they were blessed. The acquisition of dharma is secured with small trouble in Kali age by men who wash off all their sins by the water in being intent on service to dvijas and women also secure the same without trouble by service to their husbands. Therefore all these three are regarded by me as most blessed".'

21. *Matsya Purāṇa* 144.78, *Brahma Purāṇa* 229.52; Kane, op. cit., Vol. III, p. 892; also see Patrick Olivelle, *The Āśrama System: The History and Hermeneutics of a Religious Institution*, New York and Oxford: Oxford University Press, 1993, p. 236, note 53.

CHAPTER 6

Freedom of Conscience and Hinduism

I

Article 18 of the Universal Declaration of Human Rights runs as follows:

> *Article 18*
>
> Everyone has the right to freedom of thought, conscience and religion; this right includes freedom to change his religion or belief, and freedom, either alone or in community with others and in public or private, to manifest his religion or belief in teaching, practice, worship and observance.

The Hindu response to this provision is a complex one. The complexity lies in its complete sympathy with providing for freedom of belief and practice and yet some reservations regarding the freedom to change one's religion or belief.

II

The support for religious freedom, religious variety, and religious pluralism can be found in Hinduism in both theory and practice, as well as in the practice of theory and the theory of practice.

The general Hindu theory in the matter of freedom of conscience was succinctly and elegantly stated by S. Radhakrishnan in 1926, although it was formulated ages ago.[1] He told his audience while delivering the Upton lectures at Manchester College, Oxford:

> The Hindu philosophy of religion starts from and returns to an experimental basis. Only this basis is as wide as human nature itself. Other religious systems start with this or that particular experimental datum. Hinduism was not betrayed into this situation on account of its adherence to fact. The Hindu thinker readily admits other points of view than his own and considers them to be just as worthy of attention. If the whole race of man, in every land, of every colour, and every stage of culture, is the offspring of God, then we must admit that, in the vast compass of his providence, all are being trained by his wisdom and supported by his

love to reach within the limits of their powers knowledge of the Supreme. When the Hindu found that different people aimed at and achieved God-realization in different ways, he generously recognized them all and justified their place in the course of history. He used the distinctive scriptures of the different groups for their uplift since they remain the source, almost the only source, for the development of their tastes and talents, for the enrichment of their thought and life, for the appeal to their emotions and the inspiration of their efforts.[2]

In practise we find as early as the time of the *Kūrma Purāṇa* that 'the Hindu thinkers reckoned with the striking fact that men and women dwelling in India belonged to different communities, worshipped different gods, and practised different rites.'[3] This is even truer today. 'Today there is a greater variety of religions in India than in any other country in the world, but one is hard pressed to decide whether this is the result of the tolerant attitude of Hinduism or the result of the diversity of races and religions in India.'[4]

The practice of the theory resulted in the acceptance of many forms of divinity and the acceptance of a variety of approaches towards spiritual perfection, with or without reservations. Every tradition which helps man to lift his soul to God is held up as worthy of adherence.

'The Vedas, the Sāṁkhya, the Yoga, the Pāśupata and the Vaiṣṇava creeds, each of them is encouraged in some place or other. Some think that this is better, or that is better owing to differences of taste, but all men reach unto you, the Supreme, even as all rivers, however zigzag their courses may be, reach the sea.' Hinduism is therefore not a definite dogmatic creed, but a vast, complex, but subtly unified mass of spiritual thought and realization. Its tradition of the godward endeavour of the human spirit has been continuously enlarging though the ages.[5]

Another manifestation of this theory in practice was the acceptance of a wide variety of scriptures.

Hinduism is the religion not only of the Vedas but also of the Epics and the Purāṇas. By accepting the significance of the different intuitions of reality and the different scriptures of the peoples living in India (sarvāgamaprāmāṇya), Hinduism has come to be a tapestry of the most variegated tissues and almost endless diversity of hues. The Purāṇas with their wild chronology and weird stories are mainly imaginative literature, but were treated as a part of the sacred tradition for the simple reason that some people took interest in them. The Tantras, which deal especially with yogic sādhanā or discipline and have influenced the lives of some communities from the time of the Ṛg Veda, are accepted as a part of the sacred literature and many Hindu ceremonies show traces of the Tantrik worship.[6]

One may cite the following example from the life of the modern Hindu mystic of Bengal, Rāmakṛṣṇa Paramahaṁsa (1836–1886), which illustrates the practice of the theory. Left-handed Tantra, called *vāmācāra*, is not considered exactly respectable by most Hindus and Rāmakṛṣṇa, although he 'did not accept the *vāmācāra* as the reputable way'[7] still nevertheless accepted it as a way.

> Why should we hate them? Theirs is also a way to God, though it is unclean. A house may have many entrances—the main entrance, the back door and the gate for the *bhangi* who comes to sweep the unclean places of the home. These cults are like this door. It does not really matter by which door one enters; once inside the house, all reach the same place. Should one imitate these people or mix with them? Certainly not![8]

For the theory of the practice let us consider just one example—that of the Hindu philosophical school of Advaita Vedānta as expounded by one of India's leading modern philosophers, K.C. Bhattacharyya:

> Toleration is to Advaita Vedānta a religion in itself; no one who realizes what any religion is to its votary can himself be indifferent to it. The claim of a religion on its votary is nothing outside the religion and is itself as sacred to others as the religion is sacred to him. While then an individual owes special allegiance to his own religion or *svadharma*, which chooses him rather than is chosen by him, he feels that the religion of others is not only sacred to them but to himself also. This, in fact, is the practical aspect of the Advaitic view of all individual selves being the one self. The oneness is not contemplated in the empirical region, and there is no prescription of universal brotherhood in the sense that the happiness of others is to be promoted as though it were one's own happiness. There is indeed the duty to relieve distress, but such work is to be performed as duty rather than as a matter of altruistic enjoyment, the dry detached attitude of duty being consonant with the spirit of the religion of *jñāna*. The brotherhood that is practically recognized in this religion is the brotherhood of spirits realizing their *svadharma*, the *dharma* of being sacred to all. If, then, in this view it is irreligious to change one's faith, it is only natural to revere faiths other than one's own. To tolerate them merely in a non-committal or patronizing spirit would be an impiety, and to revile then would be diabolical. The form in which the truth is intuited by an individual is cosmically determined and not constructed to him, and the relativity of truth to the spiritual status of the knower is itself absolute. Even the illusory object in this view is a mystical creation (*prātibhāsika-sṛṣṭi*), the three grades of reality that are recognized—the illusory, the relational, and the transcendental—being in fact grades of this absolute relativity.[9]

III

The modern Hindu position, however, despite its emphasis on tolerance, is in some ways critical of the right of freedom of conscience inasmuch as it includes the freedom to change one's religion or belief, or religious conversion, in other words.

Two contradictory points call for recognition here. The first of these is that the person whom many consider the greatest Hindu of modern times, Mahatma Gandhi (1869–1948) was *opposed* to conversion. The second is that, nevertheless, the Indian Constitution provides for it. It is important not to overlook this contradiction for it could surface again in the context of human rights and Hinduism.

The question naturally arises: why would a person like Mahatma Gandhi be opposed to religious conversion? The clue is contained in the following conversation with C.F. Andrews.

EQUALITY OF RELIGIONS

C.F. Andrews: 'What would you say to a man who after considerable thought and prayer said that he could not have his peace and salvation except by becoming a Christian?'

Gandhiji: 'I would say if a non-Christian (say a Hindu) came to a Christian and made that statement, he should ask him to become a good Hindu rather than find goodness in change of faith.'

C.F. Andrews: 'I cannot in this go the whole length with you, though you know my position. I discarded the position that there is no salvation except through Christ long ago. But supposing the Oxford Group Movement people changed the life of your son, and he felt like being converted, what would you say?'

Gandhiji: 'I would say that the Oxford Group may change the lives of as many people as they like, but not their religion. They can draw their attention to the best in their respective religions and change their lives by asking them to live according to them. There came to me a man, the son of *brahmana* parents, who said his reading of your book had led him to embrace Christianity. I asked him if he thought that the religion of his forefathers was wrong. He said, 'No.' Then I said: 'Is there any difficulty about your accepting the Bible as one of the great books of the world and Christ as one of the great teachers?' I said to him that you never through your books asked Indians to take up the Bible and embrace Christianity, and that he had misread your book—unless of course your position is like that of the late M. Mahomed Ali's, viz. that 'a believing Mussulman however bad his life, is better than a good Hindu.'

C.F.A.: 'I do not accept M. Mahomed Ali's position at all. But I do say that if a person really needs a change of faith I should not stand in his way.'

Gandhiji: 'But don't you see that you do not even give him a chance? You do not even cross-examine him. Supposing a Christian came to me and said he wanted to declare himself a Hindu, I should say to him: 'No.' What the *Bhagawata* offers the Bible also offers. You have not yet made the attempt to find it out. Make the attempt and be a good Christian.''

C.F.A.: 'I don't know. If someone earnestly says he will become a good Christian, I should say, 'You may become one,' though you know that I have in my own life strongly dissuaded ardent enthusiasts who came to me. I said to them, 'Certainly not on *my* account will you do anything of the kind.' But human nature does require a concrete faith.

Gandhiji: If a person wants to believe in the Bible let him say so, but why should he discard his own religion? *This proselytization will mean no peace in the world.* Religion is a very personal matter. We should by living the life according to our lights share the best with one another, thus adding to the sum total of human efforts to reach God.' 'Consider,' continued Gandhiji, 'whether you are going to accept the position of mutual toleration or of equality of all religions. My position is that all the great religions are fundamentally equal. We must have innate respect for other religions as we have for our own. Mind you, not mutual toleration, but equal respect.'[10]

A much more strong statement on this point from Mahatma Gandhi is also forthcoming.

There is in Hinduism room enough for Jesus, as there is for Mohammed, Zoroaster and Moses. For me the different religions are beautiful flowers from the same garden, or they are branches of the same majestic tree. Therefore they are equally true, though being received and interpreted through human instruments equally imperfect. It is impossible for me to reconcile myself to the idea of conversion after the style that goes on in India and elsewhere today. *It is an error, which is perhaps the greatest impediment to the world's progress towards peace.* 'Warring creeds' is a blasphemous expression. And it fitly describes the state of things in India, the mother, as I believe her to be, of Religion or religions. If she is truly the mother, the motherhood is on trial. Why should a Christian want to convert a Hindu to Christianity and vice versa? Why should he not be satisfied if the Hindu is a good or godly man! If the morals of a man are a matter of no concern, the form of worship in a particular manner in a church, a mosque or a temple is an empty formula; it may even be a hindrance to individual or social growth, and insistence on a particular form or repetition of a credo may be a potent cause of violent quarrels leading to bloodshed and ending in utter disbelief in Religion, i.e. God Himself.[11]

IV

Hindu thought thus challenges us to undertake a fresh assessment of what religious freedom itself means.[12]

What is Religion?

In order to undertake such an assessment one must ask two prior questions: (1) what exactly is meant by *freedom* of religion and (2) what is religion? In this investigation the vexed question of what religion is will not be addressed, as it is an issue which needs to be examined in its own right. The importance of the point, however, must be briefly recognized in atonement for not addressing it. The existence of the celebrated First Amendment to the American Constitution did not adequately safeguard the freedom of religion of American Indians, it can be argued, precisely because its application was hamstrung by an inadequate concept of religion.[13] Similarly, a recent legislative effort in Russia tries to restrict freedom of religion in Russia to 'traditional religion'.[14] The dual experience of the USA and Russia, in different historical periods, underlines the important bearing the way religion is conceptualized has on the concept of freedom of religion. The definition of religion in the proposed legislation drawn up in the wake of the Aum Shinrikyo episode in Japan reinforces the point. The following English translation of the definition of religion according to the Proposed Basic Law as reported in *Sekai Nippo* of 24 January 1996 was offered to the writer:

> This law defines religion as an innate condition of the individual, wherein that person, based on the individual's conviction and faith, is led to observe and practice the doctrines, commandments or precepts pertaining to an existence or law, which supersedes human rationality.

The definition of religion in the above formulation seems excessively individualistic and is likely to complicate the exercise of freedom of religion. If accepted, it might once again provide an instance of how the definition of the word religion complicates the question of free exercise thereof.[15]

What is Freedom?

The spotlight may now be turned on *freedom* rather than religion, in the expression 'freedom of religion'. This done, the term assumes several dimensions. 'Freedom', in the context of religion, could mean several things such as: (1) freedom *of* religion, in the sense of being able to choose one's religion; (2) freedom *from* religion, in the sense of not being placed under any obligation to subscribe to any religion; and (3) freedom *to* religion, in the sense of freedom to engage in various forms of religious activities such as freedom to practise, to preach, to propagate, or to proselytize, and so on.

A prominent sense, however, which the term seems to possess in the Universal Declaration of Human Rights, is the sense of freedom *to change* one's religion. This dimension of freedom of religion, therefore, may now be subjected to further scrutiny.

Freedom as Freedom to Convert

The point may be examined by contextualizing it within the field of religious studies. Such an examination suggests the perspective that at least six kinds of freedom can be identified lurking underneath the otherwise innocuous right to change one's religion. These could be spelled out as follows: (1) the right to *change* one's religion; (2) the right to *retain* one's religion; (3) the right to *ask* someone to change one's religion; (4) the right not to be *asked* to change one's religion; (5) the right to *appropriate* the items of another religion, such as symbols, scriptures, and so on; and (6) the right not to have such items of one's own religion *appropriated* by another.

Thus when the right to 'freedom to change one's religion' is unpacked as a universal human right, a lot more comes to light than might have been apparent at first sight. The significance of this point may be elaborated by the example of Christianity.

(1) Christianity encourages others to convert to Christianity, so it may seem fair to assume that Christianity as a religion would be favourably disposed towards the exercise of this right. This might indeed well be true in an inter-religious context. In recent years, however, the unfettered exercise of this right has assumed the dimension of an intra-faith problem within Christianity. Leaders of the Russian Orthodox Church[16] are resentful of Protestant missionary activity being carried on in Russia, especially as the Protestant missions have evangelical resources at their disposal, which cannot be matched by the Orthodox Church. Similarly, the Catholic Church in Latin America is resentful of Pentecostal missionary activity directed at its members. The point goes beyond mere dislike at losing someone of one's flock. Such a sentiment is only human. What is problematical is the asymmetrical access to resources between the competing groups, which seems to violate one's sense of justice.[17]

(2) This second right becomes problematical in relation to Christianity in two opposite cases—when one is not permitted the right to change and when the change is not as total as the Church might

wish. The first case can be illustrated with the example of Islam. According to the classical interpretation of Islamic law, the punishment for apostasy in Islam is death. In other words, Islam denies to its adherents the right to change their religion. It thus absolutizes the right to retain one's religion. At the opposite end of the spectrum one encounters cases where the Christian Church has not allowed the adherents of other religions to retain their religions, through such measures as promoting the adoption of non-Christian children in Christian families. Such revelations recently caused a stir in Canada.

(3) The right to ask someone to change one's religion is accepted as a God-given right within Christianity and accepted in its secular incarnation as the right to convert. However, the question arises: is this an unbridled right or is there a point after which persuasion begins to amount to coercion? The illuminating property of an extreme, even absurd, case is cited here. Until a few years ago, the Mormons or more properly the Church of the Latter Day Saints, even 'converted' the dead of other sects to their persuasion without consulting the 'dead'. This bizarre episode points to the need for establishing the right to be asked to convert to a religion. In a less bizarre way this, it is alleged, happens constantly in Third World countries where Christian orphanages regularly bring up orphaned children, born into other religions, as Christians.

(4) The right *not* to be asked to change one's religion is obviously in apparent conflict with the right to be asked to change one's religion. These two rights need to be reconciled, in principle at least, even if in practice this issue has not reached flashpoint. However, while it is true that this is not an issue at the national or the international level, some portents in that direction are beginning to appear on the American campuses, where 'student evangelical groups are active'.[18] In response to complaints of harassment by other non-Christians, the following rule-of-thumb is now in force. An evangelist has the right to make his or her pitch *once*, but if the other party thereafter indicates lack of interest in the matter, further pursuit of the 'quarry' could invite a charge of harassment.[19]

(5) For a long time now the right to appropriate the items of another religion has lain dormant but a flashback in history suffices to disclose its potential relevance. Christianity is one of the few

religions of the world which has adopted virtually the entire scripture of another religion as its own—namely, the so-called Hebrew Bible. Do the Christians possess the right to do so, or does such adoption violate the rights of the Jews? Is it possible that the right to appropriate the texts of another religion will move to the forefront of the public debate as religions become more syncretic and an increasing number of people in the world start practising multiple religious participation? A recent example: an item of public property in California started betraying such a likeness to the stylized symbol of Śiva, that it became an object of veneration until it was removed by the public authorities. Were the rights of its worshippers violated?

(6) The matching right to the previous one is the right *not* to have the items of one's religion appropriated by others. In recent times, for instance, the followers of the native American tradition have been objecting to the unlicensed incorporation of their religious objects by various religious movements associated with the New Age. In India, the adoption of the Hindu mendicant lifestyle by Christian monks—saffron robes and all—has also begun to raise eyebrows.

Three points emerge clearly from the foregoing discussion: (1) that the right to change one's religion is not intuitively obvious to everyone as a fundamental human right; (2) that the right has several dimensions to it and is a multi-layered rather than a seamless right; and (3) that each level requires the reconciliation of two competing rights rather than the unilateral proclamation of a single majestic right to freedom of religion. The following matrix will help to clarify the last point:

Freedom of Religion

Right to convert	Right *not* to convert
Right to be made an object of proselytization	Right *not* to be made any object of proselytization
Right to assimilate another's religious universe	Right to autonomy over one's own religious universe

The discussion hitherto, although laced with suitable illustrations from historical data or contemporary observation, was essentially theoretical in nature. It may now be complemented with a practical discussion of the even greater complexity the principle of freedom of religion acquires in the field, even when attention is confined to only one dimension of it—namely, the right to conversion. Examples drawn from Nepal, India, and Japan will be used to illustrate the point.

The law in Nepal *forbids* conversion from one religion to another. In this respect the basic law survives unaltered through the various formulations of the Nepalese Constitution and may be recounted in its original formulation:

> Every citizen, subject to the current traditions, shall practice and profess his own religion as handed down from ancient times, provided that no person shall be entitled to convert another person to his religion.[20]

On the face of it, this flagrantly goes against the concept of religious freedom as expressed in the right to change one's religion. However, the king of Nepal commended this law to the then vice-president of India, S. Radhakrishnan, precisely on the ground that it upheld freedom of religion, for it left each religion free to develop without interference by other religions. The ecumenical argument could be elaborated as follows. All religious endeavours:

> lead finally to the same goal, and the only ultimate heresy is to fail to realize that fact. Conversion is a waste of time, an exchanging of one path up the mist-shrouded mountain for another; indeed, it may be worse, since there are sound cultural reasons for remaining within one's own ancestral fold.[21]

A little reflection makes it clear that the difference in these two formulations of the *same* right to freedom of religion arises from the fact that in one case the level engaged is that of *individual* rights and in the other that of *group* rights. If religious freedom is to have meaning for the individual, the individual should be free to choose his or her religion. However, in relation to a group, the right to freedom of religion naturally acquires a different connotation—the right of this group to continue practising its own religion. A difference in quantity (in the number of followers involved) has led to a difference in the quality of the formulation of the right of religious freedom, in the best Marxian intellectual tradition!

By contrast, India allows for conversion as an expression of freedom of religion. It is noteworthy that, by contrast with Nepal, India is less 'Hindu' in the sense that while over 80 per cent of the Indian population is statistically classified as Hindu, the figure for Nepal is over 90 per cent and, further, that Hinduism is more homogeneous in Nepal than in India, in the sense that, in Nepal, Hindu identity takes precedence over such other identities as that of caste, and so on, much more markedly than in India. In other words, in Nepal, Hindus have a stronger group identity than in India—which may go some way towards explaining the *different* expressions of the *same* freedom of religion, which is enshrined in the Indian Constitution as follows:

> Subject to public order, morality and health and to the other provisions of this part, all persons are equally entitled to freedom of conscience and the right freely to profess, practise and propagate religion.[22]

The application of the principle of freedom of religion, when viewed as freedom of conversion, may now be examined in the context of Japan. The key provision involved is Article 20 of the Constitution of Japan, which runs as follows:

> Freedom of religion is guaranteed to all. No religious organization shall receive privileges from the state, nor exercise political authority. No person shall be compelled to participate in any religious act, celebration, rite or practice. The state and its organs shall refrain from religious education or any other religious activities.[23]

It is striking that whereas the constitutional statement enshrining the freedom of religion in the Indian Constitution is *subject* to 'public order, morality and health', in the Japanese Constitution it is not subject to any such provision. One could then say that while freedom of religion is granted only conditionally under the Indian Constitution, it is granted unconditionally under the Japanese.

What significance does this difference possess for the conceptualization of religious freedom as a universal human right? Precisely this that a thin membrane is placed over religious freedom in one case, while leaving it fully exposed to the atmosphere in the other in the bazaar of religious freedom. If the provisions of freedom of religion are violated in the two cases, it attracts the intervention of the state sooner under its 'conditional' provision than the unconditional one. This conclusion is obvious but the examples which serve to illustrate the working of this conclusion in public life remain striking. One could argue, for instance, that this accounts for the alacrity with which the Indian government could ban Salman Rushdie's *The Satanic Verses* in India out of fear of disturbance of public order on the one hand, and the cautious pace with which the Japanese government proceeded against the Aum Shinrikyo on the other. In the former case a limitation to religious freedom was recognized in the very granting of it, while in the latter case the limitation lay outside of it—in the realm of secular crime.

Religion: East and West

The issue of individual versus group rights was raised earlier in the context of freedom of religion and that point may now be pursued further, especially in the light of the fact that emphasis on group rights is increasingly being recognized, and indeed advocated, as an Asian value.[24]

In this context, it is of prime importance that the close connection between the allied concepts of Western thought—'the separation of Church and State' and 'freedom of religion' be clearly grasped. In *nuce*, the concept of religious freedom is a 'secular' concept and the following diagram helps to demonstrate why this is so.

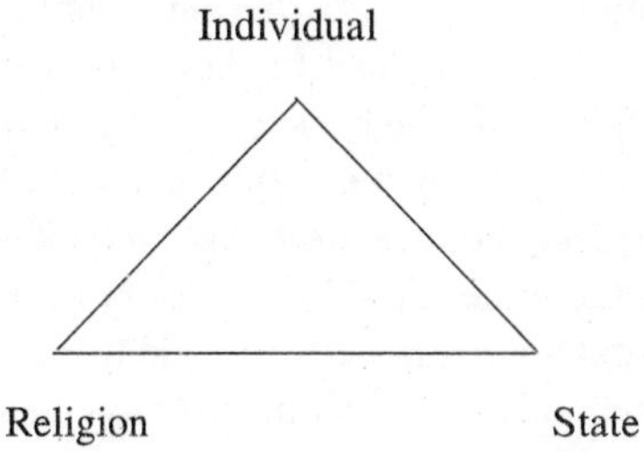

This diagram presents three sets of relationships visually:

1. Religion and the individual
   (freedom of religion)
2. State and the individual
   (citizenship)
3. State and religion
   (separation of State and religion).[25]

The essence of this depiction lies in its portrayal of the individual as relating to the state in the public capacity of a citizen and to religion in the private capacity of a believer of any religion or none. The flatter the triangle the more 'secular' the state of affairs.

If the concept of freedom of religion is associated with such a concept of the secular, two points need to be recognized: (1) that such a concept of the secular arose in a historical context and (2) that the historical context of some non-Western countries, such as India or Japan, for instance, may be different. From this it does not automatically follow that the

Western concept of the secular does not apply to them; but it does seem to follow that the differences in historical circumstances, if any, need to be taken into account in this context.

There seem to be at least five ways in which the historical background of India, for instance, differs from the Western on this point. (1) The concept of the secular, and of religious, freedom associated with it arose in an interdenominational context in the West, while the reality in India is characterized by *inter-religiosity*. In other words, denominational pluralism within Christianity gave rise to the secular idea and one must ask the question whether it can be applied, as such, to a context of religious rather than just Christian pluralism, to secure religious freedom. The case of Japan seems analogous. (2) Prior to the secular developments in the West, religious minorities in the West were subjected to religious persecution. The rise of the secular idea, therefore, gave rise to the concept of minority rights. Earlier on, minorities had been deprived of their rights. This was atoned for in the new dispensation and their rights were safeguarded. The basic context here was that of the past oppression of the minority by the majority. Indian historical experience, however, is different in this respect. Arguably, it is one of oppression of the majority by the minorities. The majority of the Hindus were under minority rule from approximately AD 1200 to AD 1947. From 1200 until 1800, it can be maintained, a Muslim minority ruled over them, and thereafter a Christian. Thus while Western history represents a case of the oppression of the minorities by the majority until the modern period, the experience of India has been different and, if anything, reverse. One must, therefore, ask the question whether this difference in the nature of their historical experience has a bearing on how minority rights are to be assessed as a constituent element of religious freedom. (3) In the West, since the Enlightenment in any case, the concept of religious affiliation has been dominated by the idea that one person can belong only to one religion or none—that religious affiliation is a one-to-one relationship, monogamous if you will. While this idea has been present in India since the arrival of Islam, the dominant Indian idea, at least in relation to Indian religions, has been one which allowed for multiple religious participation (if they are individually demarcated) or syncretism (if they are not). This has obvious implications for the idea that religious freedom involves the freedom of changing from one religion to another. The idea could still be applied in the Indian case, in the sense that one should be free to change adherence to 'one religion' from adherence to a 'cluster of religions' but clearly this understanding is not on all fours with the

Western. It may even be possible to argue that the doctrine of San-Chao in Sung China and the current Japanese multiple affiliation in large numbers with Shinto and Buddhism as well as Christianity, represents a continuation of the same trend. In fact the argument could also be developed a little further: that the arrival of Islam and Western Christianity in India and Marxism in China has in fact rendered this Asian value dormant in these cultures. Be that as it may, it is clear that the concept of religious freedom will acquire a different flavour in such a context. (4) The Western secular idea has promoted religious tolerance. The main theatre of tolerance, however, has been the public sphere. It is in the interface among themselves in their public faces that the individuals or religious bodies are required to display tolerance because coercion is the sole monopoly of the state in a secular state, which may never be placed at the disposal of a religion. In their private persona they are not required to manifest any tolerance. Although they well might do so in private too, the crux of the matter is that irrespective of their benign or otherwise private visage, their public persona must be tolerant. In the case of India, and perhaps Japan as well, such tolerance is also often a part of the religious tradition's own physiognomy. It need not be a mask. Thus while religious tolerance must be a public property in the West, in countries like Japan and India, apart from being public property, a good bit of it is also private currency. This means that religious tolerance, which may be purely transactional or extrinsic in nature in the context of the Western secular situation, often possesses an essential or intrinsic character in Asia. This too may not be without its significance when it comes to reviewing the application of Western secular concepts of religion, and the religious freedom, which goes with it. (5) The fifth point follows from the fourth. Religious freedom, in its Western conception, does not find its space *within* the various religions so much as in the space *between* them, *from which the state has now withdrawn*. In this sense then, religious freedom in the Western sense is founded on a secular basis. In many countries of the East, and particularly in India, to practise religion as one pleased had, in some form or other, always existed as a 'social right' quite *outside the purview of the state*. Thus, while in the West, state intervention in matters religious has come to be viewed negatively, this is not necessarily the case in India, where at least the 'Hindu' state does not carry such a negative historical burden in the public imagination in relation to religion. Thus, unlike in the West, countries in the East may not be averse to the idea of the state itself acting as an active agent for promoting religious freedom, or even tolerance.

The reader may assess for himself or herself the individual force of these arguments. I would like to take their collective force into account to point out that the prospect of religious freedom is drastically affected in the West and in India when they are taken into account. The point is best illustrated by an analytical manipulation of the celebrated First Amendment of the American Constitution: 'Congress shall make no law respecting an establishment of religion or prohibiting the free exercise thereof.'[26] This amendment does two things: it forbids the establishment of a state religion, but it also allows religions to freely exercise themselves in the political sphere. Now consider the following scenario. A party, such as the 'Christian Right', by utilizing the free exercise clause, wins the election and comes to power with such an overwhelming majority as to be potentially in a position to declare the USA a Christian State, *but* for the Amendment! It may or may not then attempt to do so. In the case of India, however, should a Hindu Right come to power on the same terms, it may not be in a position to do so on account of its *own* concept of freedom of religion rather than a Western secular one.

CONCLUSION

The foregoing analysis, in its present stage, enables one to draw at least two conclusions—a general conclusion and a specific one—regarding religious freedom as a universal human right. The general conclusion is that, in order to be truly universal, the concept of freedom of religion must take the Asian religious experience more comprehensively into account. The specific conclusion is the right to convert from one's religion, as an expression of freedom must also be accompanied by an equally clear enunciation of the *right to retain one's religion.*

An additional contribution which Hindu thought makes to the discourse on human rights is to draw attention to the fact that whether religious freedom is ensured or not will depend on the rules of engagement depending on whether the parties involved are:

(1) Proselytizing religions, that is, Islam and Christianity;
(2) Non-proselytizing religions, that is, Hinduism and Judaism; or
(3) Proselytizing and non-proselytizing religions, that is, Christianity and Hinduism.

While the conclusion may be presented pragmatically in the aforesaid matter, the question at the conceptual level is even more significant for human rights discourse. The remarks made by Julia Ching in this connection set the stage for developing the discussion further at the conceptual level. She begins by noting that

An important difference between East Asian religious life and that of India and the West is that its various communities are not completely separate. If you ask a Japanese, for instance, whether he or she is a believer in a particular religion, you may get the answer 'no' (even the Japanese word for 'no' is not as tightly defined a denial as is 'no' in English). However, if you ask whether he or she adheres to Shinto, Buddhism, and Confucianism, you may get the answer 'yes' (albeit again a bit noncommittal compared with the English 'yes'). Many Japanese follow more than one religion, even though they do not consider themselves very religious.[27]

This last point however is not limited to the Japanese.

Much the same can be said of the Chinese, the Koreans, or the Vietnamese. At issue is the inseparability of religion and culture in East Asia, as well as the syncretism, or combination that characterizes all major religions there. East Asians all assert the importance of cosmic and social harmony. And because harmony is highly valued, each of the religious traditions tend to meet some of the needs of the people. In spite of occasional religious conflicts, all tend to work together in a larger cultural and social context.[28]

This attitude has important implications for the concept of religion itself. Indeed,

Some scholars go so far as to say that the Chinese and Japanese have no religion, since their 'religions' do not make the exclusive claims to truth and dogma so characteristic of Western religions. Others claim that China and Japan have no religion because their civilization is basically areligious and this-worldly. Still others, while granting that religion is present in East Asian civilization, find it so entwined in the culture itself that the two have become inseparable; they hold therefore that it is useless to speak about religion in such places as China. Others are not always sure whether they should speak of 'religion' in the singular or the plural.[29]

It might then be useful to compare the concept of religion, say in China, with the prevailing conception of it. Thus Julia Ching goes on to say:

The Chinese word for 'religion' is *zongjiao*. *Zongjiao* (Japanese, *shukyo*) is actually the Japanese translation of the Western or English term 'religion'. The English term has a Latin root, referring to a bond—presumably between the human being and the divinity. But literally, the Sino-Chinese term means 'lineage-teaching', that is, the transmitted teaching of certain lineage—the names of those masters from whom they received their teaching. The accent is very much on 'receiving' rather than inventing. It should be noted that the translated term does not necessarily refer to any bond between two parties, unless we are to say that the bond is between those connected by lineage.

This is interesting, as the word *zong* resembles *zhuzong*, the Chinese word for ancestors. There is also the focus on lineage transmissions, which are always traced back to the original 'progenitor', be it that of a sect or tradition or people. For the Chinese, *zongjiao* seems inextricably interwoven with the ancestral cult. After all, the word *zong* also refers to blood lineage, i.e. ancestry. Ancient Chinese religion was in many ways an ancestral religion, involving veneration of the spirits of the deceased. So the focus is also on a relationship with the spirits—but not necessarily with the divine.[30]

This contrast in the two conceptions of religion forces her to clarify her position. She writes:

We should make our own position clear. There is ground for confusion, we grant, because of the close ties between religion and culture. It is not easy to separate religion and culture in our discussions. This does not mean, however, that East Asian civilizations are areligious. Some people dismiss customs and rituals as superstitious, but others in the same culture see them as practical means of securing benefit of life. We should be aware that definitions of these traditions in the region are fluid, compared with the roles of religions of West Asian origin, like Christianity or Islam. Moreover, we think that the word 'religion' need not be defined in exclusivist terms, in theist terms, or even in doctrinal terms.[31]

Summation

I would now like to use Article 18 of the Universal Declaration of Human Rights as the basis for advancing three propositions: (1) That the concept of religious freedom articulated in Article 18 presupposes a certain concept of religion itself, a concept associated with Western religion and culture; (2) that a different concept of religion, associated with Eastern and specially Hindu religion and culture, leads a different concept of religious freedom, ironically but not surprisingly; and (3) the clash of the two concepts might ultimately result in the abridgement of religious freedom in actual practice, India representing a case in point.

The concept of religious freedom as embedded in Article 18 presupposes that an individual can only belong to or profess one religion at a time. If one believes that one can only belong to one religion at a time, it stands to reason that religious freedom would essentially consist of one's freedom to change such affiliation by the voluntary exercise of choice.

In parts of the East, however, one encounters a somewhat different notion of religion, as illustrated by the contemporary reality of Japan. According to the 1985 census, 95 per cent of the population of Japan declared itself as followers of Shinto and 76 per cent of the same population also declared itself as Buddhist.

To turn now to India. It is well known that most modern Hindus do not regard the various religions of Indian origin—Hinduism, Buddhism, Jainism, and Sikhism—as mutually exclusive religions. If the Indian census authorities did not insist that one can only belong to one religion—significantly a British and therefore Western legacy—I would not be at all surprised if the Indian religious statistical reality began to resemble the Japanese.

What would the concept of religious freedom possibly mean in the context of such a concept of religion? I would like to propose that it would now imply the idea of multiple religious participation rather than the idea of religious conversion. Mahatma Gandhi was once asked: what if a Hindu comes to feel that he can only be saved by Jesus Christ? Gandhi's reply may be paraphrased as thus: so be it, but why should he cease to be a Hindu? (*Harijan*, 28 November 1936). Thus in the Eastern cultural context, freedom of religion means that the person is left free to explore his or her religious life without being asked to change his or her religion. Such exploration need not be confined to any one religion, and may freely embrace the entire religious and philosophical heritage of humanity.

I can now advance to, and advance, the third proposition. According to one concept of religion—described earlier as Western—freedom of religion consists of freedom to change one's religion when faced with a religious option. According to another concept of religion—described earlier as Eastern—freedom of religion consists of not having the need to do so when faced with such an option.

Recent events in India indicate that the simultaneous operation of these two concepts can lead to religious volatility. India's religious culture is heavily imbued with the concept of *dharma*, while India's political culture relies heavily on the Western conception of religion. The tensions now building up in India seem to lend support to this third proposition. A number of states in India have introduced Freedom of Religion Bills. These legislations require prior clearance from government authorities before a conversion can be carried out. Hindus are resentful because conversion is thereby still allowed; Christians are resentful because conversion is thereby impeded! Thus proponents of both Western and Eastern concepts of religion can allege that these enactments restrict religious freedom.[32]

The point the reader might specially wish to carry with him or her as he or she leaves this section is the realization that Hinduism has evolved its own concept of religious freedom which human rights discourse must take into account. This need not involve a denial of the validity of the Western conception of religious freedom. It rather points to a more general consideration: that more than one concept of religious freedom is possible; that the Western and Hindu (or even Indic and Asian) concepts of religious freedom may not always coincide. If it is true that these concepts of religious freedom are closely related to the concept of 'religion' itself as found in the West and the East, human rights discourse will have to enlarge the scope of its understanding of religious freedom to embrace, and (when they are in conflict) to reconcile various concepts of religious freedom.

V

The role of conscience in the context of religious conversion also needs to be clearly identified and examined, as the term appears in human rights documents[33] as well as the Indian Constitution, but no adequate analysis of it from an Indic point of view has been forthcoming. The Universal Declaration of Human Rights states in Article 18 that 'everyone has the right to freedom of thought, conscience and religion . . .'[34] while Article 25 of the Indian constitution guarantees freedom of religion and conscience as follows:

> Subject to public order, morality and health and to other provision of this part, all persons are equally entitled to freedom of conscience and the right to freely profess, practise and propagate religion.[35]

In decoding the meaning of the word conscience one needs to filter it through several layers, by means of drawing certain distinctions. One such distinction is between conscience versus what is binding in conscience. If, as a Roman Catholic, I accept the position of my faith that the only permissible method of family planning is the rhythm method, that position is binding in conscience for me. What my conscience finds binding is another matter, and if it does not find it so binding this fact would be a source of moral tension for me. But the crucial point to keep in mind here is the distinction between what is binding in conscience, which represents the internalization of an external faith position and what the conscience finds binding, which represents an internal moral disposition externalizing itself and reaching out to the world. As a Hindu, for instance, I might feel the need not to eat beef binding in conscience, while at the same time I might find that my conscience does not permit me to eat not just beef but any form of meat as a vegetarian. The point to note then is that my abstention from beef is capable of two overlapping but distinct interpretations—one from the fact of what is binding in conscience and the other from the fact of what my conscience binds me to.

The other distinction to bear in mind is that between what might be called an open and private conscience. If I kill my brother and it causes me to feel that I have sinned and must perform penance for it, this moral fact has an open and a private dimension. To the extent that my immoral act and my required atonement for it is a fact of public knowledge, I have an open conscience in the matter. However, in my heart of hearts I could still feel that I cannot really repent for my sin, or that the publicly prescribed atonement is not enough, or that in some curious way my brother deserved to be killed although I wish I was not the one who brought about this end. I use the expression private conscience as a term to capture the divergence between my real personal moral feelings, as compared to the recognition they are given in public.

The first distinction recognizes the distinction between conscience as such and conscience as reflecting our social norms; the second distinction recognizes the distinction between conscience as such and conscience as manifest piety. In order to identify conscience as such, as it is in itself, apart from containing elements which reflect social norms or manifest piety, one may distinguish between conscience as such and personal choices. All conscientious choices we make are personal choices, but not all personal choices are moral choices, for they could be rational or emotional as well.

The reason for introducing these three contexts in the use of the word conscience and the allied distinctions is that the concept of 'conscience' as reflected in Hindu jurisprudence covers all the three dimensions and distinctions, and any further discussion of it must proceed with this awareness.

The distinction between conscience and binding conscience helps us understand the role of conscience in a famous verse of the *Manusmṛti* (I.12) which lists four sources of *dharma* in that order: (1) Veda or *śruti* (or revelation); (2) *smṛti* (or tradition); (3) *sadācāra* (or exemplary conduct); and (4) *ātmatuṣṭi* or what is to one's moral liking. In terms of this fourfold categorization, the word *ātmatuṣṭi* (or the expression *svasya ca priyamātmanaḥ*) could be rendered as conscience—but as binding conscience, for the working of one's conscience is located here within the fourfold scheme.

The distinction between open and private conscience helps to understand its role in the *Mahābhārata* when the discussion of the appropriateness of Draupadī's marriage to all the five Pāṇḍavas presents an occasion for moral decision-making. One of the arguments Yudhiṣṭhira advances in favour of the arrangement is that he finds nothing wrong in it. His conscience is clear—in the open. The fact that Draupadī was actually won at the *svayaṁvara* by Arjuna alone and not by the five brothers, must have some moral consequence for Yudhiṣṭhira even if he chooses to disregard it.

The distinction between conscience and personal choices helps understand the role of conscience in another verse of the *Manusmṛti* (II.223) which calls upon the moral person to emulate the wholesome example set by women and a low-caste person. This may be taken as an exemplication of *sadācara* in the verse from Manu (I.12) cited earlier. The verse then goes on to say that the person may also engage in whatever his or her mind finds congenial. This part of the verse thus offers wide scope for the exercise of personal choice to the person—of which acting according to one's conscience would be an integral part.

This amount of personal latitude allowed in determining or interpreting *dharma* is often left unarticulated in discussions of *dharma*, and what is more, even when articulated, it is sometimes not recognized as such. J. Duncan M. Derrett elaborates this role of personal individual choice implicitly in two chapters in a well-known book,[36] yet fails to mention 'conscience' as a source of *dharma*. On further reflection this failure may be accounted for by the explanation being developed here—that because 'conscience' appears in formal legal Hindu discourse as related to binding conscience, its operation as private conscience and as personal choice has gone undetected.

The crucial question to be faced now is: how is this conception of Hindu conscience to be brought in relation to that dimension of human rights discourse, if at all, which speaks of 'freedom of conscience,' in the same breath as 'freedom of religion' and links these freedoms to the freedom to change one's religion. Given the fact that the general tenor of Hinduism is opposed to conversion, the question arises: how is this attitude of Hinduism to be related to its views of 'conscience'?

One way of examining this issue would be to view it in terms of the individual's conscience and its relationship to the 'conscience' of the community of which he or she is a part. One could then argue as follows: on what grounds may one say that acts of conversion are ethically reprehensible? One answer could be: because they violate conscience. This raises the issue: whose conscience? One answer could be: the individual conscience. The other could be the collective conscience, implied in such a phrase as *mahājanaparigraha*.[37] But while the focus of the individual conscience is obvious, a question arises in the case of collective conscience: whose conscience is the collective conscience? Three answers are possible to this question in accordance with how the word *mahājana* is to be understood in the expression *mahājanaparigraha*.

The first sense in which it can be taken is that of a great person, such as a Buddha, a Mahāvīra, or a Kapila. They are the people who set the norms for us which we should individually accept. It might be objected that since they are individuals, how could one derive the concept of a collective conscience in this context? The answer lies in the fact that although they may be individuals by themselves, they also left behind a community which claims to consist of the followers of these individuals. If, however, an individual accepts what they say as 'binding in conscience', this sense of the word 'conscience' ceases to be helpful in the context of conversion.

A second sense in which the word *mahājana* may be understood is as referring to the leaders of society, whose practices and teachings may collectively acquire the character of a moral force, just as an agreement among scientists acquires intellectual persuasiveness in the scientific world. This would then mean that, in view of the 'objective' status it acquires, the collective conscience may prevail in the event of any divergence from the individual conscience.

A third sense of the word *mahājana* would mean the people in general as a whole—the great body of people rather than a body of great people. Here again, however, the collective conscience, so expressed, may submerge the individual conscience as it were.

Hinduism, especially Vedantic Hinduism, distinguishes itself from other religions of Indian origin in taking the word *mahājana* in the last two senses. But it would seem that all the three senses would undercut any grounds for the exercise of individual conscience in the matter of conversion. It would still leave room for 'mass conversion' but since the basic context of the present discussion is that of individual rights, the point is not very helpful at the moment, though potentially of great significance in the context of cultural rights.

Such a conclusion, however, seems to be overdetermined. We saw earlier how one of the Hindu contexts which semantically intersects with the word conscience is that of free choice. There are instances when its voice was at odds with the chorus of collective conscience. Thus Māndhātā, an ancestor of Rāma, refused to slay an innocent person to relieve drought in his kingdom and Mahatma Gandhi opposed his parents and by extension his community, when asked to practise untouchability at the age of fourteen. They were obviously utilizing 'conscience' as a source of *dharma*.

The explanation of the Hindu opposition to conversion has to be found not in the workings of the conscience but in the more mundane aspect of its structure as a tradition. It was pointed out in the first section of this paper that the Hindu religious tradition differs from the Abrahamic religious traditions in one crucial respect: Hinduism, unlike them, allows for multiple religious participation. If freedom means freedom to cross boundaries, Hinduism presents no boundary to cross in this respect, while the Western religions do. Therefore freedom of religion for them means freedom to change one's religion. The boundary in Hinduism is represented by the decision of each individual to choose his or her own personal deity, so religious freedom in Hinduism consists of the freedom to change one's chosen deity (*iṣṭa-devatā*) rather than to change one's religion. That Hindu practice conforms to Hindu theory in this respect is confirmed by a statistical survey in Madras. Three per cent of the population of Madras is Christian yet 10 per cent of its inhabitants identified Jesus Christ as their *iṣṭa-devatā*.

The problem from the Hindu point of view is that conversion to an Abrahamic or Western religion involves a double conversion: a conversion not just to that religion but to its view of what a religion is—that religious adherence is exclusive in nature and you cannot be a member of two religions simultaneously. This observation also enables one to identify the differing dynamics between freedom of conscience and freedom of religion in a Western and an Indic context. Because the line is drawn in terms of membership of religion in Western religions, freedom of conscience manifests itself as freedom to choose one's religion and to change it; in Hinduism there is no restriction in this respect, so no question of freedom of choice arises; freedom of conscience therefore consists of the freedom to choose one's deity from among the various deities and from among the various gods and goddesses of Hinduism—or those found outside it, or not to choose any.

Notes

1. P.V. Kane, *History of Dharmaśāstra*, Poona: Bhandarkar Oriental Research Institute, 1962, Vol. V, Part II, pp. 1623–26.

2. S. Radhakrishnan, *The Hindu View of Life*, New York: The Macmillan Company, 1927, p. 19.
3. Ibid., pp. 13–14. The verse is cited as follows: *bhārateṣu striyaḥ puṁso nānāvarṇāḥ prakīrtitāḥ, nānādevārcane yuktā nānākarmāṇi kurvate.*
4 Troy Wilson Organ, *The Hindu Quest for the Perfection of Man*, pp. 77–8.
5. S. Radhakrishnan, *The Hindu View of Life*, pp. 20–1.
6. Ibid., p. 20.
7. Klaus K. Klostermaier, *A Survey of Hinduism*, Albany, NY: State University of New York Press, 1889, p. 275.
8. Cited, ibid., pp. 275–6.
9. Krishnachandra Bhattacharyya, 'The Advaita and Its Spiritual Significance', in *The Cultural Heritage of India* (ed.), Haridas Bhattacharyya, Calcutta: The Ramakrishna Mission Institute of Culture, 1953, Vol. III, pp. 251–2, emphasis added. He goes on to say (pp. 252–3):

RESPECT FOR INDIVIDUAL DIFFERENCES

The doctrine of *adhikāri-bheda* is an application of this epistemological notion of absolute relativity to the specifically religious sphere. The difference of *adhikāra* or spiritual status is not necessarily a gradation, and so far as it is a gradation it does not suggest any relation of higher and lower that implies contempt or envy. The notion of *adhikāra* in fact means in the first instance just an acceptance of fact or realism in the spiritual sphere. It is a question of duty rather than of rights in this sphere; and a person should be anxious to discover his actual status in order that he may set before himself just such duties as he can efficiently perform in spirit. It is a far greater misfortune here to over-estimate one's status than to under-estimate it. A higher status does not mean greater opportunity for spiritual work, since work here means not outward achievement, but an 'inwardizing' or deepening of the spirit. Again, from the standpoint of toleration, one not only respects the inner achievement of a person admitting an inferior status, but can whole-heartedly identify oneself with it, the highest *adhikārin* should feel it a privilege to join in the worship of the humblest. There is aristocracy in the spiritual polity, a spiritual value is achieved by the strong and is much too sacred a thing to be pooled. At the same time every individual has his sacred *svadharma* and has equal opportunity with everyone else to realize or 'inwardize' it.

The merit of Advaitavāda lies in having explicitly recognized that spiritual work is this 'inwardizing', the deepening of faith into subjective realization, the striving after self-knowledge. This work can start from any given point, any spiritual status or situation that happens to be presented. Men are intrinsically higher and lower only in respect of this inner achievement. The problem of altering traditional society, of equalizing rights in order to create opportunities for self-realization, has accordingly a subordinate place in the Advaitic scheme of life, being recognized mainly negatively as duty of abstaining from acts of conscious injustice. This scheme of life would view with positive disfavour iconoclasm in any shape or form, any violent tampering with an institution that is traditionally held to be sacred; but it would not also apparently require one to vitalize artificially such an institution if one believes—not by hearsay, but after loyally trying to work it—that it is moribund or dead. Spiritual realism would demand both reverence allowed to die a natural death or incorporated in an ideal or symbolic form in the latter. There is no room in Advaita religion for the duty of profaning one god for the glorification of another.

The idea of hustling people out of their reverence in their own spiritual interest would be scouted in this religion as a self-stultifying profanity. Social life and tradition are viewed as sacred, as a *yajña* being performed through the ages, the sacredness being the shrine of the one Self, the shadow of Eternity. It is the life of the gods, and we can help it best by merging into it, by realizing it as our subjective life. This subjective realization may sometimes come spontaneously, but so far as it can be effected by *sādhana*, it can be effected by each individual for himself. He can indeed help others in the work by education, but he can educate only in the measure he has himself realized this life. He can wish and pray that others' self-realization might by expedited; but for an *ordinary* person to suppose that he can and ought to energize and vitalize other spirits is, to the religion of Advaita, a delusion and a curious mixture of arrogance and sentimentality.

10. M.K. Gandhi, *Hindu Dharma* (ed.) Bharatan Kumarappa, Ahmedabad: Navajivan Publishing House, 1950, pp. 231–2, emphasis added. Also see Ronald W. Neufeldt, 'To Convert or Not to Convert: Legal and Political Dimensions of Conversion in Independent India', in*Religion and Law in Independent India* (ed.) Robert D. Baird, New Delhi: Manohar, 1993, pp. 313–31.
11. Ibid., p. 232, emphasis added.
12. *Twenty-Five Human Rights Documents*, New York: Columbia University, 1994, p. 8.
13. Ronald F. Thiemann, *Religion in Public Life: A Dilemma for Democracy*, Washington, DC: Georgetown University Press, 1996, pp. 164–5.
14. *Hinduism Today*, October 1997, p. 17.
15. The treatment of Scientology in Germany illustrates the point further; see *The Gazette* (Montreal), 27 January 1997, p. E7.
16. Even in the case of Catholicism, Alexy II, the head of Russia's Orthodox Church 'called for more cooperation with the Roman Catholic Church, but said he regards "as inadmissible Catholic expansionism" among the traditionally Orthodox population of Russia' (Marcus Warren, 'Nicholas II, Family Canonized', *The Gazette* (Montreal), 15 August 2000, p. B1.
17. See Harold J. Berman, 'Religious Rights in Russia in a Time of Tumultuous Transition: A Historical Theory', in *Religious Human Rights in Global Perspective: Legal Perspectives* (eds), Johan D. van der Vyer and John Witte, Jr., The Hague/Boston/London: Martinus Nijhoff Publishers, 1996, pp. 285–304; James W. Zion, 'North American Indian Perspectives on Human Rights', in *Human Rights in Cross-Cultural Perspectives: A Quest for Consensus*(ed.), in Abdullahi Ahmed An-Na'im, Philadelphia: University of Pennsylvania Press, 1992, pp. 181–220; Paul E. Sigmund, 'Religious Human Rights in Latin America', in op. cit. (eds), Johan D. van der Vyer and John Witte, Jr., pp. 467–75.
18. *The Chronicle of Higher Education*, 13 December 1996, pp. A41–2.
19. Oral communication from Reverend Scotty McLennan of Tufts University.

20. Donald Eugene Smith, *India As A Secular State*, Princeton, NJ: Princeton University Press, 1963, p. 103.
21. Eric J. Sharpe, *Comparative Religion: A History*, London: Duckworth, 1975, p. 254.
22. Cited in Eugene Smith, op. cit., p. 135.
23. T.S.Y. Lee and Osamu Nishi, *Japan*, Dobbs Ferry, New York: Oceana Publications Inc., 1999, pp. 16–17.
24. *Daily Yomiuri*, 25 August 1997, p. 5; *The Japan Times*, 29 August 1997, p. 5; etc.
25. Donald Eugene Smith, op. cit., p. 4.
26. See Ronald F. Thiemann, op. cit., p. 27.
27. Julia Ching, 'East Asian Religions', in *World Religions: Eastern Traditions* (ed.), Willard G. Oxtoby, second edition, Toronto: Oxford University Press, 2002, pp. 318.
28. Ibid.
29. Ibid.
30. Ibid., pp. 318–19.
31. Ibid., p. 319.
32. Author's testimony before the United States Commission on International Religious Freedom in his individual capacity as Professor of Comparative Religion on 18 September 2000.
33. Ian Brownlie (ed.), op. cit., p. 25.
34. Ibid.
35. Cited, Subhash C. Kashyap (ed.), *Perspectives on the Constitution*, Delhi: Shipra Publications, 1993, p. 91.
36. J. Duncan M. Derrett, op. cit., Chapters 3 and 4.
37. See Arvind Sharma, 'Minority vs. Majority Rights', in *Perspectives on the Constitution* (ed.), Subhash C. Kashyap, Delhi: Shipra Publications, 1993, p. 91.

CHAPTER 7

Universalism in India and the West

I

Hitherto in this book we have focused on human rights. It is now time to turn our attention to their description as 'universal'.[1] It is going to be the thesis of this chapter that the core concept underlying universalism differs significantly in India and the West, and further that, if this significant difference is overlooked, discourse on the issue of rights becomes warped, as two interlocuting cultures use the same word to mean different things. However, once such confusion is cleared, the discourse on universalism is enriched.

I would like to move towards the conclusion in three stages. I shall begin by identifying one sphere where the concepts of 'universal' in the two interlocuting cultures actually do converge. Then I shall try to demonstrate why the senses begin to diverge when they do, and, finally, how they diverge when they do. This will pave the way for developing the propositions outlined in the final section.

In arguing the point that the concepts of the universal in India and the West do converge in some ways, I realize that I shall, at least initially, be arguing against my own thesis. But this then is the procedure adopted in much philosophical disputation in India—to argue first against one's own thesis before arguing for it.

II

The point of convergence is provided by the fact that the discussion of the universal gives rise to similar conceptual classifications and clarifications in Indian and Western philosophy. This fact can be established by a ready reference to standard texts on Indian thought. Even if one grants that Indian thought presented in English may tend to get moulded in the categories of that language, the similarity in formulation one encounters between Western and Indian thought on the issue of universals is still sufficiently striking, as will be obvious from the following passage:

Things of a certain class bear a common name because they possess a common nature. Men, cows and swans have, severally, something in common, on account of which they bear these general names. The thought of what they have in common is called a general idea or class-concept. Now the question is: What is it that they have in common? Or, what is the something that is common in them, and is the ground of their being brought under one class and called by the same name? The first answer, which is only provisional, is that it is the class-essence corresponding to the class-concept. The Nyāya-Vaiśeṣikas would say that it is their sāmānya or generality. Or, in the words of modern Western philosophers, it is the 'universal' in them. Hence the previous question leads to a second, viz. What is sāmānya or the universal?[2]

The responses to this question, from within the realm of Indian philosophy, are capable of being reduced to three broad positions. These are often referred to as (1) the linguistic, (2) the conceptualistic, and (3) the realistic approaches to the issue of universals. These may briefly be summarized here. Buddhism espouses the linguistic view—or the nominalistic view.

According to it, the individual (svalakṣaṇa) alone is real and there is no class or universal other than the particular objects of experience. The idea of sameness that we may have with regard to a number of individuals of a certain character is due to their being called by the same name. It is only the name that is general, and the name does not stand for any positive essence that is present in all individuals. It means only that the individuals called by one name are different from those to which a different name is given. Thus certain animals are called cow, not because they possess any common essence but because they are different from all animals that are not cows. So there is no universal but the name with a negative connotation.[3]

By contrast, the Jainas and Advaitins favour a conceptualistic view of the universal.

According to them, the universal does not stand for any independent entity over and above the individuals. On the other hand, it is constituted by the essential common attributes of all individuals. So the universal is not separate from the individuals, but is identical with them in point of existence. The universal and the individual are related by way of identity. The universal has existence, not in our mind only, but also in the particular objects of experience. It does not, however, come to them from outside and is not anything like a separate 'essence', but is only their common nature.[4]

The realistic perspective on universals upheld by the Nyāya-Vaiśeṣikas differs from both these views.

> According to them, universals are eternal (nitya) entities, which are distinct from but inhere in, many individuals (anekānugata). There is the same (eka) universal in all the individuals of a class. The universal is the basis of the notion of sameness that we have with regard to all the individuals of a certain class. It is because there is one common essence present in different individuals that they are brought under a class and thought of as essentially the same. Thus sāmānya or the universal is a real entity which corresponds to a general idea of class-concept in our mind.[5]

It is clear from the above that not only is the issue of the universal formulated in a manner analogous to that in the West, the positions developed in response to it—namely, the linguistic, the conceptualistic and the realistic, can also be clearly attached to such eminently identifiable schools of Indian thought as the Buddhist, the Jaina and Advaita Vedānta, and the Nyāya-Vaiśeṣika respectively.

It was noted above that the Nyāya-Vaiśeṣika school favours a realistic approach to the question of universals. The parallel can be pushed even further down the line in terms of Western philosophy. It has been pointed out, for instance, that

> Some modern realists also hold that a 'universal is an eternal timeless entity which may be shared by many particulars'. They agree further with the Naiyāyikas in maintaining that universals do not come under existence (sattā). These do not exist in time and space, but have being and subsist in substance, attribute and action (dravya-guṇa-karmavṛtti). There is no universal subsisting in another universal, because there is but one single universal for one class of objects. If there are two or more universals in the same class of things, then they would exhibit contrary and even contradictory natures and we could not classify them one way or the other. The same individuals could have been men and cows at the same time.[6]

III

We now stand at an important crossroad when we must examine the relationship between philosophy and religion in these two traditions—the Indian and the Western. It once was and is still commonplace to claim, though a little less now than earlier, that the Indian and Western realities differ in one marked respect: that religion and philosophy part company in the West but have remained unsundered in India.[7] I do not wish to debate the point here but I do wish to allude to it for two reasons.

The first is that this observation contextualizes the point I wish to raise appropriately. The second is that it enables one to not merely contextualize but also to advance the proposition, that, while in India, the concept of universal even in religion has remained philosophical; in the West, even in modern philosophy, it has become religious.

What do I mean when I say that in the West the universal in philosophy has become religious? What I intend to say is that in Western religions, on account of their missionary nature, the distinction between the universal and the universalizable collapses; and this lack of recognition of a distinction between the two is also visible in Western thought.

In Indian philosophy, the idea of the universal relates to identifying the common feature of separate items which belong to a class; so also in Western philosophy,, but the claim that Christianity is a universal religion implies the homogenizing of all the separate items, so that they all possess not a common feature but the same feature. Alternatively, the extraction of a common feature is replaced by the imposition of a common feature. The denial of universality to the ethnic religions in Western discourse is revealing in this respect, as it suppresses the fact that they contain their own form of religious universalism. Thus both Judaism and Hinduism, typically labelled ethnic, believe in universal salvation but Christianity, which typically does not accept this idea that all are saved as such, claims that it is a universal religion. As a Jewish author, Ruth R. Wisse, has observed:

> Jewish 'parochialism' is always implicitly universal, since Jewish law recognizes both the legitimate existence of other peoples and the right of everyone who genuinely desired it to become a Jew. By contrast, universalist idealism in religion and politics is always implicitly repressive, since it expects everyone to become its particular species of universalist.[8]

IV

This point can be developed further by reviewing the manner in which moral universals have been identified in the West. Frederick Bird has pointed out in a recent survey that the search for moral universals has typically taken one of the following three paths in the West: (1) as grounded in human nature or human reason, (2) in terms of cultural commonalities, and (3) in terms of developmental models.[9]

While the strategies employed along the second and third routes are largely anthropological and psychological in orientation, those employed under the first category are philosophical. The Kantian legacy here that 'a will is genuinely good if the maxim by which it acts can be universalized'[10] has been lasting, and surfaces in the work of Alan Gewirth and Bernard Gert.[11] Many of these theories tend to distinguish between normative conventions (usually culture-bound) and authentic moral principles—which are universalizable.[12]

It is significant that when modern liberal thinkers, such as John Stuart Mill and John R. Rawls,[13] exempt parts of the Third World from the operations of their liberal philosophies, the reason for such exemption is again couched in terms of universalizability—this time the lack of it.

V

One cause of our present discontent is the failure to distinguish between these two senses of the universal, *now that both of these have crossed over to other cultures and may overlap within a culture.*

For instance, of late the universality of human rights has become a contested issue. Now, even when Indians allege that human rights are 'Western' rather than universal, it is the Western conception of 'Human Rights' and *not* its conception of universality as such which is contested by them. It is assumed by the discussants both for and against universal human rights, both in India and the West that 'universal' and 'global' are interchangeable terms.

This chapter seeks to break new ground by proposing that the concept of universality itself might not be universal, in the sense that the concept may possess different distinguishing features and further that the discussants in India and the West, who have uncritically accepted the Western configuration as paradigmatic of universalism for both India and the West, may have miscued the situation in a way seriously detrimental to productive dialogue between Hinduism and the West.

On the other hand, the secularization of the West has had its own consequence for the reconfiguration of the universal in the West. The biblical universal has assumed the following form after undergoing secularization, according to S.N. Balagangadhara:

> In the name of science and ethnology, the biblical themes have become our regular stock-in-trade: that God gave religion to humankind has become a cultural universal in the guise that all cultures have a religion; the theme that God gave one religion to humanity has taken the form and belief that all religions have something in common; that God implanted a sense of divinity is now a secular truth in the form of an anthropological, specifically human ability to have a religious experience. . . . One has become a Christian precisely to the degree Christianity ceases being specifically Christian in the process of its secularization. We

may not have had our baptisms or recognize Jesus as our saviour: but this is how we prosecute the Christians. The retribution for this is also in proportion: the pagans themselves do not know how pagan they really are. We have, it is true, no need for specifically Christian doctrines. But then, that is because all our dogmas are in fact Christian.[14]

But this modification applies only to the secularized West, not to the religious West, where universal continues to mean universalizable,[15] and Christianity continues to be evangelical. Hence the distinction between the two types of universalism hitherto examined philosophically, historically, and religiously must now be stated metaphorically, in order to liberate it from cultural contingencies. To a human being on this planet both the sky above and the earth around constitute a universal presence. However, celestial universality is seamless, while terrestrial universality comes with undulations and variations, so that the core of terrestrial universality consists of either the substance earth itself, or of the plates that underlie it. This is not the case with celestial universality, which is uniform and homogeneous. Another way to the same insight might well lie in characterizing the Western conception of universality as one of transcendental universality, and the Hindu concept as one of inclusive or immanentist universality.

VI

What, it might be asked, do we gain by distinguishing between these two forms of universalism, which I originally identified as Indian and Western, but which may henceforth be preferably described in culture-neutral terms as transcendental/immanentist or celestial/terrestrial, given the cultural interpenetration which has begun to characterize the modern world.

Theoretically the distinction sheds light on the relationship of form and function in the context of the universal. The flattening kind of universalism merges form and function in one. The more textured version allows for the possibility of different forms serving the same universal function. In fact, the same function may be served by ostensibly opposite forms: the same function of 'family concern' takes opposite forms in the elderly being looked after by the children in the West, and old Inuit parents looking after their children by walking out in the cold. The conflation of uniformity with universality is thereby avoided. In the study of religion the distinction enables more nuanced comparisons. Thus the presence of scriptures is universal in world religions and one would therefore compare the Koran with the Bible. This is a formal comparison based on a universal category. A functional comparison might involve comparing the Koran with the person of Jesus. Here the universal category is revelation but its forms differ.[16]

VII

It is indeed more in the world of 'religion' than any other that the difference between these two kinds of universalism plays itself out. The Christian Church conceives of itself as engaged in a universal mission. The category of the universal, however, has not been arguably understood within it with the required analytical nuance to enable it to conceive of its mission adequately in 'universal' terms. At the root of this difficulty lies a unidimensional understanding of the term 'universal'. The difficulty may be explained by examining two expressions in which the word universal occurs: (1) English is a universal language and (2) language is a universal phenomenon. In the first sense it means that the same language is spoken by different speakers. The emphasis here is on uniformity. In the second sense, English itself becomes one of the several languages illustrative of a wider phenomenon, namely, that human beings are *homo loquens*. Here different languages illustrate the same phenomenon. The emphasis here is on unity, not uniformity. This might initially appear to be an interesting point, but in danger of being trivial. Its ramifications, however, are far from being so; for other distinctions flow from this distinction.

(1) The two major families of religions, variously called the Western and Eastern, or Prophetic and Wisdom, or Semitic and Indic-Sinic traditions, represent this subtle but significant division. The Eastern religions allow for far more inter-religious diversity (on the 'religion is a universal phenomenon' model) than the Western traditions, which seem to work more along the lines of 'English is a universal language' metaphor (with Judaism constituting a special case). As a case of 'as within, so without', the Eastern religions also seem to allow for far more intra-religious diversity.

(2) The distinction has metaphysical ramifications beyond the global. Take the expression: 'Truth is an indivisible treasure'.[17] The Western traditions take this to mean that as truth is indivisible, and they alone have it, it is imperative for others to join their fold to have access to it, for it is indivisible. The Eastern traditions on the other hand (with the special case of Nichiren Buddhism as an exception), take it to mean that as truth

is indivisible, it cannot be divided up among religions and stands equally accessible to all.

(3) The distinction also plays a role in the formation of religious identity. This point becomes clear when one examines the way religious identity is affected by contact with religious traditions other than one's own. The point was made earlier that Eastern universalism tends to be more accepting of other religious points of view than has typically been the case with Western universalism. The differences, however, go deeper and also seem to affect not merely the fact but also the mode of such acceptance. For instance, in the case of the followers of the Western religions, it leads to the emergence of what has been called the syncretic self, while in the case of the followers of the Eastern religions it contributes to the emergence of the multiple self, (hopefully avoiding the pitfalls of multiple personality disorder or schizophrenia which lurk around issues of plural identities in both cases). This point is destined to surface again later in a slightly different context.

(4) This difference in the two forms of universalism affects not only the sense of individual self-perception of the member within a tradition; it also has a bearing on the attitude one adopts towards the direction of the tradition as a whole on the theatre of history. The attitude of Western universalism towards history is, well, historical: that is to say, history for such a religious tradition is a process in which the whole world is subject to an enveloping movement. By contrast, the approach of Eastern universalism in this context may be described as more topographical or geographical. It is concerned with identifying, and encountering in an enriching way, the new religious modality it becomes exposed to in the larger world. If the historical attitude of Western universalism may be summarized in one word as one of conquest, that of Eastern universalism may similarly be described in one word as that of quest.

(5) The distinction has social ramifications as well. The religious communities constituted by Western religions are typically constituted by different groups of people, who may be considered the same, as they subscribe to the same creed. The religious communities of the Eastern traditions typically consist of constituencies of the same people who are prepared to let others adhere to different creeds—both internally and externally. In the former the doctrine comes first, the people follow, in the latter the people come first and what these people choose to believe together comes later. This point also extends further—in the sense that 'dogma' becomes the primary concern in the Western religions (with

Judaism again constituting a special case) and praxis is secondary, while the roles are reversed in Eastern religions (with some notable exceptions).

(6) The distinction ramifies even further in the forms assumed by the interaction of these religions with other religions. Thus when the items from other religions are adopted by adherents of a Western tradition, it attracts the word syncretism; but when the followers of Eastern traditions feel favourably disposed to items in other religious traditions, or to the traditions themselves, the proper description here is not syncretism but multiple religious participation.

(7) The ramifications extend further and have implications for the methodology of religious studies. Thus the historical and social-scientific methods appear more consistent with the study of Western religions and the phenomenological, psychological, and hermeneutical methods appear more consistent with the study of Eastern religions. This may roughly correspond to the assignment of the categories of 'history' and 'nature' as holding the key for understanding the two families of religion.

(8) There is more. The way in which missionary activity manifests itself in these two sets of traditions also seems to be profoundly affected by the sense of the word 'universal' put into play by these traditions. Thus Western traditions tend to be 'guest' traditions, that is, traditions that move across cultures as guests. Christianity and Islam straddle different cultures, and Judaism found its way into even more diverse cultures. The Eastern religions, however, tend to be 'host' traditions—they culturally play host to a number of different religions. The religious histories of India, China, and Japan illustrate the point well.

(9) The two universalisms tend to harbour different approaches towards religious diversity. The universalism associated with Western religions, while it might accept that diversity is good, admits it to be so because, among other things, seemingly unrelated, religious phenomena may sometimes come together to shed spiritual light. The more pressing concern tends to be that diversity might represent deviation or, at least, parochialism. The universalism associated with Eastern religions, while it might admit that diversity carries with it the danger of a certain lack of regulation which might undermine normative considerations, attaches greater significance to the fact that religious traditions otherwise far apart, may display similarities which bring them closer in some ways than two disparate elements within the sacred canopy of the same tradition, imparting to the statistical fact that separate elements within two populations may be closer across populations than within them, a spiritual rather than random significance.

(10) The attitudes of the two universalisms in relation to conversion also tend to differ. The universalism of the Western traditions actively seeks converts (with the special exception of Judaism) for its universal imperative implies that, in order to be universal, each member of the population must subscribe to one particular tradition. This the Eastern religions find rather baffling (with the partial exception of Nichiren Buddhism) because for them it suffices that every one may belong to any one of them, that is, any one particular tradition. The Islamic doctrine of *ahl al-kitāb* imparts to the whole point an intriguing convolution.

(11) The cross-fertilization of the two universalisms constitutes a dimension all its own. The invocation of Judaism as an exception in the case of Western religions, and of Nichiren Buddhism in the case of Eastern religions highlights the fact that each cluster of traditions, and the universalism it represents, is not unfamiliar with its 'other'. This raises a crucial point for the mission or the church in our times: are the two universalisms negotiable, and if so in what ways? Strikingly, a Hindu India, which is presumably committed to the non-missionary universalism of the Eastern religions, permits conversion, while Islamic Indonesia, which is presumably committed to the missionary universalism of Western religions, restricts it.

(12) The two forms of universalisms are not without their own implication for the relationship of church and state. One would, for instance, expect the so-called ethnic religions to proclaim their own dominant religion as state religions, in keeping with their ethnic orientation. However, their attitude to the state is mediated by their brand of universalism so that paradoxically, countries characterized by the so-called ethnic religions, such as India or Japan, do not have a state religion (with Nepal constituting an exception) while Sri Lanka, Pakistan, and Bangladesh, while subscribing to the 'missionary' religions of Buddhism and Islam, have declared the relevant religions as state religion in the South Asian theatre, with Indonesia claiming to be neither a secular nor a theocratic state.

(13) Finally and contemporaneously, the dual universalism under discussion has implications for human rights discourse. This point is best explored further in the light of two human rights documents.

UNIVERSAL DECLARATION OF HUMAN RIGHTS (1948)

Article 18

Everyone has the right to freedom of thought, conscience and religion. This right includes the freedom to change his religion or belief, and freedom, either alone or in community with others in public or private, to manifest his religion or belief in teaching, practice, worship and observance.

INTERNATIONAL COVENANT ON CIVIL AND POLITICAL RIGHTS (1966)

Article 18

1. Everyone shall have the right to freedom of thought, conscience and religion. This right shall include freedom to have or adopt a religion or belief of his choice, and freedom, either individually or in community with others and in public or private, to manifest his religion of belief in worship, observance, practice and teaching.
2. No one shall be subject to coercion, which would impair his freedom to have or to adopt a religion or belief of his choice.
3. Freedom to manifest one's religion or belief may be subject only to such limitations as are prescribed by law and are necessary to protect public safety, order, health or morals, or the fundamental rights and freedoms of others.
4. The States Parties to the present Covenant undertake to have respect for the liberty of parents and, when applicable, legal guardians to ensure the religious and moral education of their children.

As it stands, Article 18 of the Universal Declaration of Human Rights (UDHR) acknowledges religious freedom as one seamless right, involving a mere dichotomy of its existence as contrasted with its absence. Its active component consists of the right to change one's religion or belief.[18] The same Article 18, as elaborated in the International Covenant of Civil and Political Rights maintains the same salience, namely, that the right to freedom is the 'freedom to have or adopt a religion or belief of choice'.[19]

A student of religion finds this formulation problematic. It was pointed out in the previous chapter that there are several religious traditions of humanity for whom freedom of religion would consist not so much of the freedom to change religion as to retain it. This is, for instance, how Judaism, Zoroastrianism, Hinduism, and the indigenous religions would historically perceive the protection of their religious freedom. The freedom to convert also poses a theological problem from the point of view of Islam,[20] in which such conversion is tantamount to apostasy. In some forms of Hinduism such conversion is even deemed wicked.[21] It was also pointed out in the previous chapter that this formulation of freedom of religion in the UDHR is not only historically and theologically but also logically questionable, as it obscures the fact that freedom of religion is not one blanket right but really involves the negotiation of two equally valid rights: (1) the right of someone to proselytize and (2) the right of one not to be made an object of proselytization.[22] By blurring these two rights it poses a serious challenge to religious peace. The conception of a blanket right to conversion poses problems not only inter-religiously, but also intra-religiously, as demonstrated by the reaction to Protestant missionary activity in Russia and Latin America. The fact that the problems caused by the present formulation of the right are almost as universal as the right itself claims to be, lends credibility to the present concern and highlights the need to problematize our current understanding of it.

The present formulation, with its bias in favour of missionary religions, imposes a Western conception of religion on the rest of the world. It thereby seriously compromises and even undermines the stipulated universality of human rights discourse already under attack,[23] unless it is rectified. For it is the Western view of religion which, even when downgraded culturally, pervades the prevailing view of religion. It has been forcefully suggested that even those who are aware of this bias cannot escape it, because it permeates the linguistic structures which shape their thought.

VIII

The great challenge of the twenty-first century is going to be: how will members of the world community deal with a type of universalism other than its own? Can one universe sustain two universalisms?

This section may be read as a plea for mutual accommodation in human rights discourse, if the claim of such discourse to universality is to retain its credibility. It might be helpful to refer to an accommodation which has already been made in this connection in one stream of universalism, referred to as Western in cultural terms, which could also be described as Abrahamic in religious terms. The reader will have noticed that the right to *change* one's religion, as found in Article 18 of the Universal Declaration of Human Rights, does *not* appear as such in the International Covenant on Civil and Political Rights (1966). The corresponding expression takes the form of right to *adopt* a religion.[24]

The subtle nature of the change should not conceal its significance. Some Islamic nations had actually abstained from endorsing the Universal Declaration of Human Rights because Islam does not permit one to 'change' one's religion. Such a change is punishable by death according to the sharī'ah. Hence, in order to accommodate the objection, the word 'change' was dropped in the Covenant and replaced by the word 'adopt'.[25]

One might be tempted to ask: what difference does it make? Is it not a case of

What's in a name? That
Which we call a rose,
By any other name
Would smell as sweet.

In this case, far from not mattering at all, it matters a great deal. When one 'changes' one's religion, it normally involves two operations: (1) the *giving up* or abandoning of one religion and (2) the *taking on* or accepting of another religion.

It is the 'giving up' of Islam which attracts the death penalty according to the sharī'ah. As this is the clear implication of the word 'change', it was considered objectionable from the Islamic point of view. By contrast, the word 'adoption' indicates the acceptance of something new, *without entailing the rejection of something else*. Hence this altered formulation could pass muster and was adopted. A simple example might help clarify the point. Let us suppose that a person, on account of being on affectionate terms with a particular family for a long time 'adopts' this other family as his or her own. This does not mean that one has abandoned one's own family. If, however, one changed (exchanged) the new family for the old, the situation would differ radically.

One can relate to a certain impatience with such minutiae on the part of the reader; the reader might also, however, wish to appreciate the fact through the foregoing discussion that a word can also, far from not mattering, be a matter of life and death, as this example illustrates. Why, sometimes a diphthong can make a lot of difference. It has been said the difference between the Athanasian and the Arian position on the exact nature of the father-son relationship in early Christianity could be described as a 'battle over a Greek diphthong, the Athanasians calling the son *homousian* (of the same substance) in contrast to the Arian *homoiousian* (of similar substance)'.[26]

This example of the substitution of the word *change* by *adopt* illustrates the need of being sensitive to differences in understanding even within one 'stream of universalism'; how much more then the need of bringing another whole stream of universalism into the picture?

The fact that such a change was indeed made in the transition from Declaration to Covenant proves that such changes can be made. The change now being advocated is the incorporation of the word 'retention' (i.e., the right to retain one's religion) in the documents on human rights.

NOTES

1. On the use of this word in relation to the Declaration of Human Rights, See Mary Ann Glendon, op. cit., p. 161.
2. Satischandra Chatterjee and Dhirendramohan Datta, *An Introduction to Indian Philosophy*, Calcutta: University of Calcutta: 1966, p. 235.
3. Ibid., p. 235.
4. Ibid., p. 236.
5. Ibid.
6. Ibid., pp. 236–7.
7. Ibid., Chapter 1.
8. Ruth R. Wisse, *If I am Not For Myself*, New York: The Free Press, 1992, p. 179.
9. Frederick Bird, 'Moral Universals', *Journal of Religious Pluralism*, Vol. III, 1993, pp. 29–83.
10. Ibid., p. 37.
11. Ibid., pp. 37–8.
12. Ibid., p. 40.
13. Upendra Baxi, 'From Human Rights to the Right to be Human', in *Rethinking Human Rights* (eds), Smitu Kothari and Harsh Sethi, New York: New Horizons Press, 1991, p. 152.
14. S.N. Balagangadhara, *The Heathen in his Blindness: Asia, the West and Dynamic of Religion*, Leiden, New York, and Koln: E.J. Brill, 1994, pp. 246–7.
15. In the less glamourous formulation even 'so-called internationalism is only an extension of narrow . . . nationalism', Jawaharlal Nehru, *The Discovery of India*, New York: The John Day Company, 1946, p. 41.
16. 'Muslims believe that the *Qur'ān* is an immutable heavenly book, preserved by God in the "Mother of the Book" or the source of all revelation. In fact, there is an interesting theological parallel, between Christ and the *Qur'ān*. For Christians, Christ is the eternal word of God, made incarnate in a certain moment in time, as stated in the prologue to John's Gospel. For Muslims, the *Qur'ān* is quite an accurate proclamation, within earthly history, of the eternal word of God: 'This surely is a glorious *Qur'ān*, preserved in a well-guarded tablet' (Q.85:21–2), Mahmoud M. Ayoub, 'The Islamic Tradition', in *World Religions: Western Traditions* (ed.), Willard G. Oxtoby, second edition, Toronto: Oxford University Press, 2002, p. 355.
17. See Louis Renou (ed.), *Hinduism*, New York: George Braziller, 1962, p. 56; R.C. Zaehner (ed.), *The Concise Encyclopaedia of Living Faiths*, Boston: Beacon Press, 1967, p. 16.
18. *Twenty-Five Human Rights Documents*, New York: Centre for the Study of Human Rights, Columbia University, 1994, p. 8.
19. Ibid., p. 21.
20. Robert Traer, *Faith in Human Rights*, Washington, DC: Georgetown University Press, 1991, p. 118.
21. Eric J. Sharpe, *Comparative Religion: A History*, London: Duckworth, 1986, pp. 255–6.

22. See *The Gazette*, Montreal, 14 June 1996, p. E8.
23. See Mary Ann Glendon, op. cit., Chapter 12.
24. *Twenty-Five Human Rights Documents* (op. cit., p. 21).
25. For an account on how this change came about and its implications, see Bahiyyih G. Tahzib, *Freedom of Religion or Belief: Ensuring Effective International Legal Protection* (The Hague/Boston/London: Martinus Nijhoff Publishers, 1996), pp. 84–7. I am indebted to Professor Brian D. Lepard for this reference.
26. Willard G. Oxtoby, 'The Christian Tradition', in *World Religions: Western Traditions* (ed.), Willard G. Oxtoby, second edition, Toronto: Oxford University Press, 2002, p. 229.

CHAPTER 8

A Human Rights Contribution to Hinduism and a Hindu Contribution to Human Rights

What can Human Rights discourse Contribute to Hinduism?

I

I would like to begin by stating that human rights discourse can make a positive contribution to the discourse of Hinduism. Once such a statement is made the next thought likely to cross our minds is that this statement is too trite to be taken seriously as Hinduism, at first glance, seems opposed to human rights. All one needs to do to be confirmed in this view is to scan the discourse of Hinduism with the searchlight of human rights norms. Such an effort will spotlight the glaring shortcomings of Hinduism in the form of the evils of the caste system, the treatment of women down to that of female foetuses and so on. So the great contribution human rights discourse can make in relation to the discourse of Hinduism, or discourse around Hinduism, is to expose the shortcomings of Hinduism to popular attention. While this task in itself has a negative dimension to it, its effect will be positive. It will tell Hindus what is wrong with their religion and how they might go around rectifying it, or even abandoning it.

When I raise the question of how human rights discourse can contribute to the discourse on Hinduism, however, I have something more than this in mind. I value the critique human rights discourse offers of Hindu practices and associated doctrines. This critique now has been in existence for over half a century and, if anything, is becoming even more intense. This book, however, aims at approaching the relationship between Hinduism and human rights at a conceptual level. It is therefore at the conceptual level that I shall try to probe the issue as I proceed. The fact that I shall not be addressing the issue of human rights violations within Hinduism should not be taken to mean that I do not attach importance to it; the fact that I shall not focus on it does not mean either that it is considered inconsequential by me, or is inconsequential. It only means that the focus of my interest at the moment lies elsewhere.

II

Now that the nature of the present task has been identified, I would like to focus on the concept of 'rights' itself, as in 'Human Rights', and try to examine how viewing Hindu ethical discourse from this perspective might enrich the discourse on Hinduism.

In order to achieve such an outcome I would like to proceed by asking the following four questions. (1) Are 'rights' discourse and 'duties' discourse comparable? (2) Are they comparable in such a way that one might ask of them the following question: (if the two are comparable, then) is it possible to discuss the pros and cons of utilizing one form of such discourse over another? And are there certain circumstances in which one form may be preferred to another? (3) If 'rights' and 'duties' discourses are comparable, could the category of *dharma* be placed in the matrix of this discussion to determine if there exists any analogous rights discourse associated with it, and if not, can such discourse be associated with it on the strength of the comparability of rights/duties discourse? (4) If there are certain situations in which rights discourse is preferable to duty discourse , and if the category of *dharma* is capable of mediating both rights as well as duties discourse, is the *dharma* discourse capable of shifting into such a semantic gear?

ARE 'RIGHTS' AND 'DUTIES' DISCOURSE COMPARABLE?

I

I would first like to begin by focusing on the concept of rights from a comparative perspective. It has been claimed that the concept of rights is a secular and Western concept. If this is indeed so, our understanding may turn out to be more complex than might be apparent at first sight. In order to pursue this point two questions might be raised: (1) what exactly is meant by rights in current discourse and (2) do other religions and cultures possess such a concept (or an analogous one), or are they devoid of it?

What are rights? Modern discourse seems to offer four main ways of looking at rights: (1) rights as liberties, (2) rights as claims, (3) rights as entitlements, and (4) rights as trumps. If we use the term reproductive rights, for instance, to refer to the cluster of 'rights to family planning, contraception, and abortion', it might also be of interest to determine the nature of this right from these four points of view.

Rights as Liberties

Rights as liberties are associated with civil and political rights, such as the right against unlawful detention, or interference with privacy, and so on. In sum: 'Liberty rights, with which civil and political rights are associated, are negative rights in that they offer certain protections but do not necessarily generate duties, other than the duties to refrain from coercion or interference.'[1]

The right to marry and raise a family, as part of the umbrella term reproductive rights, seems to belong here.

Rights as Claims

By comparison with rights as liberties, 'Rights as claims involve a subject of the right (the person who is making the claim), what the subject has a right to, and who has responsibility for fulfilling the duty implied in the claim.'[2]

The right to due process is a good example of such a concept of rights. The right to practice contraception and abortion seems to belong here.

Rights as Entitlements

'Rights as entitlements view the nature of rights not as against someone, but as for something'.[3] A good example of this is provided by the rights of children, where the 'specific bearer of duty for the right may not be clear, but the obligation to provide protection is nevertheless valid'.[4] The right to have access to *facilities* for exercising the right to contraception and abortion seems to fall under this rubric.

Rights as Trumps

Rights as trumps are a way of dealing with conflict among rights. 'All rights talk signifies the moral weightiness of the liberty, negative or positive claim, entitlement, duty or obligation. But when there is a conflict in serious moral claims, trumps signify that some rights, while not absolute, are nevertheless based on more compelling moral grounds.'[5] Such a view of rights might be helpful in 'negotiating the tension between biotic rights and human reproductive rights. Human reproductive rights could trump biotic rights for the first child, or even the second. But beyond replacement, biotic rights could then trump',[6] where biotic rights may involve restorative measures to preserve a species from extinction, for instance,[7] or the protection of the biosphere.

The question of abrogation of reproductive rights under certain circumstances, or conversely their ability to ace other rights in certain cases, may belong here.

If one examines these four concepts of rights closely, one finds that they contain some elements in common. These are (1) an entitlement and (2) an entitlement to remedy, when that entitlement is disregarded. The fact that we have a category called rights as entitlement should not obscure the fact that *all* rights involve entitlements. Unless one is entitled to liberties, or claims, one cannot claim them as rights. Similarly, rights as trumps means that some rights possess a more compelling claim or entitlement than others. Perhaps another clarifying insight here consists of the realization that rights are like legal claims, whose violation involves punishment or compensation. The corresponding question to ask in relation to non-Western societies and cultures then is: through which category do people make claims in these cultures, such that their violation involves punishment or compensation?

The answer is duty. In most of the traditional cultures the entitlement of others, or their claims on us, are articulated as our duties towards them and failure to perform one's duty involves atonement (in terms of conscience) or shame (in terms of society) or in some cases, even compensation. In duties then we seem to possess an analogue to rights.

In fact an even stronger statement might be possible. Duty discourse and rights discourse are not only comparable, to a certain extent they may even be convertible. The fact that the word duties crops up in the discussion of all the views of human rights lends credence to this view.[8] This does not mean that rights and duties are coextensive, because duties can extend beyond rights. For instance, 'some duties could precede the attribution of rights',[9] just as 'there could be duties not grounded in rights'.[10] Nevertheless though not coextensive, rights and duties are correlative in that (someone's) rights are related to (someone's) duty.

Three claims can be made, at this stage, on the nature of the relationship between rights and duties, each stronger than the other. One could begin by claiming that rights and duties are *comparable* entities. One can then go on to make the stronger claim that the two are *convertible*. Finally, one could claim that the two are *coextensive* for the light it sheds on the claim that they are convertible. Consider the case of infants. Infants, in relation to parents, have rights without duties. And parents, in relation to infants, have duties without rights. Parents, however, could also be said to possess rights, in the sense that they have a right not to have the infant taken away from them. This right however is *not* in the form of direct reciprocation for duties performed for the infant, but rather in relation to the state. It could now be argued that when the infant grows up and becomes an adult, parents do have a right to be looked after by the children and this right is indeed located in one who is now an 'infant' and *not* the state (although the state may have the obligation to *enforce* the right). In this sense the two *are* mutually implicative. The case of animals provides another possible example. Animals may have rights against human beings (as in animal rights), without corresponding duties, although in the case of some kinds of animals, such as draught animals, animals do have a 'duty' towards the owner, although the implication of the concept to animals is obviously problematical. There is no need to carry the exercise further because its purpose is served: even if rights and duties are not coextensive or cannot be correlated all the way, their mutual implication is difficult to deny. This is confirmed by the historical fact that the first Indian to use the English language in a major way in moral and religious discourse had no difficulty in making the switch. One has here Raja Rammohan Roy in mind, who, already in the early part of the nineteenth century, was talking about encroachment on the *rights* of Indian women.

II

Is it possible to develop this point further? In our search for a non-Western analogue to the concept of rights we have come up with the concept of duties. Is that all? Does our investigation cease here, or is it capable of being carried further?

Let us select another culture for a closer comparison with the Western, as, for instance, the Hindu. We can now place two major systems of moral discourse side by side, and survey them in depth. Once this is done one finds that each of these forms its own pattern in which rights and duties respectively find a place. We also find that the patterns differ, and further, that such differences shed light on each other.

The results of the comparison can only be summarized here.[11] While both the modern Western and the traditional Hindu worlds seem equally keen to do the right thing, the attempt to do so seems to have led them in different directions—in the direction of rights in the West, and the direction of righteousness in India. With the recognition of the individual in the

West as 'the autonomous possessor of his own person and capacities', his rights were 'now conceived essentially as the instrument for the protection of the individual and her property from the rest of society in the form of entitlements, while individual interests (were) identified prior to and independently of any moral or social bonds'.[12] Such socio-economic individualism was morally recast by Kant. With him, 'a rationally based concept of self-respect . . . breaks free of a notion of rights that in effect equate them with privileges of membership in a civic or religious organisation. It is in such a world that the idea of human rights, rights by virtue of the moral nature of human beings alone comes to the fore'.[13] This results in a separation of 'two senses of right, namely righteousness and entitlement' in Western thought, or, more accurately, the locus of the two ceases to be identical. Hindu thought, however, developed along different lines. Within it *dharma* constitutes the key category. *Dharma* 'is the order of the entire reality . . . which both keeps the world together and maintains each thing according to its nature'.[14] This carries two major implications:

> (1) the two senses of right, namely righteousness and entitlement are brought together in the Indian conception in contrast to their separation in western thought, and (2) with this convergence, the primary category is not that of moral principle but of a primordial order that is neither exclusively moral or exclusively cosmological but both together at once.[15]

This concept of order is also holistic by its very nature, encompassing the 'three worlds' of the individual, society, and cosmos, as it were. Rights and duties, nevertheless, do remain comparable, as it is the location of the two which is affected by this further argument rather than the relationship itself. Human Rights discourse, however, by definition, prefers rights discourse over duty discourse. This raises the possibility: could it be that Hinduism would benefit by favouring rights discourse in place of the duty discourse which is said to characterize it?

What are the Pros and Cons of 'Rights' and 'Duties' Discourse?

Thus it has often been pointed out that duties discourse and rights discourse can overlap and indeed that the two may be interchangeable. Alison Dundes Renteln writes:

> Chapter 2 begins by exploring the traditional notion of human rights. After clarifying the idea of a right, I discuss some of the conceptual problems associated with human rights. In particular, I challenge the claim made by some human-rights scholars that moral systems, which are duty-based, cannot accommodate

human rights. If, for example, the members of a given society have a duty to take care of the elderly, then the elderly could be said to have the right to proper care. The point is that just because the rubric of some peoples is not that of rights does not mean that human rights cannot be universal.[16]

Given this equivalence between the two it might be worth examining the reasons for preferring one over the other, or the circumstances in which this might be desirable.

Reasons for Preferring Rights Idiom

(1) There are no duties without rights. This point may be argued as follows:

To live in a world of duties will be worse than to live in a world of rights. In the world of duties, when people sometimes do not perform their duties, we cannot even claim that they *should* do their duties. For we can make such a claim only when we are living in a world of rights (and corresponding duties). I have a binding obligation to do my duty to you only when you have a right claim upon me. But where you do not have a right on me, I may or may not do my duty.[17]

(2) Duties idiom lends itself to deontological exploitation. This may be particularly true in the context of Hinduism. Even a sympathetic observer such as Louis Renou remarks:

If Hinduism is studied superficially or unilaterally, one might be tempted to see in it as chaos of irrational religious practices and superstitions and degradation through magic and verbalism. The economic dysfunction engendered by certain religious prohibitions or by the entire caste system has been pointed out. The caste system has been held responsible for social stagnation, while extensive criticism has been offered of negative tendencies, excessive non-violence and certain deplorable customs such as the burning of widows in past time and child marriage, which is still sometimes practiced. It is evident that there is both good and evil in a religious context which has been allowed to go its own way for more than two thousand years *without any internal checks* while it retained an attitude approaching defiance which became even more audacious in the face of the temptations offered by the modern world.[18]

The absence of 'internal checks' may be accounted for by the absence of rights talk. In any case, Louis Renou goes on to say, in a passage also cited earlier:

But ambivalence is characteristic of India: for her, what is the good of killing her cows if she has to lose her soul? A factor in social and psychical equilibrium is found in the notion of *dharma* with its rigorous justice and the 'truth' which it implies (the Indians insist on the attitude of truthfulness as others insist on an 'attitude of consciousness'). An important consequence of this is tolerance, non-violence considered and active virtue; this is a manner of acting which must be respected—even in the political sphere—*regardless of the attitude of others*. In this perhaps is to be found the most spectacular contribution, which India has made to the modern world and the most worthy reply to Marxism and its materialism.[19]

Although Renou's comments are appreciative, it is easy to see how this sublime unilateralism renders one liable to deception and exploitation.

(3) Rights idiom may be necessary to ensure the compliance with obligations. It may thus be argued that

... my obligations sometimes consist of nothing more than 'feeling bound' and these 'binding feelings' do not issue forth in the actual performance of obligations unless others make their rights-claim upon us. Rights-claims, in other words, act as an impetus for the discharge of my obligations which otherwise would remain in the realm of feelings.[20]

However, at the same time,

People would be less willing to perform their obligation unless the rights-holder makes the claim that others perform their obligations. For example, a debtor has an obligation to the creditor to return something he borrowed. If this obligation is founded only on the right of the creditor, then the debtor *may* not sometimes discharge his obligations unless the creditor demand that the debt be repaid. The reason for this hesitation in discharging one's obligation is obvious, since the obligation of the debtor arises as a consequence of the right of the creditor, and since the creditor has the freedom not to exercise his right, the debtor may 'wait and see' whether the creditor will 'make the first move' and demand that the debt be repaid.[21]

(4) Rights idiom provides more freedom to the individual. This becomes apparent when we compare the worldviews associated with the two forms of discourse.

A world of obligations is a world in which everyone is bound, and therefore is inconsistent with freedom which is an important human value. A world of rights, on the other hand, gives the individual some freedom to exercise or not to exercise his rights.[22]

(5) Rights idiom may be required to ensure that the state discharge its duties towards the people. For

... problems arise in a 'pure' world of obligations, without any rights. To repeat, in an imperfect world like ours, if some people fail to perform their obligations we cannot, as a matter of right, insist that they ought to perform their obligations. Take, for example, the mutual obligations of a king to his subjects and the subjects to the king. If the king fails to perform his obligations to the subjects, the subjects may not perform *their* obligations to the king. What the subjects cannot do is to *make demands* on the king that he discharge his obligations because they are *entitled* to them, for 'demanding', 'claiming', 'being entitled', etc. flow from the concepts of rights and not obligations.[23]

Reasons for Preferring Duties Idiom

(1) There can be no rights without duties. This point may be argued as follows:

> . . . the world of obligations is logically prior to the world of rights. To say that X has a right to 'A' means not only that X is entitled to A; that X can make claims against others, if he so chooses; but also[that] others are required to do according to X's pursuit of A. The obligations of others do not arise as a consequence of X's claims.[24]

Rama Rao Pappu, however, admits that one could choose to 'ignore . . . the logical priority of obligations and maintain . . . that obligations are the logical consequences of rights'.[25]

(2) Rights are claimed against others (individual, state) whereas the obligations of human beings pertain *both* to 'man-as-such towards himself and others'.[26] Thus the duties idiom provides for a broader base and goal for human development.

> Unlike the Western individualism, a person is never conceived in the East as an isolated monad who enjoys his rights in isolation. In the East, the individual is one who is *essentially* related to other persons—in fact, to the whole universe—and the relationship between persons is conceived in terms of mutual obligations. In Confucian thought, for example, 'the basic social relations are between (1) rulers and subjects, (2) parents and children, (3) husband and wife, (4) older and younger brother and (5) friend and friend.' In Indian thought, likewise, the concept of man is the concept of a *dharmic* person or 'obligatory man'. To be a person is to incur certain *ṛṇas* (debts) and to be in a *dharmic* (obligatory) relationship with other persons. Some of the *dharmas* or obligations of man are *sādhāraṇa-dharmas* (i.e. obligations pertaining to man-as-such towards himself and others).[27]

(3) Duties idiom is morally superior because it enshrines the idea of 'the progressive assumption of obligations to others, *whether or not others claim their rights.* A child, for instance, first develops a sense

of obligation towards his parents, brothers, and sisters, before he realizes or claims that he may have rights against them, or that he has obligations to them because they have rights against him'.[28]

(4) It is also morally superior because duties idiom addresses a wider world. Thus altruistic duties are not viewed as 'stopping short at mankind, but as including within their scope sub-human beings which are regarded as having rights though no duties'.[29] This argument suffers from some limitations: (1) What it really questions is a correspondence view of rights and duties. (2) Moreover, it can be used to argue the opposite that as beings can have rights but no duties, rights idiom is broader in scope than duties idiom.

However in general it does seem to be the case that the world of obligations is wider than the world of rights. It is now widely recognized that rights and obligations are not correlatives, that though every right implies a corresponding duty, not every duty or obligation implies a corresponding right. Thus we have obligations to be kind, charitable, benevolent, and so on though there are no corresponding rights to receive kindness or charity. Some philosophers also maintain that we have obligations to sub-human beings, to nature and to environment, though they do not have corresponding rights on us.[30]

(5) Rights-centredness leads to self-centredness. This point may be developed as follows:

. . . because every individual is a possessor of rights, he thinks of others discharging their obligations to him. 'What do others owe me?' 'Should I not compel others to perform their obligations?' are the foremost concerns in the world of rights. When the individual asks these questions, he makes himself the centre of attention and making the demand on others, he may not care whether others have the ability or capacity to discharge their obligations to him. Some of the problems with the economic and welfare rights contained in the Universal Declaration arise because they do not take into consideration the abilities or capacities of other individuals/nations into account.[31]

How does *Dharma* Fit into 'Rights' and 'Duties' Discourse?

It has usually been held that *dharma* talk corresponds to duty discourse rather than rights discourse. Thus, for instance, it was *rāja-dharma*—the king's duty—to rule and to rule well, but the subjects had no right to be ruled over fairly or justly. The *prajā-dharma* was their duty to be loyal. It could be argued that there was no way, in terms of *dharma* talk, of enforcing their rights. This point comes out in clear relief in Hartmut

Scharfe's discussion of the deposition of an (undesirable) king, both in an epic and Arthashastric context, as well as in historic times. In relation to the former context he writes:

In the period of epics, the dharmasūtra-s and the Arthaśāstra, the people seem to have lost most of their influence on the king's tenure; it may be more than a coincidence that at about the same time they had also lost their right to bear arms. Mbh XII 60, 19ff. does, however, grant the people the moral right to rebel against a king who fails to fulfill his duty to protect the people, and kill him like a mad dog. Invariably the rationale behind an uprising is this failure of the king rather than the people's assertion of any inalienable citizens' rights being violated. In Arthaśāstra I 17, 39 the king's agents warn a rebellious prince that even if his attack on the king should succeed, he would be 'destroyed by the people like a single clod of earth (which the plowman breaks up with a thick club)'. The king himself is warned to control his temper because 'kings under the influence of anger are known to have been killed by risings among the subjects (*prakṛti-kopa*)', while he, on the other hand, attempts to have his enemy's administrators killed by popular uprisings. Such uprisings are mentioned as an ever present threat, but the author of this state manual never endorses them as a political strategy for the state whose king and courtiers he tries to counsel. Actually, there is no recorded uprising in pre-Muslim India after the Vedic period, i.e., for almost two millennia. For the Arthaśāstra, the most serious revolt was that of the innermost circle of officers (i.e. ministers, *purohita*, commander of the army and crown prince), whereas the 'inner revolt', apparently of the people caused little concern. If others were enemies 'not just beyond the frontiers but in the capital, in the government, in the council chamber, in the kitchen, under the bed, in it,' each subsequent one was more cause for concern. In the ninth century, the commentator Medhātithi (on Manu VII 198) held that effective dissension in the enemy camp was achievable only if the rival king's family members were to go against him.

In the context of historical times, Hartmut Scharfe goes on to say:

In historic times, people more likely vented their anger by failing to support an unpopular king or by actively supporting his rivals or even outside enemies when an opportunity arose. A king that is honoured by his people is respected even by his foreign enemies, whereas one that is despised will be overpowered. The most potent independent action of the people, however, was emigration to another kingdom. A constant shortage of manpower led kings to entice residents of other states to migrate; an unpopular king could thus suffer severe losses in his state's population and revenue. The most common theme of political justice in our brahminical texts is the fervent if somewhat irrational belief that righteous brahmins bring about the fall of an unrighteous king, and that unjust coercion or punishment strikes down the unjust king directly, or that violations of righteousness lead to hell.[32]

The crux of the matter turns out to be that

There was no legal way to remove a bad king. Even the traditional freedom of peasants to turn their backs on oppressive taxes and move away was curtailed by zamindars and tax-collectors in the Benares region in the latter part of the 18th century. Interruptions in a dynastic line (besides those caused by foreign conquest) were mostly due to palace intrigues involving the royal family, ministers and other courtiers. The overthrow of the rulers by brahmins—through armed force if need be—in the Śukranīti IV 7,332f. (early 19th century) may be a traditional cliché, or it may refer to the saṁnyāsin movement in Bengal.[33]

It could be argued however that this interpretation is too one-sided. For we also read:

The king who harasses his subjects loses his life, family and kingdom. Moreover stories of kings killed for their tyranny are found in the ancient literature. For example, Vena, who was jealous of the gods, wanted sacrificial offerings to be made to himself (and not to the gods) and violated dharma, was killed by the brāhmaṇas (Śāntiparva 59.93–5, Bhāgavatapurāṇa IV.14). The Anuśāsanaparva (61.32–3) solemnly sanctions the killing of a king in certain circumstances. 'The people should gird themselves up and kill a cruel king who does not protect subjects, who extracts taxes and simply robs them of their wealth, who gives no lead. Such a king is Kali (evil and strife) incarnate. That king who after declaring 'I shall protect you' does not protect his subjects should be killed (by the people) after forming a confederacy, like a dog that is afflicted with madness.' Manu (VII.27–8) states that the great principle of *daṇḍa* if properly wielded conduces to the advancement of the three *puruṣārthas*, but if a voluptuous, mean and unjust king wields it, it recoils on his head and destroys the king together with his relations. Kām. 2.38 makes it clear that *daṇḍa* foolishly wielded might exasperate even hermits. The Śāntiparva 92.19 recommends that a king who has false and very wicked ministers and who puts down dharma should be killed by the people. Even as early as the Tai. S. II 3. 1 it appears that kings were driven away, while the Śatapatha Brāhmaṇa (XII.9.3.1 and 3) mentions a king Duṣṭarītu Pauṁsāyana who had been expelled from the kingdom which had descended to him through ten ancestors. The Sautrāmaṇi *iṣṭi* is prescribed as a rite for a king to regain a kingdom from which he had been driven away (vide H. Dh. Vol. II., p. 1227). Śānti 92. 6 and 9, Manu VII. 27 and 34, Yaj. I. 356 appear to justify at least deposing a king, if not tyrannicide.

P.V. Kane goes on to say:

Similarly, the Śukranītisāra (II.274–5) states that a king, though of a noble pedigree, should be abandoned, if he violates dharma, if he hates good qualities (in others), lines of policy and the army and if his conduct would lead to the destruction of the kingdom and that the family priest with the consent of the principal officers of state should place on the throne another scion of the royal family who is possessed of the requisite virtues. Nārada props up the theory of divine right by stating that the king secures dominion over (lit. purchases) his subjects by his austerities (performed in former lives) and therefore the king is their lord (prakīrṇaka 25). Śukranīti I.20 also brings in the doctrine of Karma 'the king holds the earth by the actions of his former lives and by his austerities.' Compare Manu VII.111–12, Śānti 78.36. The Śukranītisāra (IV.7 332–3) says that brāhmaṇas may even fight and destroy an oppressive kṣatriya king and would thereby incur no sin. The Yaśastilaka (III., p. 431) gives examples of kings killed by their subjects, one a Kaliṅga king who made a barber his commander-in-chief. In fact in all works on polity we find comparatively little about the king's rights and special privileges, but on the other hand the greatest emphasis is laid on the king's duties and responsibilities.[34]

One hesitates to test the patience of the reader further. It is easy to become pedantic in one's eagerness to document differing points of view fully but the point is a subtle one. The situation which seems to emerge is that rights exist, but there is little rights talk. It is also possible to argue that Hindu subjects displayed an increasing reluctance to avail of their right to dispose of a bad king as duty discourse became pervasive.

I would now like to propose that by exclusively understanding *dharma* as duties, many scholars have overlooked the *rights* dimension of the word *dharma*. This will pave the way for the discussion which awaits us in the next section. I provide two illustrations to substantiate my point.

The first example is one with which we are already familiar. A passage from the *Bṛhadāraṇyaka Upaniṣad* (I.4.14) was cited in an earlier chapter, in which the following expression occurred: 'so that a weak man hopes (to defeat) a strong man by means of justice (*dharma*) as one does through a king'.[35] We may supplement this translation of S. Radhakrishnan by that of Robert Ernest Hume: 'So a weak man controls a strong man by law, just as if by a king.'[36] It is however a more recent translation which helps one make the point more decidedly: 'Therefore a weaker man makes demands of a stronger man by appealing to the law, just as one does by appealing to a king.'[37]

It is difficult not to see the word *dharma* here freighted with the semantic weight of the word right.

One could even venture the view that when the word *dharma* is used in a relationship which *involves a claim against one in a higher position*, it has the connotation of a right. The following example might lend support to the view. The *smṛti* texts regularly describe the professional duties of the four *varṇa*s. Thus *Manusmṛti* (I.88–92):

88. To Brāhmaṇas he assigned teaching and studying (the Veda), sacrificing for their own benefit and for others, giving and accepting (of alms).
89. The Kshatriya he commanded to protect the people, to bestow gifts, to offer sacrifices, to study (the Veda), and to abstain from attaching himself to sensual pleasures;
90. The Vaiśya to tend cattle, to bestow gifts, to offer sacrifices, to study (the Veda), to trade, to lend money, and to cultivate land.
91. One occupation only the lord prescribed to Śūdra, to serve meekly even these (other) three castes.

These are the duties assigned to the *varṇas* in normal times. *Manusmṛti* also takes up the question of how these four *varṇa*s are to pursue their vocation in 'times of troubles' (or *āpad-dharma*). The general principle laid down is that the higher *varṇa* may resort to the professions of the lower *varṇa* in such a time, with due restrictions and precautions. Now the question arises: if, in extremis, the *brāhmaṇa* can resort to the vocation of *kṣatriya*, the *kṣatriya* to that of a *vaiśya* and the *vaiśya* to that of a *śūdra*; where does the *śūdra* turn to in a crisis?

If a śūdra was unable to maintain himself and his family by serving*dvijas*, he was allowed to maintain himself by having recourse to crafts like carpentry or drawing or painting pictures etc. Nārada (ṛṇadāna 58) allowed him to perform the work of kṣatriyas and vaiśyas in times of distress. Yāj. (I.120) also says that, if unable to maintain himself by the service of *dvijas*, the śūdra may carry on the profession of a vaiśya or may take to the various crafts. The Mahābhārata allowed a śūdra who could not maintain himself by the service of higher varṇas to resort to the avocation of a vaiśya, to rearing cattle and to crafts.[38]

What is worth noting here is that *śūdra* is allowed to adopt the professions of a higher*varṇa*: that of a*vaiśya*, and even of a*kṣatriya*. But in normal times it is the *duty* of the *śūdra* to serve them; then how are we now going to describe this*āpad-dharma* of a*śūdra*? It seems to me that 'right' is the appropriate word here. Thus one may say that in times of crisis a *śūdra* has the right to adopt the profession of a *vaiśya*.

Can *Dharma* Make the Semantic Gear Shift from 'Duty' Discourse to 'Rights' Discourse?

It just did—in the illustration cited above, in the light of the fact that when one discusses *dharma* in the context of times of distress (ā*pad-dharma*) the word *dharma* does take on the meaning of a right.

The above discussion borders on the esoteric, but is significant for it converts what is usually perceived as a problem into a puzzle. What has often been perceived as a problem is the fact that the Hindus did not have a word for rights, no conception of rights and so on. And this problem was exemplified by the word *dharma* which means duty, a word central to their discourse. It now becomes clear that at least in two situations it doubled for rights: (1) when the person in a hierarchically lower position in terms of status or power appealed to *dharma*, the word took on the connotation of a right; (2) in times of crisis, one acquired the right—as *āpad-dharma*—to perform certain actions one was not entitled to in normal times. *Given the fact that from* AD *1200 Hinduism faced such a crisis brought on by foreign rule*, the puzzle now is as to why the word *dharma* did not more palpably acquire the sense of *right*? One possible explanation of why this did not happen could well be that the whole socio-political structure in which the word now functioned prevented this from happening because one segment of the architectonics of the fourfold class system in which it functioned had gone 'foreign'. The *kśatriya* had been eliminated and replaced by foreign rule, which did not subscribe to the system, unlike earlier foreign rulers such as the Śakas who presumably did so once they became part of the system. The new rulers were just not part of the system or did not share the same frame of reference. Irfan Habib describes the situation in its broadest and most fundamental form as follows:

> There were the religious traditions coming from ancient India, which by Mughal times began to be described under the term 'Hindu'. The author of *Dabistān-i-Mazāhib* is hard put to describe what the beliefs of a Hindu are and ultimately he takes shelter in a very convenient position but the only possible position—Hindus are those who have been arguing with each other within the same framework of argument over the centuries. If they recognise each other as persons whom we can either support or oppose in a religious argument, then both parties are Hindus. The Jains, although they rejected Brahmanism, were still Hindus because they were arguing and polemicising with Brahmins. Such arguments were not taking place between Hindus and Muslims. The Muslims did not share any basic terminology with the others. Muslims did their own framework, an ideological framework, the semitic framework.[39]

But now with an Indian rather than a foreign government in place, the original semantic thrust towards 'rights' contained in *dharma* can be restored, and even magnified. This is not to say that one must use that very word to denote it—if the word *adhikāra* has become the current locution for rights in Indian languages there is no need to abandon it. One could use the expression *dharmādhikāra* if one wanted to combine the modernity of tradition with the tradition of modernity in a single expression.

But what contribution does human rights discourse make here to Hindu discourse? Just this that by detaching the concept of a right from that of duty in its own evolution, it alerts us to the danger that duty discourse can subvert rights assertion and thus makes two contributions: (1) it alerts us to this danger in modern Hindu discourse and (2) it enables the rights component of the duty-rights coupling in the term*dharma* to be clearly grasped. The second point is clear. But how great the potential danger of duty discourse subverting rights discourse is, can be gauged from the fact that the British argued against Hindu participation in the drive to do away with British rule on the ground that it was immoral for them as Hindus to do so, for it was their *dharma* to be loyal to the ruler. One can foresee a would-be dictator in India invoking the same argument.

III

What can Hinduism Contribute to Human Rights Discourse?

The contribution Hindu discourse can make to human rights discourse has already been indicated in an earlier section. It has to do with the concept of 'religion' with which human rights discourse operates. Although it is nowhere stated as such, human rights discourse seems to operate with the idea that belonging to a religion involves exclusive adherence to a single religious tradition.

Such a concept of religion is historically and geographically restricted. It is historically restricted in the sense that it is essentially Abrahamic. However, people in Abrahamic times, and before Abraham, also followed certain religions and practices which may or may not have involved mutual exclusion. It is more likely that they involved separation rather than exclusion. That is to say, people carried out their practices separately, without the sense that others were being deliberately included or excluded.

It could be maintained that the Jews enacted on a social scale what Abraham had accomplished at the personal level, when they occupied Canaan. Abraham had wiped out with past faith and adopted a new one for himself and his family. The Hebrews wiped out the earlier occupants of Canaan and adopted the new land as their own.

The other Abrahamic religions repeated the same pattern over larger territories. Elimination of earlier peoples was partially substituted by conversion but a break with the past was necessary. With the passage of time Judaism developed a different attitude in the matter but its ethnic restraint on its universalism was removed by Christianity, which ultimately went on to spread over Europe and beyond. Islam followed the same pattern. Such exclusiveness was internal as well as external: Judaism, Christianity, and Islam also differentiated themselves from each other, just as they differentiated themselves from others.

In the course of its emergence the modern West distanced itself from Christianity in some ways, but not from its ideal of religion as something involving exclusive adherence. The secular discourse of religion accepted it axiomatically. Ironically, the concept is even more potent in its secular version. For the focus of Christianity was God, and religion, while closely associated with God, could never replace God. But in a godless society 'religion' becomes God. The Universal Declaration of Human Rights speaks not of God but of religion.

The Abrahamic notion of religion as implying exclusive adherence is historically limited, in the sense that there was a 'religion' living and being practised in some sense, before the Abrahamic religions 'terminated' it. Some form of religious life must have prevailed in the Roman Empire before it became Christian, as also in Arabia before it became Muslim, or in Canaan before it was taken over by the Hebrews. The point simply is that an 'exclusive concept of religion' does not give us a full purchase on the religious life of humanity.

But even more to the point—such a concept is not representative of the religious life of humanity as it is lived around the globe. So to operate with such a concept in a document, which purports to be universal, is likely to lead to grave problems. To avoid these, the protocols developed under the human rights tradition must clearly recognize (1) the right to multiple religious participation and (2) the right to retain one's religion. Such would be a Hindu contribution to human rights discourse.

This is how Hinduism can make a contribution towards one article of the Universal Declaration of Human Rights, namely Article 18. This paves the way to the question: can Hinduism also make a contribution of an even more general order to human rights discourse?

What follows now is an attempt to answer this question. One may begin with the concept of 'Universal Human Rights' itself. In the expression: 'Universal Human Rights', each of the three terms can be problematized; and furthermore can be problematized individually as well as collectively.

First, the word universal. No moral or ethical system, or even political or economic system *consciously* claims to be unjust, at least in the sense of being founded on injustice. So justice would appear to qualify as some kind of a universal, or at least the appeal to it. However, as soon as one descends from the heights of pure principle and attempts to flesh it out in terms of actual contents, differences surface. Take the death penalty, for instance: is it just or unjust?

Now the second word: human. As soon as one raises the question: what makes human beings human, differences surface again. The answers cover a whole range of opinion varying from the theological to the biological.

The third word 'rights' poses its own set of problems. For instance, one might raise the question: is the concept legal or moral in nature? If the concept is considered legal, that is to say, if rights are positivistic in nature, what the law gives the law can take away. If the concept is considered to be moral in nature, the problem posed by different moralities, not necessarily convergent in nature, arises.

This is how each of the words can be said to be problematical when taken individually. Let us now examine the expression collectively by asking the question: what is *universal* in *human* beings that entitles them to *rights*?

Body and mind could be said to be in the universal possession of all human beings, but when spelled out in such an unqualified way they are too broad to serve as useful categories to anchor human rights in. Indeed, the concept of rights itself seems to suffer from a similar vagueness. For instance, when we say that something is a human right, we often mean that it ought to be a legal right.

Very briefly then, appeal to universal human rights does not seem to resolve anything; one needs to re-solve everything—what is meant by *universal*, by *human*, and by *rights*.

As an illustration of how the Hindu tradition might help us think more clearly and even helpfully in such matters, let me choose one category and demonstrate the result, which follows from examining it in the light of the Hindu tradition. Let me focus on the category of *universal* for this purpose.

One can think of three specific contexts in which the word universal occurs within the Hindu tradition, which it might be useful to take into account. The first of these contexts is provided by the *Yogasūtra* of Patañjali.[40] The system of yoga as espoused by Patañjali consists of eight parts or limbs. The first two are technically called *yama* and *niyama*, and constitute the moral preparation for following the path of yoga, as it were. *Yama* consists of five rules: *ahiṁsā* (non-injury), *satya* (truth), *asteya* (non-stealing), *brahmacarya* (celibacy), and *aparigraha* (non-possession), whereas *niyama* consists of the following five: *śauca* (purity), *santoṣa* (contentment), *tapas* (austerity), *svādhyāya* (study), and *īśvara-praṇidhāna* (devotion to God). It has been said that 'the five *yamas* and the five *niyamas* together constitute all that is necessary for a perfect moral and religious life. They are, so to say, the ten commandments of yoga'.[41]

The time has come to redeem oneself in terms of this somewhat dull recitation by pointing out that according to the text of Patañjali (II. 31) 'These universal moral principles, unrestricted by conditions of birth, place, time or circumstance, are the great vow of yoga.'[42] That is to say, they are unbounded by time and space and are thus universal.

Another context is provided by the discussion of the concept of the 'universal' in the schools of Hindu thought (technically called *darśanas*).[43] Compendia on Hindu philosophical systems have linked the discussion of the universal in Hindu thought to three orientations: realistic, conceptualistic, and nominal, as noted in an earlier chapter.

According to the Nyāya-Vaiśeṣika school the universal is eternal. It exists apart from the individuals, but inheres in them. This constitutes the realistic understanding of the universal. According to the school of Advaita Vedānta the universal exists but 'does not stand for an independent entity over and above the individuals'.[44] This constitutes the conceptualistic understanding of the universal. According to the Buddhist school the universal is a linguistic category. 'Thus certain animals are called cow, not because they possess any common essence but because they are different from all animals that are not cows.'[45] This constitutes the nominal understanding of the universal.

Yet another context in which the term occurs in Hinduism is that of Hindu Law, in the body of literature technically known as *dharmaśāstra*. Parts of this literature deal with the duties and obligations incumbent upon people. In this context it distinguishes between two sets of duties and obligations—specific and general. Specific duties and obligations are those specific to one's station in life (*varṇa*) and one's stage in life (*āśrama*). General duties are common to all in all stations and stages and thus called *sāmānya dharma* as distinguished from *varṇāśrama dharma*.[46] Thus it is the duty of the farmer to till the soil and of the student to study but the duty to control one's temper applies to both.

I would like to now derive three aphoristic statements based on the discussion of the universal in Hinduism, so as to lift up these insights above their context-bound nature to see what light they might shed on human rights discourse. These aphoristic insights may be formulated as follows:

(1) We have intimations of an absolute, but that does not mean that we possess an absolute intimation.
(2) That fact that we all speak a language does not mean either that we speak 'language' or that we speak no language at all.
(3) All human beings possess a sense of right and wrong but not necessarily the same sense of right and wrong.

From these the following implications in the context of the universality of human rights may be derived: (1) current human rights discourse tends to conflate the universal with the absolute. In the case of the absolute one proceeds from top downwards—it is spelled out. In the case of the universal one may proceed from bottom upwards—it is built up. (2) Current human rights discourse waves the flag of universalism, failing to distinguish between universality and universalizability. Whether universal rights are universal or not is one debate, but whether they are universalizable is another and more relevant debate. This point is not unconnected with the previous one. (3) Ironically, the specificity of a case may contribute to its universality. It is remarkable how, among a group of people drawn from different religious and cultural backgrounds engaged in a debate on universality in the abstract, agreement is often forthcoming on a specific instance as to whether it constitutes a violation of human rights.[47] Conclusion: all the three points made above converge on the need to evolve a universal out of the various individuals or particulars. Such a negotiated universal may lack the transcendental majesty of an apodictically proclaimed universal but its immanent inclusiveness might ensure its practical acceptance.

NOTES

1. Carol S. Robb, op. cit., p. 289.
2. Ibid.
3. Ibid., p. 290.
4. Ibid.
5. Ibid., p. 291.
6. Ibid.
7. Ibid., pp. 290–1.
8. Ibid., pp. 289–91.
9. Ibid., p. 291.
10. Ibid.

11. See Joseph Prabhu, 'Dharma as an Alternative to Human Rights', in *Studies in Orientology: Essays in Memory of Prof. A. Basham* (eds), S.K. Maity, Upendra Thakur, and A.K. Narian, Agra, India: Y.K. Publishers, 1998, pp. 174–9.
12. Ibid., p. 176.
13. Ibid.
14. Ibid., p. 178.
15. Ibid. The two senses are explained earlier by Prabhu as follows (ibid., p. 175): 'I start with the notion of human rights. The term "right" has two senses, one connoting righteousness or conformity to some standard as when we say, for example, that it is right that X should visit her grandmother who is ill; the second connoting entitlement, as when I say that I have a right to privacy. Now, while there may be cases where the two senses converge, such that, for example, it is both right and a matter of right to keep a contractual promise, the two concepts are by no means synonymous. Thus, if I am being mugged and you happen to be a bystander, it is right that you help me, but I have no right to your help. The same asymmetry prevails in the matter of duties and rights. In spite of the fact that rights have an essentially relational character, such that A has a right to something with respect to other parties, the obligation created by the relationship may well conflict with what these other parties regard as their duty in the situation. The classic example here is civil disobedience.'
16. Alison Dundes Renteln, *International Human Rights*, Newbury Park, California: Sage, 1990, p. 12.
17. S.S. Rama Rao Pappu, 'The Idea of Human Rights', *International Review of History and Political Science*, Vol. VI, No. 4, November 1969, p. 7.
18. Louis Renou (ed.), *Hinduism*, New York: George Braziller, 1962, p. 55, emphasis added.
19. Ibid., pp. 55–6.
20. S.S. Rama Rao Pappu, 'Human Rights and Human Obligations: An East-West Perspective', *Philosophy and Social Action*, Vol. 8, No. 4, 1982, pp. 19–20.
21. Ibid., pp. 22–3.
22. Ibid., p. 20.
23. Ibid., pp. 20–1.
24. Ibid., p. 22.
25. Ibid.
26. Ibid., p. 15. Emphasis added.
27. Ibid.
28. Ibid. Emphasis added.
29. M. Hiriyanna, *Essentials of Indian Philosophy*, p. 38.
30. S.S. Rama Rao Pappu, 'Human Rights and Human Obligations: An East-West Perspective', p. 23.
31. Ibid., pp. 23–4.
32. Peter Scharfe, op. cit., p. 68. He goes on to say (ibid., p. 69): 'In the millennium before the Muslim conquest the role of the people diminished further. "Whatever a king does is right, that is a settled rule. . . . As a husband though feeble

must be constantly worshipped by his wives, in the same way a ruler though worthless must be (constantly) worshipped by his subjects", declares the Nārada-smṛti XVIII 21f. For the Kashmiri historian Kalhaṇa, the people exercise influence mainly through their moral power. The wicked king "at last found his death through the superior effect of his subjects' merit", and the fact that the bad king Harṣa "was never shot at with an arrow and killed—that must be due to . . . the sinfulness of his subjects". Occasionally this historian sees divine interference: "That a king of such wickedness was not killed by a rising of his subjects, can only be due to his having been protected by the gods who caused him to act in this manner".'

How much the king has become a *force majeure* at the end of this period can be seen in a remark found in two state manuals, where a ritual against the six plagues (*īti*) is taught: *ītayaḥ* ('plagues') is well known, viz. deluge, drought, rats, locusts, parrots, and kings that are too near [to their subjects] (and thus able to satisfy their greed) are known as the six plagues.' Compared to the list of calamities in the much older Arthaśāstra, the king stands out as an addition. The depravity of some kings made for useful slogans in the campaign of the king's relatives or of state officers who tried to usurp power, but there was no legal way to remove a bad king".

33. Ibid., p. 69. He goes on to say (ibid., p. 69–70): 'While incompetent rulers could lose throne and life, well organized states often managed to weather a weak reign, and bad kings were made bearable by capable advisors. The sadistic 'Mad Avanti' (Unmattāvanti) held on to his rule over Kashmir for two years (AD 937–939), until he died from an incurable disease, after murdering his own family and untold other people, shamelessly humoured and entertained by his worthless courtiers: one of them "danced in the royal assembly with his loin-cloth taken off"; Virūpākṣa II (AD 1465–1485) of Vijayanagar was, according to the Portuguese traveller Nuniz 'given over to vice, caring for nothing but women, and to fuddle himself with drink'. The state suffered severe losses and recovered only through the bravery and loyalty of provincial governors. Still, only after twenty years did this king's rule come to an end when he was murdered by his eldest son. In the 16th century, Rāo Surthān of Būndi in Rājasthān was deposed and banished by his nobles for his sadistic excesses in the worship of Kālī.'
34. P.V. Kane, op. cit., Vol. III, second edition, pp. 26–7.
35. S. Radhakrishnan (ed.), *The Principal Upaniṣads*, p. 170.
36. Robert Ernest Hume, tr., *The Thirteen Principal Upaniṣads*, London: Oxford University Press, 1968 [1877], p. 84.
37. Patrick Olivelle, *The Early Upaniṣads*, New York and Oxford: Oxford University Press, 1998, p. 51.
38. P.V. Kane, op. cit., Vol. II, Part I, pp. 120–1.
39. Cited, Shashi Joshi and Bhagwan Josh, *Struggle for Hegemony in India: 1920–1947*, New Delhi: Sage Publications, 1994, p. 185.
40. Barbara Stoler Miller, *Yoga: Discipline of Freedom: The Yoga Sūtra Attributed to Patañjali*, Berkeley: University of California Press, 1995.

41. T.M.P. Mahadevan, *Outlines of Hinduism*, Bombay: Chetana Limited, 1971, p. 111.
42. Barbara Stoler Miller, op. cit., p. 53.
43. See Satischandra Chatterjee and Dhirendramohan Datta, *An Introduction to Indian Philosophy*, Calcutta: University of Calcutta, 1950.
44. Ibid., p. 240.
45. Ibid.
46. See P. V. Kane, op. cit., Vol. V, Part II, second edition, pp. 1632–3.
47. Mary Ann Glendon, op. cit., p. 222.

APPENDIX I

Universal Declaration of Human Rights

Adopted and Proclaimed by United Nations General Assembly Resolution 217 (III) On 10 December 1948

PREAMBLE

Whereas recognition of the inherent dignity and of the equal and inalienable rights of all members of the human family is the foundation of freedom, justice and peace in the world,

Whereas disregard and contempt for human rights have resulted in barbarous acts which have outraged the conscience of mankind, and the advent of a world in which human beings shall enjoy freedom of speech and belief and freedom from fear and want has been proclaimed as the highest aspiration of the common people,

Whereas it is essential, if man is not to be compelled to have recourse, as a last resort, to rebellion against tyranny and oppression, that human rights should be protected by the rule of law,

Whereas it is essential to promote the development of friendly relations between nations,

Whereas the peoples of the United Nations have in the Charter reaffirmed their faith in fundamental human rights, in the dignity and worth of the human person and in the equal rights of men and women and have determined to promote social progress and better standards of life in larger freedom,

Whereas Member States have pledged themselves to achieve, in co-operation with the United Nations, the promotion of universal respect for and observance of human rights and fundamental freedoms,

Whereas a common understanding of these rights and freedoms is of the greatest importance for the full realisation of this pledge,

Now, therefore,
The General Assembly

Proclaims this Universal Declaration of Human Rights as a common standard of achievement for all peoples and all nations, to the end that every individual and every organ of society, keeping this Declaration constantly in mind, shall strive by teaching and education to promote respect for these rights and freedoms and by progressive measures, national and international, to secure their universal and effective recognition and observance, both among the peoples of Member States themselves and among the peoples of territories under their jurisdiction.

Article 1

All human beings are born free and equal in dignity and rights. They are endowed with reason and conscience and should act towards one another in a spirit of brotherhood.

Article 2

Everyone is entitled to all the rights and freedoms set forth in this Declaration, without distinction of any kind, such as race, colour, sex, language, religion, political or other opinion, national or social origin, property, birth or other status.

Furthermore, no distinction shall be made on the basis of the political, jurisdictional or international status of the country or territory to which a person belongs, whether it be independent, trust, non-self-governing or under any other limitation of sovereignty.

Article 3

Everyone has the right to life, liberty and security of person.

Article 4

No one shall be held in slavery or servitude; slavery and the slave trade shall be prohibited in all their forms.

Article 5

No one shall be subjected to torture or to cruel, inhuman or degrading treatment or punishment.

Article 6

Everyone has the right to recognition everywhere as a person before the law.

Article 7

All are equal before the law and are entitled without any discrimination to equal protection of the law. All are entitled to equal protection against any discrimination in violation of this Declaration and against any incitement to such discrimination.

Article 8

Everyone has the right to an effective remedy by the competent national tribunals for acts violating the fundamental rights granted him by the constitution or by law.

Article 9

No one shall be subjected to arbitrary arrest, detention or exile.

Article 10

Everyone is entitled in full equality to a fair and public hearing by an independent and impartial tribunal, in the determination of his rights and obligations and of any criminal charge against him.

Article 11

(1) Everyone charged with a penal offence has the right to be presumed innocent until proved guilty according to law in a public trial at which he has had all the guarantees necessary for his defence.
(2) No one shall be held guilty of any penal offence on account of any act or omission which did not constitute a penal offence, under national or international law, at the time when it was committed. Nor shall a heavier penalty be imposed than the one that was applicable at the time the penal offence was committed.

Article 12

No one shall be subjected to arbitrary interference with his privacy, family, home or correspondence, nor to attacks upon his honour and reputation. Everyone has the right to the protection of the law against such interference or attacks.

Article 13

(1) Everyone has the right to freedom of movement and residence within the borders of each State.
(2) Everyone has the right to leave any country, including his own, and to return to his country.

Article 14

(1) Everyone has the right to seek and to enjoy in other countries asylum from persecution.
(2) This right may not be invoked in the case of prosecutions genuinely arising from non-political crimes or from acts contrary to the purposes and principles of the United Nations.

Article 15

(1) Everyone has the right to a nationality.
(2) No one shall be arbitrarily deprived of his nationality nor denied the right to change his nationality.

Article 16

(1) Men and women of full age, without any limitation due to race, nationality or religion, have the right to marry and to found a family. They are entitled to equal rights as to marriage, during marriage and at its dissolution.
(2) Marriage shall be entered into only with the free and full consent of the intending spouses.
(3) The family is the natural and fundamental group unit of society and is entitled to protection by society and the State.

Article 17

(1) Everyone has the right to own property alone as well as in association with others.
(2) No one shall be arbitrarily deprived of his property.

Article 18

Everyone has the right to freedom of thought, conscience and religion; this right includes freedom to change his religion or belief, and freedom, either alone or in community with others and in public or private, to manifest his religion or belief in teaching, practice, worship and observance.

Article 19

Everyone has the right to freedom of opinion and expression; this right includes freedom to hold opinions without interference and to seek, receive and impart information and ideas through any media and regardless of frontiers.

Article 20

(1) Everyone has the right to freedom of peaceful assembly and association.
(2) No one may be compelled to belong to an association.

Article 21

(1) Everyone has the right to take part in the government of his country, directly or through freely chosen representatives.
(2) Everyone has the right to equal access to public service in his country.
(3) The will of the people shall be the basis of the authority of government; this will shall be expressed in periodic and genuine elections which shall be by universal and equal suffrage and shall be held by secret vote or by equivalent free voting procedures.

Article 22

Everyone, as a member of society, has the right to social security and is entitled to realization, through national effort and international co-operation and in accordance with the organization and resources of each State, of the economic, social and cultural rights indispensable for his dignity and the free development of his personality.

Article 23

(1) Everyone has the right to work, to free choice of employment, to just and favorable conditions of work and to protection against unemployment.
(2) Everyone, without discrimination, has the right to equal pay for equal work.
(3) Everyone who works has the right to just and favourable remuneration ensuring for himself and his family an existence worthy of human dignity, and supplemented, if necessary, by other means of social protection.

(4) Everyone has the right to form and to join trade unions for the protection of his interest.

Article 24

Everyone has the right to rest and leisure, including reasonable limitation of working hours and periodic holidays with pay.

Article 25

(1) Everyone has the right to a standard of living adequate for the health and well-being of himself and his family, including food, clothing, housing and medical care and necessary social services, and the right to security in the event of unemployment, sickness, disability, widowhood, old age or other lack of livelihood in circumstances beyond his control.
(2) Motherhood and childhood are entitled to special care and assistance. All children, whether born in or out of wedlock, shall enjoy the same social protection.

Article 26

(1) Everyone has the right to education. Education shall be free, at least in the elementary and fundamental stages. Elementary education shall be compulsory. Technical and professional education shall be made generally available and higher education shall be equally accessible to all on the basis of merit.
(2) Education shall be directed to the full development of the human personality and to the strengthening of respect for human rights and fundamental freedoms. It shall promote understanding, tolerance and friendship among all nations, racial or religious groups, and shall further the activities of the United Nations for the maintenance of peace.
(3) Parents have a prior right to choose the kind of education that shall be given to their children.

Article 27

(1) Everyone has the right freely to participate in the cultural life of the community, to enjoy the arts and to share in scientific advancement and its benefits.
(2) Everyone has the right to the protection of the moral and material interests resulting from any scientific, literary or artistic production of which he is the author.

Article 28

Everyone is entitled to a social and international order in which the rights and freedoms set forth in this Declaration can be fully realized.

Article 29

(1) Everyone has duties to the community in which alone the free and full development of his personality is possible.
(2) In the exercise of his rights and freedoms, everyone shall be subject only to such limitations as are determined by law solely for the purpose of securing due recognition and respect for the rights and freedoms of others and of meeting the just requirements of morality, public order and the general welfare in a democratic society.
(3) The rights and freedoms may in no case be exercised contrary to the purposes and principles of the United Nations.

Article 30

Nothing in this Declaration may be interpreted as implying for any State, group or person any right to engage in any activity or to perform any act aimed at the destruction of any of the rights and freedoms set forth herein.

Source: Tad Stahnke and J. Paul Martin (eds), *Religion and Human Right: Basic Documents*, New York: Centre for the Study of Human Rights, Columbia University, 1998, pp. 57–60.

APPENDIX II

A Universal Declaration of Human Rights by the Hindus[1]

Whereas the secular and the sacred are the two main avenues whereby human beings are led to affirm that there is more to life than life itself;

Whereas the Universal Declaration of Human Rights, as adopted by the General Assembly of the United Nations on 10 December 1948 draws mainly upon only one of them as a resource;

Whereas at the time of the adoption of the Universal Declaration of Human Rights religion had retreated from the public square but has since reappeared in a major way;

Whereas religions are meant to serve humanity and not humanity to serve religion;

Whereas one must not idealize the actual but strive to realize the ideal;

Whereas the various communities constituting the peoples of the world must exchange not only ideas but also ideals;

Whereas not to compensate victims of imperialism, racism, casteism, and sexism is itself imperialist, racist, casteist, and sexist;

Whereas any further exclusion of world's religions as positive resources for human rights is obnoxious to the evidence of daily life;

Whereas rights are independent of duties in their protection but integrally related to them in conception and execution;

Whereas in the case of human beings in general, rights and duties are correlative; subhuman creatures may have rights without corresponding duties and in exceptional cases, persons, like mothers in relation to infants, duties without corresponding rights;

Whereas rights can serve both as ends in themselves (*upeya*) and as means (*upāya*) to ends and to each other;

Whereas a Hindu is like any other human being, only more so;

Whereas to be a Hindu is to possess the natural right to pursue the good (*dharma*); goods (*artha*); the good life (*kāma*); and the highest good (*mokṣa*), like all other human beings, as children of the same earth and descended from the same Manu;

Whereas Hindus subscribe to universal norms such as non-violence (*ahiṁsā*); truth (*satya*); non-appropriation (*asteya*); purity (*śauca*), and self-restraint (*indriyanigrahaḥ*) which find their expressions in rights and duties in relation to oneself, to others, and the state; and that, in relation to the state, non-violence denotes the right of protection against arbitrary conduct; truth denotes presumption of innocence until proven guilty; non-appropriation denotes right to property; purity denotes freedom from pollution, and self-restraint denotes the right that the organs of the state do not compromise the privacy and dignity of the individual.

Now, therefore, on this, Sunday Twenty-Seventh Day of June, One Thousand Nine Hundred Ninety-Nine the Hindu community, as assembled at the Hindu Mission of Canada (Quebec), at 955 Bellechasse, Montreal, adopts this Declaration, as heaven and earth are our father and mother and all people brothers and sisters.

Article 1

All human beings have the right to be treated as human beings and have the duty to treat everyone as a human being.

Article 2

Everyone has the right to freedom from violence, in any of its forms, individual or collective; whether based on race, religion, gender, caste, or class, or nation, or arising from any other cause.

Article 3

(1) Everyone has the right to food.
(2) Everyone has the right to life, longevity, and liveability and the right to food, clothing and shelter required to sustain them.
(3) Everyone has the duty to support and sustain the life, longevity, and liveability of all.

Article 4

(1) No one shall be subjected to slavery or servitude, forced labour, bonded labour, or child labour. Slavery and the slave trade shall be prohibited in all its forms.

(2) No one shall subject anyone to slavery or servitude in any of its forms.

Article 5

(1) No one shall be subjected to torture or to cruel, inhuman, or degrading treatment or punishment, inflicted either physically or mentally, whether on secular or religious grounds, inside the home or outside it.
(2) No one shall subject anybody to such treatment.

Article 6

(1) Everyone has a right to recognition everywhere as a person before law; and by everyone everywhere as a human being deserving humane treatment, even when law and order has broken down.
(2) Everyone has the duty to treat everyone else as a human being both in the eyes of law and one's own.

Article 7

All are equal before law and entitled to equal protection before law without any discrimination on grounds of race, religion, caste, class, nationality, sex, and sexual orientation. It is the right of everyone to be so treated and the duty of everyone to so treat others.

Article 8

(1) Everybody has the right to demand restitution for historical, social, economic, cultural, and other wrongs in the present and compensation for such wrongs committed in the past, provided that the victims shall always have the right to forgive the victimizers.
(2) Everybody has the duty to prevent the perpetuation of historical, social, economic, cultural, and other wrongs.

Article 9

(1) No one shall be subjected to arbitrary arrest, detention or exile by the state or by anyone else. The attempt to proselytize against the will of the person shall amount to arbitrary detention, so also the detention, against their will, of teenage children by the parents, and among spouses.
(2) It is the duty of everyone to secure everyone's liberty.

Article 10

Everybody has the right to public trial when facing criminal charges and it is the duty of the state to ensure it. Everyone who cannot afford a lawyer must be provided one by the state.

Article 11

Everyone charged with a penal offence has the right to be considered innocent by everyone until proven guilty.

Article 12

(1) Everyone has the right to privacy. This right includes the right not to be subjected to arbitrary interference with one's privacy; or of one's family, home or correspondence.
(2) Everyone has the right to one's good name.
(3) It is the duty of everyone to protect the privacy and reputation of everyone else.
(4) Everyone has the right not to have one's religion misrepresented in the media or the academia.
(5) It is the duty of the follower of every religion to ensure that no religion is misrepresented in the media or the academia.

Article 13

(1) Everyone has the right to freedom of movement and residence anywhere in the world.
(2) Everyone has the duty to abide by the laws and regulations applicable in that part of the world.

Article 14

Everyone has the right to seek and secure asylum in any country from any form of persecution, religious or otherwise, and the right not to be deported. It is the duty of every country to provide such asylum.

Article 15

(1) Everyone has the right to a nationality;
(2) No one shall be arbitrarily deprived of one's nationality nor denied the right to change one's nationality.
(3) Everyone has the duty to promote the emergence of a federal but single global government—The Parliament of Humanity.

Article 16

(1) Everyone has the right to marriage.

(2) Parties to a marriage have the right to retain and practise their own religion or ideology within a marriage.
(3) Everyone has the right to raise a family.
(4) Everyone has the right to renounce the world and join a monastery, provided that one shall do so after making adequate arrangement for one's dependants.
(5) Marriage and monasticism are two of the most successful institutional innovations of humanity and are entitled to protection by the society and the state.
(6) Motherhood and childhood are entitled to special care and assistance. It is the duty of everyone to extend special consideration to mothers and children.
(7) Everyone shall promote the outlook that the entire world constitutes a single family.

Article 17

(1) Everyone has the right to own property, alone as well as in association with others. An association also has a similar right to own property.
(2) Everyone has a right not to be deprived of property arbitrarily. It is the duty of everyone not to deprive others of their property arbitrarily, or appropriate it in an unauthorized manner. Property shall be understood to mean material as well as intellectual, aesthetic and spiritual property.

Article 18

(1) There shall be no compulsion in religion. It is a matter of choice.
(2) Everyone has the right to retain one's religion and to change one's religion.
(3) All human beings are entitled to participate in all the religions of the world as much as their own, for all are legatees of the religious heritage of humanity.
(4) Everyone has the duty to promote peace and tolerance among religions and ideologies.

Article19

(1) Everyone has the right to freedom of opinion and expression, where the term expression includes the language one speaks; the food one eats; the clothes one wears; the religion one practises and professes, provided that one conforms generally to the accustomed rules of decorum recognized in the neighbourhood.

(2) It is the duty of everyone to ensure that everyone enjoys such freedom.

Article 20

(1) Everyone has the right to freedom of assembly and association, and the duty to do so peacefully.
(2) No one may be compelled to belong to an association, or to leave one without due process.

Article 21

(1) Everybody over the age of eighteen has the right to vote, to elect or be elected and thus to take part in the government or governance of the country, directly or indirectly.
(2) Everyone has the right of equal access to public service in and the duty to provide such access.
(3) It is the duty of everyone to participate in the political process.

Article 22

Everyone, as a member of society, has a right to social security and a duty to contribute to it.

Article 23

(1) Everyone has the right to work and seek gainful employment.
(2) It is the duty of the state and society to ensure that everyone is gainfully employed.
(3) Everyone has the right to equal pay for equal work and a duty to offer equal pay for equal work.
(4) Everyone has the right for just remuneration for one's work and the duty to offer just recompense for work done.
(5) Everyone has the right to form and to join trade unions for the protection of one's interests.

Article 24

(1) Everyone has the right to work and to rest, including the right to support while seeking work and the right to periodic holidays with pay.
(2) The right to rest extends to the earth itself.

Article 25

(1) Everyone has the right to health and to universal medical insurance. It is the duty of the state or society to provide it.

(2) Every child has the right to an unencumbered childhood and it is the duty of the parents, society and state to provide it.

Article 26

Everyone has the right to free education and the right to equality of opportunity for any form of education involving restricted enrolment.

Article 27

(1) Everyone has the right to freely participate in the cultural life of the community and the right to freely contribute to it.
(2) Everyone has the right to share in scientific advances and their benefits, the duty to disseminate them, and wherever possible, contribute to such advance.
(3) Everyone has the right to the protection of their cultural heritage. It is the duty of everyone to protect and enrich everyone's heritage, including one's own.

Article 28

Everyone has the right to socio-economic and political order at a global, national, regional, and local level which enables the realization of social, political, economic, racial and gender justice and the duty to give precedence to universal, national, regional and local interests in that order.

Article 29

(1) One is duty-bound, when asserting one's rights, to take the rights of other human beings; of past, present, and future generations; the rights of humanity; and the rights of nature and the earth into account.
(2) One is duty-bound, when asserting one's rights, to prefer non-violence over violence.

Article 30

As the entire earth constitutes one extended family, all human beings possess unrestricted right of freedom of movement across all countries, nations and states all over the world.

Article 31

All human beings possess the right to due compensation should aforesaid rights be violated, irrespective of whether the violation occurs in the past, present, or future.

Article 32

(1) Everyone has the right over his or her body and mind to use it in any manner one wishes.
(2) Everyone has the duty to use his or her body and mind to further the well-being of all.
(3) One's body and mind possess the right not to be abused by oneself, as the right of the part against the whole.
(4) It is one's duty to cultivate one's body and mind.

Article 33

(1) Everyone has the right to require the formation of a supervisory committee within one's community, defined religiously or otherwise, to monitor the implementation of the articles of this Declaration; and to serve on it and present one's case before such a committee.
(2) It is everyone's duty to ensure that such a committee satisfactorily supervises the implementation of these articles.

Note

1. Composed by Professor G.C. Pande, at the International Symposium on Indian Studies, held at Kovalam in Kerala, 28 November–2 December 1994.

APPENDIX III

A Universal Declaration of Human Rights by the Hindus: A Sanskrit Text

हिन्दूधर्मप्रभवा मानवाधिकाराः अथवा अधिकारपञ्चविंशतिका

१) उपक्रमः

दशार्धवर्षसाहस्री चतुरूनशतोत्तरा ।
कलेर्यदा व्यतीताथ काले वहति दारुणे ।।१।।

देशजात्यादिसङ्घानां सम्मर्दे वृद्धिमागते ।
त्राणार्थं मानवा धर्मं जिज्ञासन्ते स्म भूयसा ।।२।।

श्रियानन्तपुरे रम्ये विद्वांसो भिन्नजातयः ।
विचारार्थं विशेषेण नानादिग्भ्यः समागताः ।।३।।

तत्रारविन्दगोविन्दौ हिन्दूधर्मगवेषकौ ।
विवेकेन विचारेण युगबोधानुरूपतः ।।४।।

"हिन्दूदृशा जनाः कुत्र धर्मतोऽधिकृता इति" ।
निर्णयं यमनुप्राप्तौ श्रुतिस्मृत्याद्यवेक्षणात् ।।५।।

निबध्यतेऽत्र तत्सारं संक्षेपेण शुभेच्छया ।
आलोकयन्तु सुधियो निर्मत्सरतयैव तत् ।।६।।

२) प्रवेशः

हिन्दूदृशा समाः सर्वे मानवा मानवत्वतः ।
मनोरपत्यभूता हि पृथिव्याः सूनवस्तथा ।।७।।

विवेको लक्षणं तेषां धर्मबुद्ध्यपराभिधः ।
ततः स्वभावसिद्धानां धर्माणामत्र संग्रहः ।।८।।

३) उपेयाधिकरणम्

धर्मार्थकाममोक्षा यत् पुरुषार्थतया मताः ।
साधने मानवास्तेषां स्वभावादधिकारिणः ।।९।।

४) उपायाधिकरणम् धर्माधिकाराः

वरणे स्वेष्टमार्गस्य स्वधर्मपालने तथा ।
अभिसन्धिं विहायैव स्वतंत्राः सर्वमानवाः ।।१०।।

धर्मस्य पालनात्पूर्वं यतो ज्ञानमपेक्ष्यते ।
सर्वेऽधिकारिणस्तस्माद् ज्ञानार्जने प्रशिक्षणात् ।।११।।

सर्वत्र सर्वदा चैव सर्वे स्युरधिकारिणः ।
धर्मक्षेत्रेषु सर्वेषां प्रवेशः स्यादवारितः ।।१२।।

समता सर्ववर्णानां स्त्रीणां च पुरुषैः सह ।
सहकारितया सिद्धा भेदस्यौपाधिकत्वतः ।।१३।।

अर्थाधिकाराः

स्वप्राणरक्षणे चैव स्वस्वत्वरक्षणे तथा ।
तदर्थं सम्यगाजीवे सर्वे स्युरधिकारिणः ।।१४।।

हितार्थं स्वस्य सर्वस्य सुखार्थमुदयाय च ।
स्वराज्यस्थापने सर्वे सौराज्ये चाधिकारिणः ।।१५।।

सौराज्यमुच्यतां तद्धि यत्र लभ्यं यथारुचि ।
आहारवसनावासचिकित्साशिक्षणादिकम् ।।१६।।

अधिराज्यमधिकाराः

अहिंसा परमो धर्म इत्युक्तेर्गम्यतेऽर्थतः ।
सर्वस्य स्वाङ्गरक्षायामसूनां चैव रक्षणे ।।१७।।

अधिकारस्तथायुष्ये जीवमात्राविहिंसने।
अन्यायबन्धनात् त्राणे तथा चाविधिपूर्वकात् ।।१८।।

लाभित्वे प्रातिनिध्यस्य व्यवहारेऽप्यशुल्कके ।
अदण्ड्यत्वे च ऋते न्यायात्परीक्ष्यैव यथाविधि ।।१९।।

समत्वे व्यवहारस्य दण्डस्य धर्मतस्तथा ।
युक्तत्वे निष्क्रये दाप्ये मिथ्याबन्धनदण्डयोः ।।२०।।

कामाधिकाराः

सर्वे धर्माविरोधेन नीतेश्चैवाविरोधतः ।
स्वच्छन्दाधिकाराः स्युः सर्वेषां सुखसेवने ।।२१।।

मोक्षाधिकाराः

स्वप्रकृत्यनुसारेण सर्वे निजविवेकतः ।
स्वेष्टमार्गेण मोक्षस्य साधने चाधिकारिणः ।।२२।।

४) उपसंहारः

विवेकाल्लक्ष्यते धर्मो नीतिर्धर्मानुसारिणी ।
राज्यं नीतिप्रतिष्ठं चेत्तदायत्ताधिकारिता ।।२३।।

क्षतिदाप्याधिकाराणां त्रिकालानवबाधिता ।
सर्वसाक्षी यतो न्यायः सर्वालोकी सनातनः ।।२४।।

धर्मे चार्थे च कामे च मोक्षेऽपि च यथाविधि ।
निःसीमानि हि राष्ट्राणि सर्वगम्या वसुन्धरा ।।२५।।

(Professor G.C. Pande)

APPENDIX IV

The Caste System and Race

The relation between the caste system and race, or casteism and racism if you will, cannot be without interest from the point of view of human rights discourse.

A salient fact with which one might commence the examination of their relationship consists of the realization that until around the middle of the nineteenth century, Hindu society looked upon itself as a living whole, existing in organic cohesion. In other words, to the extent that the Hindu reality could be described in terms of such a vocabulary, the Hindus constituted one race. There was no doubt an awareness of distinctions in very broad terms among such types of people as *ārya, draviḍa, kirāta*, and *niṣāda*, four words which broadly conform to the racial types subsequently identified as Aryan, Dravidian, Mongoloid, and Proto-Australoid.[1] But the awareness of such distinctions was at the same time more diffuse and more integrated. It was more diffuse in the sense that the distinctions were finer. Let us take the category *Draviḍa*, for instance. One spoke of the *Pañca-Draviḍa*s or the five classes of Brahmins in the south—a category, which was paired off with that of the *Pañca-Gauḍa*s or the five classes of Brahmins in the north. Professor D.C. Sircar points out that

> The Brahmanical society of South India is usually divided into five classes called the *Pañca-Draviḍa*. These classes are (1) Draviḍa (Tamil), (2) Karṇāṭa (Kannada), (3) Gurjara (Gujarati), (4) Mahārāṣtra and (5) Tailanga (Telugu). This classification is based on linguistic division of the South Indian Brāhmaṇas. Although the population of North India can hardly be divided into five linguistic groups with propriety, an attempt was made in imitation of the South Indian classification to classify the Brāhmaṇa society of Northern India into the same number of subdivisions. Strangely, however, the common name applied to the five classes of Northern Brāhmaṇas was Gauḍa as Draviḍa is the general name of southern Brāhmaṇas. The divisions of the Northern Brāhmaṇas are: (1) Sārasvata (associated with the valley of the Sarasvatī in the Punjab), (2) Kānyakubja (in Uttar

Pradesh), (3) Gauḍa (in Bengal), (4) Maithila (in North Bihar) and (5) Utkala (in Orissa). In these cases, therefore, the name Draviḍa indicates South India, while Gauḍa signifies North India. We know that the name Gauḍa, originally applied to a part of Bengal, was often used to indicate all the countries of Eastern India. Thus the East Indian style of Sanskrit composition as well as the medieval East Indian alphabet came to be called after Gauḍa. A further expansion of the connotation of the name to indicate the whole of North India is suggested by the classification of Brāhmaṇas referred to above.[2]

It was also more integrated in the sense that, howsoever divided the Hindu society may have been internally, it was conceptually integrated under the *varṇa* scheme, within which the *jātī*s had also been subsumed. Underlying this was the belief that the people of this land belonged to this land. There may have been some dim awareness of the fact that different people may have entered the country in the past but the perception that all were now part of one integrated whole superseded such information. Thus all Hindus were of one race, if subdivided into various castes. It is worthwhile noting here that the consequence of explaining *jāti* by intermarriage among the *varṇa*s made them all of one 'blood'.

This picture was radically changed by the growth of Western Indology, central to whose depiction of India was the fact of an Aryan invasion of India. These invaders then occupied the land and pushed its earlier inhabitants, the Dravidians, deep into the south. It was claimed that the physical features and language of the invaders were markedly different from that of the Dravidians, and so was their religion. Hinduism as a religion was then depicted as arising out of a synthesis of Aryan and Dravidian religions, and Hindu social organization was then described as arising out of an attempt on the part of the victorious but numerically fewer Aryans to maintain, first, their dominance and, then, their hegemony over the earlier inhabitants. The caste system was the outcome of this effort at social engineering.

This is the regnant view in modern scholarship (though now under challenge).[3] A.L. Basham recapitulates it as follows:

There is evidence to show that when the Aryans first came to India—at least five hundred years before the composition of the *Puruṣasūkta*—there was a class distinction between patricians and plebeians within the Vedic tribes. A special class of priest, forgotten by the time of this hymn, may also have existed in those days. But the original Aryan class system seems to have been much looser than the four *varṇas*, or classes, of the brahmanic scheme. Originally there were occasional promotions from a lower to a higher class, and intermarriage seems to have been permitted, as indeed it had been in India for centuries. From then on, however, even down to the present day, the four rigid classes formed the norm of Aryan and Hindu society. That norm has not always been followed in fact, but in theory it is eternal and inviolable.[4]

He goes on to say:

Thus, nearly three thousand years ago, the Aryans tried to establish a fairly strictly partitioned social system. With the sanction of their religion they largely succeeded in doing this, and the four *varṇa*s became the social norm. The word *varṇa* also means colour, and the pigmentation of the skin may have a hand in the evolution of the system. In the *Ṛg-veda* there is reference to 'the colour of the Aryans' and 'the colour of the Dāsas', the latter being a term for the indigenous inhabitants of northwestern India, a term that soon came to mean slave or serf. We are not told explicitly what the colours were, but it is assumed that the phrases refer to fair and dark skins respectively. Probably the Aryans, when they first entered India, though they were far from being Nordic blondes, had skins and hair little if at all darker than those of the modern European, especially in the Mediterranean areas; the indigenous inhabitants, on the other hand, were probably various shades of brown. The *varṇa* system may reflect an attempt to prevent further miscegenation, which was looked on as very objectionable. Though nowadays many Indians, influenced by egalitarian ideas, are strongly opposed to segregation, the sense of colour is still very strong in India.[5]

An important link in this chain of argument is the connection which is established between the Dāsas and Dasyus of Vedic Hinduism and the *śūdra*s of classical Hinduism. As Ram Sharan Sharma writes:

In 1847 it was suggested by Roth that the śūdras might have been outside the pale of Aryan society. Since then it has usually been held that the fourth varṇa of Brahmanical society was mainly formed by the non-Aryan population, who were reduced to that position by the Aryan conquerors. This view continues to derive support from the analogy of conflict between the white-coloured Europeans and the non-white population of Asia and Africa.[6]

As must be clear from Professor Basham's summary, four elements were crucial for the equation of the native peoples (as *śūdra*s) with the enemies of the Aryans mentioned in the *ṚgVeda*, the foundational text of the conquering Aryans: (1) differences in colour or complexion, (2) differences in physiognomy, (3) differences in religious practices, and (4) differences in language.

The fact that the *ṚgVeda* describes the Aryans or the *āryavarṇa* as fair and the *dāsavarṇa* as dark seemed to clinch the issue.[7] The fact that the 'caste system' itself was described as a system of *varṇa* (or colour) seemed to clinch the issue even more so. The physical features of the enemies of the Aryans similarly seemed to match those of the native population. The enemies were described as snub-nosed. The fact that they were described as of unintelligible speech reinforced the divide by pointing to differences in language, while the criticism of their religious practices pointed to differences in religion.

This is how the caste system, which in the Hindu mind had no racial component to it, acquired one through the labours of modern Western Indology. And this racial origin of caste system has now led to the suggestion that it is/was a form of racism.

II

In terms of the caste system, the people who constitute the bottom of it and therefore the worst sufferers under such a dispensation would be the former untouchables. There is some discussion in the literature on the subject whether they constituted a 'fifth' class on their own, or are to be subsumed under the *śūdra*s. This, however, has little bearing on the abject nature of their status. It would also seem to be the case that as the worst-off people under the system they might be inclined to endorse the theory of the racial origin of the caste system thus presented, as it maximizes the clout that they could gain from victimhood which is so effective a position to be in, in a liberal polity such as that of present-day India, which has constitutionalized affirmative action for the former untouchables. The equation of caste with race, in other words whether true or not, would serve their political interests, as it would double their claim to victimhood and consequently to compensation.

It therefore must occasion some surprise that the challenge to the theory of the racial origin of the caste system has come from Dr B.R. Ambedkar, who was himself an untouchable, suffered as one, played a major role in the framing of the Indian Constitution (which abolished untouchability and instituted affirmative action) and who, towards the end of his life, abandoned Hinduism and converted to Buddhism. His arguments against the theory certainly deserve serious consideration in the light of his biographical background, a theory that he himself summarizes as follows:

(1) The people who created the Vedic literature belonged to the Aryan race.
(2) This Aryan race came from outside India and invaded India.
(3) The natives of India were known as Dasas and Dasyus who were racially different from the Aryans.
(4) The Aryans were a white race. The Dasas and Dasyus were a dark race.
(5) The Aryans conquered the Dasas and Dasyus.

(6) The Dasas and Dasyus after they were conquered and enslaved were called Shudras.

(7) The Aryans cherished colour prejudice and therefore formed the *Chaturvarnya* whereby they separated the white race from the black race such as the Dasas and Dasyus.[8]

These points are examined by Dr B.R. Ambedkar and his findings are summarized below:

(1) *The people who created the Vedic literature belonged to the Aryan race.* Dr Ambedkar cautions against conflating a 'race' with a 'people' and cites Profesor W.E. Ripley to the effect that the Jews are a 'people' and not a race.[9] He also points out that although at one time it was thought that four elements constituted a race, namely, (1) form of head, (2) colour of hair and eyes, (3) colour of skin, and (4) stature, more recent opinion relies solely on anthropometry for its determination, i.e., on the cephalic and facial index. He notes that on the basis of anthropometry the 'Aryan race is described as long-headed'.[10] He also notes, however, that according to Professor Ripley both the Teutonic and the Mediterranean racial types are long-headed, so the 'question which of the two is the Aryan race still remains open'.[11] He also points out that Max Müller denies the racial connotation of the word Arya and accepts only a philological one.[12]

(2) *The Aryan race came from outside India and invaded India.* Dr Ambedkar argues that the Aryans never entered India from outside India. On the contrary he follows Professor D.S. Trivedi in citing *Ṛg Veda* X.75.5 to the effect that 'the rivers are addressed as "my Ganges, my Yamuna, my Sarasvati" and so on. No foreigner would address a river in such familiar and endearing terms unless by long association he had developed an emotion about it'.[13]

(3) *The natives of India were known as Dasas and Dasyus who were racially different from the Aryans.* Dr Ambedkar maintains, in agreement with Mr P.T. Srinivasa Iyengar, that the differences between the Aryans and the Dāsas and Dasyus were not racial but cultic. Those who claim that the differences were racial rely on two descriptions: (a) of the Dasyus as *mṛdhrvāk* and *anās* and (b) of the Dāsas as *kṛṣṇa yoni*. B.R. Ambedkar clarifies that *mṛdhrvāk*, according to its occurrence in the *ṚgVeda* (I.174.2; V.32.8; VII.6.3 and VII.18.3) means crude (as opposed to polished) speech.[14] He also points out that the word *anās* (V.29.101) can mean either 'mouthless' or 'noseless'. But as there is 'no other place where the Dasyus are described as noseless,' it is only fair to 'read it as a synonym of *mridhrvak*.'[15]

On the point of Dasas being described as black his comments are worth citing in some detail.

Turning to Dasas, it is true that they are described as *Krishna Yoni*, in Rig Veda vi.47.21. But there are various points to be considered before one can accept the inference, which is sought to be drawn from it. First is that this is the only place in the Rig Veda where the phrase *Krishna Yoni* is applied to the Dasas. Secondly, there is no certainty as to whether the phrase is used in the literal sense or in a figurative sense. Thirdly, we do not know whether it is a statement of fact or a word of abuse. Unless these points are clarified, it is not possible to accept the view that because the Dasas are spoken of as *Krishna Yoni*, they therefore belonged to a dark race.

In this connection, attention may be drawn to the following verses from the Rig Veda:

(1) *Rig Veda*, vi.22 10.—Oh, Vajri, thou has made Aryas of Dasas, good men out of bad by your power. Give us the same power so that with it we may overcome our enemies.
(2) *Rig Veda*, x.49 3, (says Indra).—I have deprived the Dasyus of the title of Aryas.
(3) *Rig Veda*, i.151. 8—Oh, Indra, find out who is an Arya and who is a Dasyu and separate them.

What do these verses indicate? They indicate that the distinction between the Aryans on the one hand and the Dasas and Dasyus on the other was not a racial distinction of colour or physiognomy. That is why a Dasa or Dasyu could become an Arya. That is why Indra was given the task to separate them from the Arya.[16]

(4) *The Aryans were a white race. The Dasas and the Dasyus were a black race*. This point has been dealt with above.

(5) *The Aryans conquered the Dasas and the Dasyus*. Dr Ambedkar presents three arguments against this proposition. He admits that in a number of hymns Dāsas and Dasyus are described as enemies of the Aryans, in which the gods are asked to smite them. However: (i) there is a 'paucity of such preferences . . . out of the 33 places in which the word occurs in the *Rig Veda* only in 8 places is it used in opposition to the Dasas and only in 7 places is it used in opposition to the word Dasyus' which is evidence of 'sporadic riots' not of 'conquest or subjugation';[17] (ii) in the following verses the Dāsas and Aryans stand as 'one united people against a common enemy':[18] vi.33.3; vii.83.1; viii.51.9 and x.102.3. The third point is best presented in some detail. Dr Ambedkar writes:

The third point to note is that whatever the degree of conflict, it was not a conflict of race. It was a conflict, which had arisen on account of difference of religions.

That this conflict was religious and not racial is evidenced by the *Rig Veda* itself. Speaking of the Dasyus, it says:

They are *avrata*, without (the Aryans) rites (R.V., i.51.8, 9; i.132. 4; iv.41, 2; vi.14. 3); *apavrata* (R.V., v.42.2), *anyavrata*, of different rites (R.V., viii.59. 11; x.22. 8), *Anagnitra*, fireless (R.V., v.189. 3) *ayajyu, ayajvan*, non-sacrifices (R.V., i.131.44; i.33.4; viii.59.11), *abramha*, without prayers (or also not having Brahmana priest (R.V., iv.15.9; x.105.8), *anrichah*, without *Riks* (R.V., x. 105.8), *Brahmadvisha,* haters of prayer (or Brahmans) (R.V., v.42.9), and *anindra*, without Indra, despisers of Indra, (R.V., i.133.1; v.2.3; vii.18.6; x.27. 6; x.48.7). 'They pour no milky draughts they heat no cauldron' (R.V., iii.53.4). They give no gifts to the Brahmana (R.V., v.7.10).

Attention may also be drawn to the *Rig Veda* x.22.8, which says:

We live in the midst of the Dasyu tribes, who do not perform sacrifices, nor believe in anything. They have their own rites and are not entitled to be called men. O! Thou, destroyer of enemies, annihilate them and injure the Dasas.

In the face of these statements from the *Rig Veda*, there is obviously no room for a theory of a military conquest by the Aryan race of the non-Aryan races of Dasas and Daryus.[19]

(6) *The Dasas and Dasyus after they were conquered and enslaved were called Shudras*. Dr Ambedkar devotes a whole chapter to this idea in the course of which he makes several points, but one may come to the point by reiterating the central thesis of the proposition, namely, that the Dāsas or Dasyus ended up as *śūdras* in the fourfold *varṇa* scheme. He begins by citing P.V. Kane in support of this thesis[20] as follows:

A clear line of demarcation was kept between the Ārya and the Śūdra in the times of the Brāhmaṇa works and even in the dharmasūtras. The Tāṇḍya Brāhmaṇa speaks of a mock fight the śūdra and ārya fight on a hide, out of the two they so arrange that the ārya colour becomes the victor. The Āp. Dh. S. (I.I.3.40–1) says that a brahmacārin, if he cannot himself eat all the food he has brought by begging, may give it to a śūdra who is a dāsa (of his teacher). The same Dharmasūtra (II.2.3.1 and 4) says 'Āryas who are pure (by bath) should prepare the food for Vaiśvadeva; . . . or śūdras supervised by āryas should prepare it. Similarly Gautama X. 69 uses the word anārya for śūdra . . .[21]

The central argument made by Dr Ambedkar in rebuttal is the following:

These stanzas which speak of the Shudra and the Arya as separate and opposed form the foundation of the theory that the Shudras are non-Aryans. To say the least, such a conclusion would be a very hasty one. Two considerations must be borne in mind before any conclusion is drawn from the aforementioned statements. In the first place, it must be borne in mind that according to what has been said before and according to the evidence of the Rig Veda, there are two categories of Aryans, the Vedic and the non-Vedic. Given this fact, it would be quite easy for an Aryan of one class to speak of an Arya of another class, as though the two were separate and opposed. Interpreted in this way, the above statements, in which Shudras are set against the Aryans, do not mean that they were not Aryas. They were Aryas of a different sect or class.[22]

Dr Ambedkar then produces several items of evidence in support of this position, some of which are summarized below. (1) At least five texts[23] make no distinction among the four *varṇas*, which supports the view that the division is not racial; (2) several texts either debate or confirm the participation of the *śūdra* in Vedic ritual, which suggests that the issues between the two groups were cultic and not racial;[24] (3) many Hindu law books, including the oldest and according to some the most conservative, allow for the transformation of *brāhmaṇas* into *śūdras* and vice versa over several generations, which is hardly conceivable if they were racially distinct groups; and (4) the *Arthaśāstra* (III.13) clearly classifies the *śūdra* with the *āryas*.[25]

(7) *The Aryans cherished colour prejudice and therefore formed the chaturvarnya whereby they separated the white race from the black race such as the Dasas and the Dasyus.* The crucial issue is whether the Aryans had a colour prejudice in favour of the white colour. Dr Ambedkar notes that one verse refers to the marriage of a dark Shyāvya with a fair Rushatī (I. 117.8) another speaks of Vandanā as possessing a golden colour (I. 117.5) and yet another asks for a son with *piśanga* (tawny) complexion (II.3.9). This evidence, combined with the fact that such a quintessentially Aryan *ṛṣi* as Kaṇva should be of dark colour (X. 31.11) and so also Dīrghatamas, makes it difficult to identify colour prejudice with the Aryans.[26]

Given the importance attached to the word *varṇa* in the whole debate, the word and its occurrence may be brought under the lens. The word occurs at twenty-two places in the *ṚgVeda*[27] according to Dr Ambedkar, who takes three tacks in this connection. His first step is to distinguish between the applications of the word to the gods and to human beings; according to him, '. . . in about 17 places the word is used in reference to deities such as Ushas, Agni, Soma, etc. and means lustre, features or colour. Being used in connection with deities, it would be unsafe to use them for ascertaining what meaning the word *varna* had in the *ṚgVeda* when applied to human beings.'[28]

Rig Veda, iii.34.5 seems to be of doubtful import. The expression 'caused Shukla Varna to increase' is capable of double interpretation. It may mean Indra made

Ushas throw her light and thereby increase the white colour, or it may mean that the hymn-maker being of white complexion, people of his i.e., of white colour increased. The second meaning would be quite far-fetched for the simple reason that the expansion of the white colour is the effect and the lightening of Ushas is the cause.

Rig Veda, ix.71.2 the expression 'abandons Asura Varna' is not clear, reading it in the light of the other stanzas in the *Sukta*. The *Sukta* belongs to Soma Pavamana. Bearing this in mind, the expression 'abandons Asura Varna' must be regarded as a description of Soma. The word Varna as used here is indicative of *roopa*. The second half of the stanza says: 'he throws away his black or dark covering and takes on lustrous covering.' From this it is clear that the word Varna is used as indicative of darkness.

Rig Veda, i.179.6 is very helpful. The stanza explains that Rishi Agastya cohabited with Lopamudra in order to obtain*praja,* children and strength and says that as a result two Varnas prospered. It is not clear from the stanza, which are the two Varnas referred to in the stanzas, although the intention is to refer to Aryas and Dasas. Be that as it may, there is no doubt that the Varna in the stanza means class and not colour.

In Rig Veda, i.104.2 and Rig Veda, ii.12.4 are the two stanzas in which the word Varna is applied to Dasa. The question is: What does the word Varna mean when applied to Dasa? Does it refer to the colour and complexion of the Dasa, or does it indicate that Dasas formed a separate class? There is no way of arriving at a positive conclusion as to which of the two meanings is correct.[29]

Dr Ambedkar then argues that perhaps this ambiguity could be cleared up by looking at the *Avesta*, a text which has been recognized as close in style and content to the *Ṛg Veda*. The form in which the word is found in the *Avesta* is *varana* or *varena*. After examining its six occurrences in the Gāthās, Dr Ambedkar concludes: 'This evidence from the Zenda Avesta as to the meaning of the word *varna* leaves no doubt that it originally meant a class holding to a particular faith and had nothing to do with colour or complexion.'[30]

Notes

1. S.K. Chatterji, 'Race-Movements and Prehistoric Culture',' in *The Vedic Age* (ed.), R.C. Majumdar, London: George Allen & Unwin Ltd., 1952, Chapter VIII.
2. D.C. Sircar, *Studies in the Geography of Ancient and Medieval India*, Delhi: Motilal Banarsidass, 1971, p. 16. Also see D. Devahuti, *Harsha: A Political Study*, Oxford: Clarendon Press, 1970, pp. 84, 194.
3. See Edwin Bryant, *The Quest for the Origins of Vedic Culture: The Indo-Aryan Migration Debate*, New York: Oxford University Press, 2001.

4. A.L. Basham, *The Origins and Development of Classical Hinduism* (edited and annotated by Kenneth G. Zysk), Boston: Beacon Press, 1989, p. 26.
5. Ibid., pp. 26–7.
6. Ram Sharan Sharma, *Śūdras in Ancient India*, Delhi: Motilal Banarsidass, 1980 [1958], p. 9.
7. Although A.L. Basham is cautious on this point, others are more forthcoming, see P.V. Kane, op. cit., vol. II, Part I, p. 25.
8. B.R. Ambedkar, *Who Were the Shudras?* Bombay: Thackers, 1970 [1946], pp. 57–8.
9. Ibid., p. 58. The following observation by P. Giles is relevant here: 'But the study of this family of languages has from the beginning been beset with a subtle fallacy. There has been throughout an almost constant confusion between the languages and the persons who spoke them. It is hardly necessary to point out that in many parts of the world the speaker of a particular language at a given time was not by lineal descent the representative of its speakers at an earlier period. In the island of Britain many persons of Welsh blood, many persons of Irish Celtic and Scottish Celtic origin speak English. It is many centuries since it was observed that Normans and English who had settled in Ireland had learned to speak the Irish language and had become more Irish than the Irish themselves. It is well known that by descent the Bulgarians are of Asiatic origin, and of an entirely different stock from the Slavs, a branch of whose language is now their mother tongue. It is therefore clear that it is impossible, without historical evidence, to be certain that the language spoken by any particular people was the language of their ancestors at a remote period. The name Indo-Germanic therefore suffers from the ambiguity that it characterizes not only languages but also peoples. As has been suggested elsewhere, it would be well to abandon both the term Indo-European and term Indo-Germanic and adopt some entirely colourless word which would indicate only the speakers of such languages. A convenient term for the speakers of the Indo-European or Indo-Germanic languages would be the Wiros, this being the word for 'men' in the great majority of the languages in question.' (P. Giles, 'The Aryans' in *The Cambridge History of India* (ed.), E.J. Rapson, Cambridge: Cambridge University Press, 1922, pp. 65–6.)
10. Ibid., p. 64.
11. Ibid.
12. Ibid., pp. 60–3. This point seems to have the support of modern scholarship. Romila Thapar notes regarding Max Müller that 'his later repeated attempts to deny the existence of an Aryan race were often ignored'. (*Ancient Indian Social History: Some Interpretations*, New Delhi: Orient Longman, Ltd., 1978, p. 224, note 2.)
13. Ibid., p. 70. The idea of an Indo-Aryan immigration is still widely accepted, although it has been pointed out that 'In fact, the accepted belief in the Indo-Aryan immigration from central Asia depends largely on the interpretation of the geographical allusions in the *Rig Veda* and *Yajurveda*. Direct testimony to the assumed fact is lacking, and no tradition of an early home beyond the

frontier survives in India' (Percival Spear[ed.], *The Oxford History of India by the Late Vincent A. Smith, C.I.E.* [fourth edition], Delhi: Oxford University Press, 1994, p. 53). Whether the Aryans are indigenous to India or entered India from outside is a contested site; for the evidence for and against see Edwin Bryant, op. cit., passim.

14. Ibid., p. 72. It also occurs in V.29.10, see Ram Sharan Sharma, op. cit., p. 15, note 8.
15. Ibid.
16. Ibid., p. 73.
17. Ibid., p. 70.
18. Ibid., p. 71.
19. Ibid.
20. Ibid., p. 112.
21. P.V. Kane, op. cit., Vol. II, Part I, second edition, p. 35. P.V. Kane argues on behalf of the Western view elsewhere as follows (op. cit., pp. 33–5): 'We shall now see what position was assigned to the śūdra in the Vedic Saṁhitās and Brāhmaṇas. In the Ṛgveda the Ārya is contradistinguished from the men "of dark skin". In the dharmasūtras we find the śūdras spoken of as "dark varṇa". Vide Ap. Dh. S. I. 9.27.11 which is the same as Baud. Dh. S.II.59. "The śūdra among men and the horse among beasts. Therefore those two, the horse and the śūdra, are the conveyances of being; therefore the śūdra is not fit (or ordained) for sacrifice" (Tai. S. VII. 1.1.6). This shows that the śūdra could not perform the Vedic sacrifices and that he was employed for carrying persons in a palanquin or otherwise. In Tai. S. V.7.6.3–4 we have "put light (glory) in our brāhmaṇas, put it in our chiefs (or kings), (put) light in vaiśyas and śūdras, put light in me by your light". This is a sure indication that the śūdra who took the place of the dāsa is here placed on the same level with the other three classes in the matter of the receipt of light from God and that far from being looked upon as an enemy, he had come to be looked upon as a member of the society (though the lowest in the scale). "The śūdra is a moving burial ground; therefore one should not study the Veda in the vicinity of a śūdra." "He created the brāhmaṇa with Gāyatrī, the rājanya with Triṣṭubh and the vaiśya with Jagatī; but he did not create the śūdra with any metre". The Tāṇḍyamahābrāhmaṇa says, "Therefore a śūdra, though he may have many beasts, is not entitled to perform sacrifice, he is godless as no deity was created after him (as in the case of the other varṇas); therefore he does not go beyond washing the feet (of the three other varṇas), since he was created from the feet" (this last being an allusion to the Puruṣasūkta X.90.12 *padbhyāṁ śūdro ajāyata*). This shows that the śūdra, however rich in cattle he might be, had to perform the menial duty of washing the feet of dvijas. The Śatapatha Br. says that "the śūdra is untruth" (S.B.E. vol. 44, p. 446) that 'śūdra is toil' (S.B.E. vol. 44, p. 410). And that a dīkṣita (one who was initiated for a Vedic sacrifice) was not to speak with a śūdra (S.B.E. vol. 26, p. 4). The Aitareya Brāhmaṇa remarks that "the śūdra is at the beck and call of others (the three varṇas), he can be made to rise at will, and he can be beaten at will". When the father of Śunaḥśepa (who had sold

Śunaḥśepa for 100 coins and had shown himself ready to kill him as a paśu for another hundred coins) urged his son to come back to him after the boy had been taken into favour by Varuṇa and Viśvāmitra, he contemptuously discarded his father's proposal with the words "one who commits an evil deed once may commit another sinful deed thereafter; you did not leave aside the śūdra's line of conduct; you did what leaves no door for reconciliation". These passages show that the śūdra, though he had ceased to be an enemy of the ārya and had been allowed to be within the pale of society, was looked down upon, was assigned a very low position, had to perform work of toil as a menial and was not allowed to perform Vedic sacrifices.'

He has proposed this basic idea earlier when he writes (op. cit., p. 33): 'The word "dāsa" in later literature means "a serf or slave". It follows that the dāsa tribes that we see opposed to the Āryas in the Ṛgveda were gradually vanquished and were then made to serve the Āryas. In the Manusmṛti (VIII. 413) the śūdra is said to have been created by God for service *(dāsya)* of the brāhmaṇa. We find in the Tai. S., the Tai. Br. And other Brāhmaṇa works that the śūdra occupies the same position that he does in the smṛtis. Therefore it is reasonable to infer that the *dāsas* or *dasyus* conquered by the Āryas were gradually transformed into the śūdra. From being enemies they were brought into friendly relations and given a very subordinate position. Traces are visible even in the Ṛgveda that friendly relations had begun to be established between certain dāsas and the priests. For example in Ṛg VIII. 46.32 we read "the singer took a hundred (cows and other gifts) from the dāsa Balbūtha and from Tarukṣa". In the Puruṣasūkta (X. 90. 12) the brāhmaṇa, kṣatriya, vaiśya and śūdra are said to have sprung from the mouth, arms, thighs and feet of the supreme Puruṣa. In the very next verse the sun and the moon are said to have been born from the eye and mind of the Puruṣa. This shows that the composer of the hymn regarded the division of society into four classes to be very ancient and to be as natural and God-ordained as the sun and the moon.'

22. B.R. Ambedkar, op. cit., p. 113.
23. *Atharva Veda* XIX. 32.8; XIX 62.1 and *Vājasaneyī Saṁhitā:* XVIII.48; XX.17 and XVIII.48.
24. *Bharadvāja Śrauta Sūtra* V.28; *Kātyayāna Śrauta Sūtra* I.4.16; *Mīmāṁsā-Sūtra* VI.1.27; etc.
25. From the point of view of Dr Ambedkar's thesis it is remarkable that even according to P.V. Kane: 'It is possible to say that Dāsas of Dasyus were some Aryan tribes that had fallen from the worship or culture of the Aryan singers of Vedic hymns', op. cit., p. 27.
26. From this point of view it is significant that 'in the earliest period we find the word varṇa associated only with dāsa and with ārya. Though the words brāhmaṇa and kśatriya occur frequently in the Ṛgveda, the word varṇa is not used in connection with them. Even in the Puruṣasūkta (Ṛgveda X.90) where the words brāhmaṇa, rājanya, vaiśya and śūdra occur the word varṇa is not used.' (P.V. Kane, op. cit., p. 27). E.J. Rapson also points out: 'Before the end of the period covered by the hymns of the Rigveda a belief in the divine origin of the

four orders of men was fully established: but there is nowhere in the Rigveda any indication of the castes into which these orders were afterwards subdivided. The word "colour" is still used in its literal sense. There are as yet only two varṇas, the light and the dark. But in the next period, the period of the Yajurveda and the Brāhmaṇas, the term denotes "a social order" independently of any distinction of colour, and we hear for the first time of mixed varṇas, the offspring of parents belonging to different social orders.' (E.J. Rapson, ed., op. cit., p. 54).

27. Ibid., p. 78.
28. Ibid.
29. Ibid., pp. 78–9.
30. Ibid., pp. 81–2.

Bibliography

Agrawala, V.S. (1968). *India as Known to Pāṇini*, Varanasi: Prithvi Prakashan.

Altekar, A.S. (1995). *The Position of Women in Hindu Civilization*, Delhi: Motilal Banarsidass.

Ambedkar, B.R. (1946). *Who Were the Shudras?*, Bombay: Thackers.

An-Na'im, Abdullahi Ahmed (1992). *Human Rights in Cross-Cultural Perspectives: A Quest for Consensus*, Philadelphia: University of Pennsylvania Press.

——— (1990). *Towards an Islamic Reformation: Civic Liberties, Human Rights and International Law*, Syracuse: Syracuse University Press.

Ashby, Philip H. (1974). *Modern Trends in Hinduism*, New York: Columbia University Press.

Baird, Robert D. (ed.) (1993). *Religion and Law in Independent India*, New Delhi: Manohar.

Balagangadhara, S.N. (1994). *The Heathen in His Blindness: Asia, the West and the Dynamic of Religion*, Leiden/New York, Köln: E.J. Brill.

Basham, A.L. (1999 [1954]). *The Wonder That Was India*, New Delhi: Rupa & Co..

——— (1989). *The Origins and Development of Classical Hinduism*, (ed.) Kenneth Zysk, Boston: Beacon Press.

Basu, B.D. (1916). *The Bṛhadāraṇyaka Upaniṣad with the Commentary of Śrī Madhvācārya*, Allahabad: The Pāṇini Office.

Baxi, Upendra (2002). *The Future of Human Rights*, New Delhi: Oxford University Press.

Beal, Samuel (tr.) (1969 [1884]). *Buddhist Records of the Western World*, Delhi: Oriental Books Reprint Corporation.

Bhattacharyya, Haridas (ed.) (1953). *The Cultural Heritage of India*, Vol. III, Calcutta: The Ramakrishna Mission Institute of Culture.

Bird, Frederick (1993). 'Moral Universals', 29–83, *The Journal of Religious Pluralism*, 3.

Bowes, Pratima (1977). *The Hindu Religious Tradition*, London: Routledge & Kegan Paul.

Brownlie, Ian (ed.) (1992), *Basic Documents on Human Rights*, Oxford: Clarendon Press.

Bryant, Edwin (2001). *The Quest for the Origins of Vedic Culture: The Indo-Aryan Migration Debate*, New York: Oxford University Press.

Carman, J.B. (1988). 'Duties and Rights in Hindu Society', in *Human Rights and The World's Religions*, (ed.) Leroy S. Rouner, 113–28, Notre Dame, Indiana: University of Notre Dame Press.

Chatterjee, Satischandra and Dhirendamohan Datta (1966). *An Introduction to Indian Philosophy*, Calcutta: University of Calcutta.

The Chronicle of Higher Education, 13 December 1996.

Connolly, Peter and Sue Hamilton (eds) (1997). *Indian Insights: Buddhism, Brahmanism and Bhakti*, London: Luzac Oriental.

de Bary, Wm. Theodore and Tu Weiming (eds) (1998). *Confucianism and Human Rights*, New York: Columbia University Press.

Derrett, J. Duncan M. (1968). *Religion, Law and State in India*, New York: Free Press.

Devahuti, D. (1970). *Harsha: A Political Study*, Oxford: Clarendon Press.

Devaraja, K.N. (1975), *Hinduism and the Modern Age*, New Delhi: Islam and the Modern Age Society.

Embree, Ainslie T. (ed.) (1988). *Sources of Indian Tradition*, second edition, New York: Columbia University Press.

——— (ed.) (1972). *The Hindu Tradition*, New York: Random House.

Forsythe, David P. (1983). *Human Rights and World Politics*, Lincoln: University of Nebraska Press.

Gandhi, M.K. (1958). *Hindu Dharma*, Ahmedabad: Navajivan Publishing House.

Glendon, Mary Ann (2001). *A World Made New: Eleanor Roosevelt and the Universal Declaration of Human Rights*, New York: Random House.

Hiriyanna, M. (1975). *Indian Conception of Values*, Mysore: Kavyalaya Publishers.

——— (1932). *Outlines of Indian Philosophy*, London: George Allen & Unwin.

Hume, Robert Ernest (tr.) (1968 [1877]). *The Thirteen Principal Upaniṣads*, London: Oxford University Press.

Ignatieff, Michael (2000). *The Rights Revolution*, Toronto: Canadian Broadcasting Corporation.

——— (1997). *The Warrior's Honor: Ethnic War and the Modern Conscience*, New York: Henry Holt and Company.

The International Bill of Human Rights (1993), New York: United Nations.

Jain, Girilal (1994). *The Hindu Phenomenon*, New Delhi: UBSPD.

Johnson, James Turner (1997). *The Holy War in Western Islamic Traditions*, University Park, PA: Pennsylvania State University Press.

——— (1981). *Just War Tradition and the Restraint of War: A Moral and Historical Inquiry*, Princeton, NJ: Princeton University Press.

Joshi, Shashi and Bhagwan Josh (1994). *Struggle for Hegemony in India: 1920–1947*, New Delhi: Sage Publications.

Kane, P.V. (1930–1962). *History of Dharmaśāstra*, five volumes, Poona: Bhandarkar Oriental Research Institute.

Kangle, R.P. (1988). *The Kauṭilīya Arthaśāstra*, three volumes, Delhi: Motilal Banarsidass.

Kashyap, Subhash C. (ed.) (1993). *Perspectives on the Constitution*, New Delhi: Shipra Publications.

Keer, Dhananjay (1971 [1954]). *Dr. Amedkar: Life and Mission*, Bombay: Popular Prakashan.

Kelsay, John and Sumner B. Twiss (eds) (1994). *Religion and Human Rights*, New York: The Project on Religion and Human Rights.

——— (1991). *Just War and Jihad: Historical and Theoretical Perspectives on War and Peace in Western Islamic Traditions*, New York: Greenwood Press.

Kinsley, Davis R. (1993). *Hinduism: A Cultural Perspective*, Englewood Cliffs, New Jersey: Prentice Hall.

Klostermaier, Klaus K. (1989). *A Survey of Hinduism*, Albany, NY: State University of New York Press.

Kothari, Smitu and Harsh Sethi (eds) (1991). *Rethinking Human Rights*, New York: New Horizons Press.

Krishna, Gopal (ed.) (1979). *Contributions to South Asian Studies*, Delhi: Oxford University Press.

Lauren, Paul Gordon (1998). *The Evolution of International Human Rights: Visions Seen*, Philadelphia: University of Pennsylvania Press.

Lee, T.S.Y. and Osamu Nishi (1999). *Japan*, Dobbs Ferry, NY: Oceana Publications Inc.

Mahadevan, T.M.P. (1971). *Outlines of Hinduism*, Bombay: Chetana.

Majumdar, R.C. (ed.) (1968). *The Age of Imperial Unity*, Bombay: Bharatiya Vidya Bhavan.

——— (ed.) (1970 [1954]). *The Classical Age*, Bombay: Bharatiya Vidya Bhavan.

——— (ed.) (1952). *The Vedic Age*, London: George Allen and Unwin.

Miller, Barbara Stoler (1996). *Yoga: Discipline of Freedom*, Berkeley: University of California Press.

Muir, J. (1972). *Original Sanskrit Texts*, Delhi: Oriental Publishers.

Murty, K. Satchidananda (1993). *Vedic Hermeneutics*, Delhi: Motilal Banarsidass.

Nehru, Jawaharlal (1946). *The Discovery of India*, New York: The John Day Company.

Nickel, James W. (1987). *Making Sense of Human Rights: Philosophical Reflections on the Universal Declaration of Human Rights*, Berkeley: University of California Press.

Olivelle, Patrick (1998). *The Early Upaniṣads*, New York and Oxford: Oxford University Press.

——— (1993). *The Āśrama System: The History and Hermeneutics of a Religious Institution*, New York and Oxford: Oxford University Press.

Organ, Troy Wilson (1974). *Hinduism: Its Historical Development*, Woodsbury, NY: Barron's Educational Series Inc.

——— (1970). *The Hindu Quest for the Perfection of Man*, Athens, Ohio: Ohio University.

Oxtoby, Willard G. (ed.) (2002): *World Religions: Western Traditions*, Toronto: Oxford University Press.

——— (ed.) (2002). *World Religions: Eastern Traditions*, Toronto: Oxford University Press.

Panda, K.B. (1977). *Sanatana Dharma and Law*, Cuttack: Naitika Punaruthan Samiti.

Panikkar, K.M. (1961). *Hindu Society at the Crossroads*, Bombay: Asia Publishing House.

Panikkar, R. (1982). 'Is the Notion of Human Rights a Western Concept?', 75–102, *Diogenes*, 120.

Pappu, S.S. Rama Rao (1982). 'Human Rights and Human Obligations: An East-West Perspective', 15–28, *Philosophy and Social Action*, 8.4.

——— (1969). 'The Idea of Human Rights', 44–50, *International Review of History and Political Science*, vol. VI, no. 4.

Patel, Ramesh H. (1991). *Philosophy of the Gita*, New York: Peter Lang.

Paul, Ellen Frankel et al. (1986). *Human Rights*, Oxford: Basil Blackwell.

Prabhu, Joseph, (1998). 'Dharma as an Alternative to Human Rights', in *Studies in Orientology: Essays in Memory of Prof. A. L. Basham* (eds), S.K. Maity, Upendra Thakur, and A.K. Narain, 174–9, Agra, India: Y.K. Publishers.

Radhakrishnan, S. (1992). *The Principal Upaniṣads*, Atlantic Highlands, NJ: Humanities Press.

——— (1927). *The Hindu View of Life*, New York: The Macmillan Company.

Rai, Lal Deosa (1995). *Human Rights in the Hindu-Buddhist Tradition*, Jaipur: Nirala Publications.

Rao, P. Nagaraja (1970). *The Four Values in Indian Philosophy and Culture*, Mysore: University of Mysore.

Rao, S.K. Ramachandra (1979). *Jivanmukti in Advaita*, Madras: JBH Publications.

Rapson, E.J. (ed.) (1922). *Ancient India*, Cambridge: Cambridge University Press.

Renou, Louis (ed.) (1962). *Hinduism*, New York: George Braziller.

——— (1951). *The Nature of Hinduism*, (tr.) Patrick Evans, New York: Walker and Company.

Renteln, Alison Dundes (1990). *International Human Rights*, Newbury Park, CA: Sage.

Robb, Carol S. (1998). 'Liberties, Claims, Entitlements, and Trumps: Reproductive Rights and Ecological Responsibilities', 283–394, *Journal of Religious Ethics*, 26.2.

Runzo, Joseph (2001). *Global Philosophy of Religions: A Short Introduction*, Oxford: One World.

Saksena, K.P. (ed.) (1994). *Human Rights: Perspectives and Challenges*, New Delhi: Lancers Books.

Sastri, K.A. Nilakanta (ed.) (1957). *The Mauryas and Satavahanas*, Bombay: Orient Longman.

Scharfe, Hartmut (1989). *The State in Indian Tradition*, Leiden: E.J. Brill.

Sen, K.M. (1961). *Hinduism*, Harmondsworth: Penguin Books.

Sharma, Arvind (1999). 'The Puruṣārthas: An Axiological Exploration of Hinduism', 223–56, *Journal of Religious Ethics*, 27:2.

Sharma, Ram Sharan (1980[1958]). *Śūdras in Ancient India*, Delhi: Motilal Banarsidass.

Sharpe, Eric J. (1986). *Comparative Religion: A History*, London: Duckworth.

Shastri, Hari Prasad (tr.) (1959). *The Ramayana of Valmiki*, London: Shanti Sadan.

Sircar, D.C. (1971). *Studies in the Geography of Ancient and Medieval India*, Delhi: Motilal Banarsidass.

Smart, Ninian and Shivesh Thakur (eds) (1993). *Ethical and Political Dilemmas of Modern India*, New York: St. Martin's Press.

Smith, Donald Eugene (1963). *India as a Secular State*, Princeton, NJ: Princeton University Press.

Spear, Percival (ed.) (1994). *The Oxford History of India*, fourth edition, New Delhi: Oxford University Press.

Stahnke, Ted and J. Paul Martin (eds) (1998). *Religion and Human Rights: Basic Documents*, New York: Center for the Study of Human Rights.

Tahzib, Bahiyyih G. (1996). *Freedom of Religion or Belief: Ensuring Effective International Legal Protection*, The Hague/Boston/London: Martinus Nijhoff Publishers.

Thapar, Romila (1978). *Ancient Indian Social History: Some Interpretations*, New Delhi: Orient Longman.

Thiemann, Ronald F. (1996). *Religion in Public Life: A Dilemma for Democracy*, Washington, DC: Georgetown University Press.

Traer, Robert (1991). *Faith in Human Rights*, Washington DC: Georgetown University Press.

Twenty-Five Human Rights Documents (1994), New York: Columbia University Press.

Twiss, Sumner B. (1998). 'Moral Grounds and Plural Cultures: Interpreting Human Rights in the International Community', 271–82, *Journal of Religious Ethics*, 26.2.

van Buitenen, J.A.B. (tr.) (1973). *The Mahābhārata*, Vol. I, Chicago and London: The University of Chicago Press.

van der Vyer, and John Witte (eds) (1996). *Religious Human Rights in Global Perspective: Legal Perspectives*, The Hague/Boston/London: Marinus Nijhoff Publishers.

Vivekananda, Swami (1970). *The Collected Works of Swami Vivekananda*, vol. 5, Calcutta: Advaita Ashrama.

Waley, Arthur (1958). *The Way and Its Power: A Study of the Tao Te Ching and Its Place in Chinese Thought*, New York: The Grove Press.

Walker, Benjamin (1968). *The Hindu World*, two volumes, New York: Frederick A. Praeger.

Wisse, Ruth R. (1992). *If I am not for Myself*, New York: The Free Press.

Zaehner, R.C. (ed.) (1967). *The Concise Encyclopedia of Living Faiths*, Boston: Beacon.

Glossary

Adhikāra	The view that one is entitled to pursue certain practices or study certain texts only after the qualification (*adhikāra*) to do so has been obtained.
Advaita Vedānta	A school of Hindu thought which claims that the ultimate teaching of the Hindu scriptures consists of non-dualism.
Ahiṁsā	Non-violence as a principle of conduct or policy.
Ahl-al Kitāb	The Arabic term for 'people with a book'—those to whom a revelation has been vouchsafed by God prior to the Koran. The term includes Jews and Christians.
Analects	One of the classics of Confucianism known as *Lun Yü* in Chinese. It consists of the sayings of Confucius, often in dialogue with his disciples.
Aṇīmāṇḍavya	A sage who became the victim of a miscarriage of justice. His story is narrated in the first canto of the *Mahābhārata*.
Āṇṭāl	A famous female devotee of Kṛṣṇa from Tamil Nadu.
Anuśāsanaparva	One of eighteen cantos or books (*parva*) which comprise the *Mahābhārata*.
Āpad-dharma	Acts one might perform in a time of crisis, which are otherwise not permitted.
Artha	The pursuit of wealth as constituting one of the four *puruṣārtha*s, including statecraft and political economy within its scope.
Ārṣa	A form of marriage in which the bride is given to the bridegroom after receiving a cow or a pair of bulls.

Arthaśāstra	A famous text on Hindu statecraft discovered in 1909, perhaps the most comprehensive and ancient text of its kind. Its authorship is attributed by tradition to Kauṭilya who is placed in the fourth century BC, although the precise age of the present text is a matter of debate.
Ārya	A word used by the people of the *ṚgVeda* to refer to themselves in recognition of their own nobility.
Aśoka	A famous king of the Mauryan dynasty who became a pacifist and patronized Buddhism, considered by many to be one of India's greatest rulers (c. third century BC).
Āśrama	The word could mean (1) a hermitage or (2) a stage of life, depending on the context.
Āśrama-dharma	The duties appropriate to one's stage in life, especially as visualized in the scheme of the four *āśramas*.
Āsura	A form of marriage in which the bride is secured for a monetary consideration.
Asura-vijaya	Conquest of another kingdom with a view to its annexation.
Ātmatuṣṭi	Moral self-satisfaction as a source of *dharma*.
Atisarga	The word means permission accorded to the daughters to choose their own bridegroom.
Bheda	The method of overcoming opposition by causing divisions in its ranks.
Brāhma	A form of marriage in which the bedecked bride is given away to a learned person of good conduct.
Brahmacarya	The first stage of life in which one prepares for the rest of it as a celibate student.
Brāhmaṇa	The first class in the fourfold division of society according to Hinduism, consisting of priests, religious scholars, and people with similar concerns.
B.R. Amdedkar (1892–1956)	Leader of the untouchables of India, who is considered the architect of the Indian Constitution.
Bṛhadāraṇyaka Upaniṣad	A major early Upaniṣad of great authority, usually assigned to around the eighth century BC.

Caturvarga	Another word for the four *puruṣārthas* considered as a quarternary.
C.F. Andrews	A British Christian priest who became a close associate of Mahatma Gandhi.
Chāndogya Upaniṣad	One of the classical Upaniṣads usually placed c. eighth century.
Dabistān-i-Mazāhib	A seventeenth century text of Mughal India which offers a strikingly accurate and refreshing account of Indian religious life during this period.
Daiva	A form of marriage in which the bride is given away to a priest in marriage.
Dāna	(1) The word means charity in general but in a marital context means the giving away of the girl in marriage.
	(2) The exercise of diplomacy through financial inducements.
Daṇḍa	Coercion as a means of conflict resolution.
Darśana	The word means visual audience in a devotional sense but as a philosophical term refers to the schools of Indian philosophy as offering 'an insight into reality' or offering a 'worldview'.
Dāsa	A class of people distinct from the Aryans with whom they had a complex pattern of relationship involving both conflict and cooperation.
Dhammapada	One of the classics of Buddhism, sometimes called the Buddhist bible. It forms part of the *Sutta-Nipāta*, considered among the oldest parts of the Theravāda canon.
Dharma	The pursuit of righteousness as an end in itself in the Hindu scheme of values.
Dharma-Vijaya	Hindu imperialism distinguishes between three types of conquest-involving ruthless extermination (*asura-vijaya*); financial extortion (*lobha-vijaya*) or the gentler form in which the defeated king accepts the conqueror's paramountcy on generous terms (*dharma vijaya*). King Aśoka evolved

	his own version of *dharma vijaya*, which emphasized pacifism.
Draupadī	Draupadī was the common wife of the five Pāṇḍavas, which is quite unusual. The case therefore has been much remarked upon in both ancient and modern times.
Draviḍa	According to the regnant view in the nineteenth century, the Draviḍas were believed to be the original inhabitants of India who were overcome and assimilated by the Aryans, but the theory has now been virtually abandoned.
Dvāpara Yuga	The third of the four ages in which the cosmic decline continues.
Gāndharva	A form of marriage in which the two parties voluntarily enter into marriage without family intermediation.
Gārhasthya	The second stage of life spent as a householder and in raising a family.
Gītā	A text of 700 verses which appears as an inset in the*Mahābhārata*. Also known as the*Bhagavadgītā*, it is one of Hinduism's popular scriptures.
Gospel of Mark	One of the four Gospels which form part of the New Testament and narrate the life, deeds, and words of Jesus Christ.
Guṇas	The word primarily meaning 'quality', possesses several meanings in Sanskrit, often stated in a set of three, as *sattva*, *rajas*, and *tamas*.
Ḥadīth	Words or deeds of the Prophet Muhammad as constituting a basis for Islamic law.
Harijan	A word used by Mahatma Gandhi to refer to the class of people otherwise known as the untouchables.
Iṣṭa-Devatā	The deity of one's choice which could be any one out of the vast Hindu pantheon, or even from beyond it.
Jāti	A group to which one belongs by birth, such birth often determining the nature of one's occupation and the social circle to which one belongs.

Kali Yuga	The last of the four ages in which cosmic decline hits rock bottom.
Kalpa	A period of time consisting of 1000 *mahāyugas*, and symbolic of a vast expanse of time.
Kāma	One of the four goals of human life (or *puruśārtha*s) covering its hedonic and aesthetic dimensions.
Kauṭilya	A famous figure in ancient India who brought about the downfall of the Nanda dynasty through his protégé Candragupta Maurya (c. fourth century BC).
Kirāta	The Sanskrit terms said to correspond to the Mongoloid element as a component of India's racial make-up.
K.M. Panikkar (1894–1963)	A leading historian of modern India, author of the pioneering work entitled *Asia and Western Dominance*.
Kṛta Yuga	The first and best of the four ages in which righteousness and happiness prevail; also known as *Satya Yuga*.
Kṣatriya	The second class in the fourfold division of society according to Hinduism, consisting of kings, warriors, bureaucrats, and people with similar concerns.
Lobha-vijaya	Conquest of another kingdom motivated by greed.
Mahābhārata	One of the two major epics of Hinduism, the other being the *Rāmāyaṇa* which it far exceeds in length.
Mahājanaparigraha	The consensus of the people in general, or the general consensus of leading people, as the basis of according the status of scripture to a text.
Mahatma Gandhi (1869–1948)	Leader of India's non-violent struggle for emancipation from the British colonial rule.
Manu	An abbreviation for the *Manusmṛti* (when not referring to an individual by that name). The *Manusmṛti* is perhaps best known among the *smṛti*s and usually assigned to a time between the second century BC to AD second century.
Mātsyanyāya	Hindu metaphorical expression for anarchy.

Medhātithi — A famous ninth-century commentator on the *Manusmṛti*.

Mīmāṁsā — The school of Hindu thought which attaches fundamental importance to the ritual portions of the Vedas and to the ritualistic dimension of the religious life.

Mleccha — The word for an outsider to the pale of Vedic life, either because of loss of such status or lack of acceptance within it, particularly on account of being a foreigner.

Mokṣa — The search for salvation or liberation as an aspect of human endeavour, and therefore spiritual in orientation in contrast to *dharma, artha*, and *kāma*.

Nārada — A wandering sage, who is a popular figure in the *Purāṇas*.

Nāradasmṛti — A *smṛti* text usually placed in the Gupta period, based on the extant *Manusmṛti* but dealing with judicial procedure and a king's legal role in more detail.

Nichiren Buddhism — The form of Buddhism associated with the name of Nichiren (1222–82) known for its militant and missionary spirit. This form of Buddhism accords a special status to the *Lotus Sūtra*.

Niṣāda — The Sanskrit term said to correspond to the Negrito and/or proto-Australoid elements in India's racial composition.

Nivṛtti — The mode of life characterized by passive disengagement from affairs of the world.

Nyāya-Vaiśeṣika — A school of Hindu philosophy characterized by realism and pluralism.

Paiśāca — A form of marriage in which the bride is seduced while asleep, intoxicated, or otherwise not in control of her senses.

Pañca-Draviḍa — A classification of the Brahmins of the south as originating from the five regions of Tamil Nadu, Karnataka, Andhra, Maharashtra, and Gujarat.

Pañca-Gauḍa	Five classes of *Brāhmaṇas* in North India, probably identified in imitation of the five classes of Brahmins in the south known as *Pañca-Draviḍa*.
Pāṇini	The name of a grammarian of Sanskrit language usually placed in the fifth century BC and author of the *Aṣṭādhyāyī*—a text enormously influential in subsequent history.
Patañjali	The putative authorship of the *Yoga-sūtra*, an influential text usually assigned to the fifth century.
Prajā-dharma	The duties and moral obligations of the subjects to the king, as distinguished from those of the king (*rāja-dharma*).
Prājāpatya	A form of marriage in which the bride and the bridegroom come together to perform their common religious duties.
Pravṛtti	The mode of life characterized by active engagement in affairs of the world.
Purāṇas	Class of books in Hinduism which deal with the lives of gods and heroes and other celestial matters, usually listed as consisting of eighteen major and eighteen minor works.
Puruṣārtha	A collective term for the four goals of life (*dharma, artha, kāma, mokṣa*) whose pursuit is considered legitimate in Hindu axiology.
Puruṣārtha-catuṣṭaya	The four goals of human endeavour identified as (1) *dharma*, (2) *artha*, (3) *kāma*, and (4) *mokṣa.*
Rāja-dharma	The special duties and moral obligations of kingship, or the state by extension.
Raja Rammohan Roy (1772/74–1833)	Often called the Father of modern India, Roy was the first modern Indian to engage the West and to welcome the positive aspects of Western civilization.
Rākṣasa	A form of marriage in which the bride is abducted.
Rāma	A famous king of Hindu mythology, considered an incarnation of Viṣṇu.

Rāmakṛṣṇa Paramahaṁsa (1836–1886)	A highly regarded saint of modern Hinduism who experimented spiritually with various forms of Hinduism and even other religions.
Rāmāyaṇa	One of the two major epics of Hinduism, which narrates the life of Rāma, an incarnation of Viṣṇu.
Rāmāyaṇa of Tulsīdās	A seventeenth-century rendering in Hindi of the *Rāmāyaṇa* story extraordinarily popular in North India.
ṚgVeda	The first and earliest of the four Vedas, the foundational scriptures of Hinduism.
Sadācāra	Normative conduct as a source of *dharma*.
Sādhana	The spiritual quest.
Sādhāraṇa-dharma	Duties common to all human beings irrespective of their station in life or stage in life.
Sāma	Conciliation as a means of conflict resolution.
Samañña-phala Sutta	Or the Discourse of the Fruits of Asceticism. It forms part of the *Sutta Piṭaka* and is significant on account of the fact that non-Buddhist teachers and their teachings are referred to therein.
Śambūka	A *śūdra* sage who is beheaded by Rāma for practising austerities not permitted to *śūdras* in the Tretā Age.
San-Chao	The Chinese term of the 'Three Teachings' of Confucianism, Taoism and Buddhism—specially when viewed non-exclusively.
Śaṅkara/Śaṁkara	A famous Hindu philosopher, usually placed c. eighth century, whose formulation of Advaita Vedānta became paradigmatic for later generations.
Sannyāsa	The last stage of life in which all connection with the world is cast aside as one focuses solely on spiritual matters.
Śānti-Parva	One of the eighteen cantos or books into which the *Mahābhārata* is divided.
Satyam	Hindu word for truth or reality.

Smṛti	A class of works whose author is known and which therefore represent tradition, as distinguished from *śruti* which consists of the revealed word.
S. Radhakrishnan (1888–1975)	A famous philosopher and statesmen of modern India, who wrote extensively on Hinduism and comparative religion and went on to become the president of India.
Śruti	The Vedas, specially when considered as constituting an aural revelation or an oral transmission.
Śūdra	The last class in the fourfold division of society according to Hinduism, consisting of workers, domestics, labourers, and serfs.
Svadharma	A polysemic word which literally means one's own *dharma*, whose exact connotation may vary with the concept of self-identity involved.
Swami Vivekananda (1863–1902)	A disciple of Rāmakṛṣṇa who went on to become an extremely influential spokesman of modern Hinduism.
Talmud	An authoritative compendium of Jewish belief and practice from the point of view of Rabbinic Judaism.
Tapas	The word means heat, specially when generated by austerities and hard work, as a form of latent potency.
Tretā Yuga	The second of the four ages in which cosmic decline sets in.
Upaniṣads	A body of texts also known as Vedānta, which constitute the final section of the Vedas.
Vaiśya	The third class in the fourfold division of society according to Hinduism, consisting of agriculturalists, merchants, artisans, and similar professions.
Vānaprasthya	The third stage of life in which one goes into retirement with one's wife, abandoning conjugal relations.
Varṇa	The term denotes one of the classes constituting the fourfold classification of society, in Hinduism into *Brāhmaṇa*s, *Kṣatriya*s, *Vaiśya*s, and *Śūdra*s.
Varṇa-dharma	The duties appropriate to one's station in life,

specially as established by the fourfold division of Hindu society into *varṇa*s.

Varṇa-saṅkara The word refers to the confusion of classes, which is said to result from immorality, miscegenation, or abdication of assigned vocation.

Varṇāśrama Dharma The duties incumbent on one as a member of a *varṇa* and as one passing through a well-defined phase of life called *āśrama*.

Vedas The foundational scriptures of Hinduism, comparable to the Bible and the Koran.

Vemana A medieval poet-saint of Andhra Pradesh.

Vidura A sagely figure in the *Mahābhārata*. He represents Dharma, who was born a *sūdra* as a result of being cursed by an Anī-māṇḍanya for not dispensing justice in proportion to the crime.

Vikraya The word means sale in general, but in a domestic context means the selling of children, especially daughters.

Xuanzang (Hiuen-Tsiang) A Chinese traveller who visited India in the seventh century during the reign of King Harṣa and left behind a valuable account of his travels.

Yāska A Vedic exegete, usually assigned to the fifth century BC.

Yudhiṣṭhira The eldest of the five brothers collectively known as the Pāṇḍavas, whose fratricidal struggle with their cousins known as Kauravas constitutes the kernel of the *Mahābhārata* epic.

Yugas The Hindu temporal doctrine according to which the cosmos undergo repetitive cycles of determined durations, characterized by the succession of four *yuga*s (or ages) called *kṛta*, *tretā*, *dvāpara*, and *kali*, in that order. This entire period comprising the four *yuga*s is called a *mahāyuga*.

Index

Kṛṣṇa, cult of, as child-god 39
Kṛta yuga 85, 87
  dharma in 86
kṣātra-dharma 24
Kṣatriya/Kshatriya class 51, 57, 59, 61, 62, 150
  dharma to protect people 32, 63
Kūrma Purāṇa 97

Lauren, Paul Gordon 32, 37
legal view, of human rights 4–5, 8, 12
lobha-vijaya 45
Locke, John 7, 10

Mahābhārata 5, 16, 24, 25, 40, 60, 61, 67, 68, 69
  on duties assigned to *varṇas* 150
  on role of conscience 116
  Śānti Parva of 68, 69
mahājana 117
mahājanaparigraha, on collective conscience 117
Maithila Brāhmaṇas 179
Majumdar, R.C. 42
Mānasollāsa 44
mānava dharma 60
mānava-jāti 69–71
  rights of 70
Manavantara 86
Manusmṛti 18, 23, 25, 44, 60, 73n, 86, 148
  on duties of *varṇas* 149–50
  on role of conscience 115
  varṇa and caste in 66
marriage, in Hinduism 79, 81–2
  types of 81–2
Marx, Karl 32
Marxism 144
  in China 109
  and materialism 59
'mass conversion' 117
Matsya Purāṇa, śūdra varṇa in 92
Maurya, Chandragupta 46
Mauryan Dynasty 46
Medhātithi 147
Megasthenes 43, 46
Mill, John Stuart 7, 126
Mīmāṁsa school 10, 14, 93n
minority rights, in the West 108, 109
mridhrvak 182
'missionary' religions 131, 133
Mitākṣarā Yāj 14
mokṣa (liberation) 10, 13, 16, 21
moral agency 6
moral basis/view, of human rights 5–7, 9, 11
morality, and human rights 6, 7, 8, 11, 16, 19, 60
Müller, Max 182, 187n
Murty, K. Satchidananda 80

nānāvarṇa 21
Nāradasmṛti 12, 158n
nation state, concept of 65, 71
nationalism 15
nationality, based on birth 63–4
'natural law' 89, 90
Nehru, Jawaharlal 18
Nepal, Hindu identity in 106
  religious conversion forbidden in 105
Nepalese Constitution, on conversion 105
Nichiren Buddhism 128, 131
Nirukta 81
niṣāda/Proto-Australoid race 178
nivṛtti, and *pravṛtti* phases of life 83
niyama 154, 155
non-proselytizing religions 110
non-violence 59, 60
Norweign Constitution, of 1815 31
Nyāya-Vaiśeṣika 155
  view on universals 123, 124

order, concept of 142
Organ, Troy Wilson 15, 16